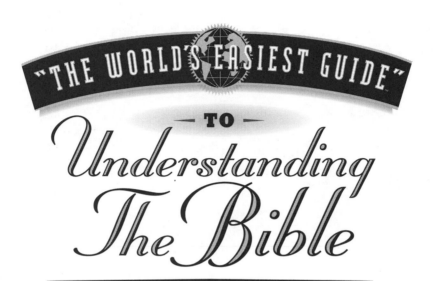

"THE WORLD'S EASIEST GUIDE"

TO

Understanding The Bible

Stan Campbell is a veteran writer who has authored more than 30 Bible-related books—most recently *The Complete Idiot's Guide to the Book of Revelation* and a new, revised edition of *The Complete Idiot's Guide to the Bible.* Many of his writing opportunities have grown out of his more than 20 years in youth ministry with his wife, Pam.

"THE WORLD'S EASIEST GUIDE"

TO
Understanding The Bible

STAN CAMPBELL

NORTHFIELD PUBLISHING
Chicago

All Scripture quotations, unless otherwise indicated, are taken from the *Holy Bible, New International Version.*® NIV® Copyright © 1973, 1978, 1984 by International Bible Society. Used by permission of Zondervan Publishing House. All rights reserved.

Scripture quotations marked NASB are taken from the *New American Standard Bible*®, Copyright © The Lockman Foundation 1960, 1962, 1963, 1968, 1971, 1972, 1973, 1975, 1977, 1995. Used by permission.

Scripture quotations marked NKJV are taken from the *New King James Version.* Copyright © 1982, 1992 by Thomas Nelson, Inc. Used by permission. All rights reserved.

Scripture quotations marked TLB are taken from *The Living Bible* copyright © 1971. Used by permission of Tyndale House Publishers, Inc., Wheaton, Illinois 60189. All rights reserved.

Scripture quotations marked *The Message* are from *The Message,* copyright © by Eugene H. Peterson 1993, 1994, 1995. Used by permission of NavPress Publishing Group.

Editors: James Bell Jr.
James Vincent

Campbell, Stan.
    "The world's easiest guide" to understanding the Bible / Stan Campbell.
      p. cm.
    Includes index.
    ISBN 1-881273-23-7
    1. Bible--Introductions. I. Title

BS475.3 C36 2002
220.6'1--dc21   2002071899

ISBN: 1-881273-23-7
1 3 5 7 9 10 8 6 4 2
Printed in the United States of America

Table of Contents

continued on next page

PART ONE

About the Bible

We've been told the Bible is a pretty special Book, but we may not know exactly why. So before we start ruffling through its pages, perhaps we need to consider how those pages got there in the first place, why the Bible stands out among other books on the shelf, how we can best prepare to read it, and why many would-be readers find the Bible intimidating.

The first four chapters of this guide will attempt to do just that. You'll discover why many people feel the need to respond to the teachings of the Bible more than any of the other reading options you'll find in your library or bookstore. And you'll see why it is considered more trustworthy, accurate, and inspired than other works.

You don't necessarily have to know all these things to read and appreciate the writings of Scripture. But since our goal in this guide is to *understand* the Bible, these opening chapters will provide a helpful background. After you know how the Bible came to exist in the first place and why it is deemed to be so important, you're likely to get considerably more from your reading of it.

The Least-Read Best-Seller Ever?

SNAPSHOT

Once upon a time, a scientist determined to help the hungry and homeless people he saw each day as he went to work. He devoted himself to creating a device that could manipulate certain molecules and actually manufacture food out of subatomic particles in the air. And rather than rush to write scientific papers or seek fame and fortune, he chose instead to give away his device to someone who really needed it.

On his way to work the next day, he carried his pocket-sized invention. A man stood on the corner with a "Will Work for Food" sign, so the scientist asked if he was hungry. "I'm starving," the man said. "I haven't had anything substantial in almost a week."

The scientist smiled, handed the man the device, and explained how it worked. "All you do," he said,

SNEAK PREVIEW

1. Many people own a Bible, yet they never use it as a helpful or reliable resource for coping with the challenges of life.
2. It's not as hard to understand the Bible (at a basic level, at least) as many people think.
3. A working knowledge of the Bible is helpful for lots of practical life issues, not just for establishing doctrine and theology.

"is key in numbers to get whatever food you want. Here's a list with a thousand different possibilities, including chicken soup, T-bone steaks, baked manicotti, double cheeseburgers, fries, hot fudge sundaes, and just about anything else you can think of."

The man on the street hit the numbers for ham, eggs over easy, hash browns, and coffee. Each item appeared in turn. The man devoured the food on the spot and was shocked beyond words when the scientist insisted that he keep the device. The scientist then went on his way, determined to create another device and write out the instructions so the machines could be mass-produced to feed the hungry people of the world. He was still working on his second model two weeks later when, on his way to work, he saw the guy to whom he had given the first device. The man was back on the streets, begging for food.

The scientist was alarmed. He stopped and asked the man, "What's wrong? Did the food device malfunction? Did you lose it? Was it stolen?"

"No," answered the man. "I still have it, and it works fine. It's back in the alley in a shopping cart with all my other possessions."

"Then why are you begging for food?" asked the bewildered scientist.

The man replied, "Well, I tried most of the things that the machine can manufacture, and it's some of the most delicious stuff I've ever eaten. But it just seems too easy to press a button and get whatever I want. Sometimes I'd just rather provide for myself, you know? When I go through garbage cans or beg for food, I never know what I'm going to get. For instance, last month I found the remains of a bucket of chicken. It had a slight green tinge to it, but I was so hungry that it tasted dumpster-licking good. Later I was sick for three days straight, but it was satisfying to know I was taking care of myself. Your machine just makes it too easy."

The scientist walked away, dismayed. He never finished his second device. Instead, he went into the field of behavioral psychology to try to understand what makes people act in such strange ways. In the meantime, the needy person is still hungry, while the wonderful device is out there somewhere—lying unused in an alley . . . or perhaps collecting dust in a motel room drawer.

* * * * * * * * * * * * * * *

You'll find a lot of parables in the Bible, but not this one. This parable of the benevolent scientist was written because of the way people *respond to* the Bible. Many will confess that too often they relate to the needy, hungry person. While few of us ever go hungry in a physical sense, *spiritual* hunger is something else altogether.

Would You Like to Use a Lifeline?

Most of us own a Bible, a divinely inspired collection of writings (more on that in the next chapter) in which God provides a vast feast of blessings, promises, hopes, assurances, encouragements, warnings, guidelines—essentially everything we need to navigate this perilous obstacle course we call *life*. In most cases, the material is clearly stated and simple to understand. But to be honest, many of us are all too willing to "wing it." We find ourselves in difficult circumstances and rather than consulting the wisdom that the Lord of the universe has seen fit to provide us, we attempt to handle things using our own strength and smarts.

Or maybe we act instinctively and don't even consider the tremendous resource at our disposal. Or—dare we confess it—we have a good idea what God wants us to do, yet blunder on with what we *feel* like doing anyway.

The Bible is called a lamp to our feet and a light for our path (Psalm 119:105). Yet to activate the most powerful of our lamps and flashlights, we must go to the effort of turning them on. If we want God's light to shine in our dark worlds, we have to actually open the Bible and read what He has to say to us.

We scoff at people on *Who Wants to Be a Millionaire?* who don't use their lifelines and end up leaving early because they didn't know as much as they thought they did. Yet all they lose is a big wad of cash. We miss out on much more if we neglect the lifeline of God's Word so readily at our disposal.

Do We Really Need Another Book About the Bible?

The Bible is the world's all-time best-seller. In addition, it has inspired untold thousands of additional works and ministries. A recent search of "Holy Bible" on a popular Internet search engine came up with well over one million Web sites. As for products, another book-selling site lists a choice of 32,000 titles connected with "Bible," though the number reflects the recent trend to publish "bartenders bibles," "golf bibles," "computer bibles," and such, which have nothing to do with Scripture. Yet for each of these, there is certainly hundreds of other unlisted titles about the Bible that are no longer in print. So do we really need *another* book about the Bible?

The author must confess to personally contributing several dozen books to the mélange of books about the Bible—many now in that infamous "out of print" category. After trying to simplify something to that extent, you may wonder if obsession drives me to now shoot for the distinction of *The World's Easiest Guide to Understanding the Bible.*

I had similar qualms about the need for yet another "dumbed down" explanation of the Bible. But I can tell you exactly what convinced me to address this vital topic yet again.

You Don't Know Jo? Nah!

I recalled an incident from my youth ministry experience. After writing Bible studies for junior highers and high schoolers for fifteen-plus years, I thought I had a pretty good idea what to expect from students and how to challenge them without assuming they know more than they do.

One evening we were playing our own version of *Pictionary* using Bible references. The group was divided into teams, and a representative from each team was assigned something to draw, the winner being the person whose team was first to guess correctly what was being drawn. After each round, we would quickly review the significance of the person or event drawn. And since our group included a number of people who were quite new to many of the Bible stories, I was being careful not to assign any obscure or unfamiliar topics—or so I thought.

Imagine my surprise when the assigned word was *Jonah* and one of the senior boys whispered to me, "I don't know who that is." At the time, I quietly advised him to draw a big fish with a person inside, and I think his team even won the point. And not long afterward we held a weekend retreat based on the story of Jonah. But the incident has ever since redefined my suppositions about general Bible knowledge.

Most people in my baby boomer generation had a certain degree of Bible knowledge, whether or not they eventually opted for church involvement. It comes as no surprise that we can't make the same assumptions today. Yet I still register a certain degree of shock when faced with the harsh realization that someone can go all the way through high school and never be introduced to the character of Jonah. You'd think that if the name didn't come up as a Bible reference, the question would be raised in some secular context, such as a reading of *Moby Dick*. (One chapter is titled "Jonah Historically Regarded.") And for a generation that hasn't necessarily come into contact with Jonah, what *other* Bible basics are they missing—things that people like me assume *everybody* knows?

So these recent realizations, coupled with the invitation to contribute a book to this World's Easiest Guide series, has challenged me to address the Bible at an even more basic level than ever before. After all, it wasn't my student's fault that he had never been exposed to Scripture. He was not a rebellious kid or a slow learner. He was a good student in a good school system. And during youth group gatherings and retreats, he was as quick to detect spiritual insights as any of the other group members. Yet somewhere along the way his parents had not gotten him involved in Sunday school classes, and the school system had apparently made no mention of a (I had always assumed) well-known Old Testament figure named Jonah.

It will be a primary goal of this book to not only expose you to the start-to-finish flow of action in the Bible, but also to help you learn to get more out of the Bible on your own. This guide may only scratch the surface of what's in the Bible, but it will give you some suggestions and starting points for further study. Personally, I hope you read this guide, give it to someone else who can use it, and then pick up your Bible and use what you've learned. This guide is only successful if it connects you with the only Book that matters.

The Bad News . . . The Good News

Even though the Bible is a best-seller, and even though hundreds of thousands of books *about* the Bible have been printed throughout the centuries, many of us still aren't coming into personal contact with Scripture. Perhaps we don't have Bibles in the home; more likely, we're not regularly reading the ones we have, or we're not understanding what we read.

Some Christians are quite alarmed that children and teenagers are not being trained in the truths of Scripture, and numerous books exist to sound warnings and call for various actions to be taken. My approach in *this* book, however, is to concede that Bible literacy may indeed be at an all-time low—for whatever the reasons. That's the bad news.

But the good news is that many people are coming to realize their lack of knowledge about the Bible, and they're eager to learn. It's simply that the challenge of coming to the Bible as an adult, trying to make up for lost time, can seem an insurmountable challenge. Those who grow up reading Bible stories and attending Sunday school and vacation Bible school have a tremendous head start. As teenagers and adults, it's simply a matter of filling in some gaps, going a little deeper, and learning to apply Scripture to their own lives. Yet for adults who approach with little, if any, experience, the Bible looms before them as a big, thick, intimidating book. Is it really worth the effort to start *now* to try to read, remember, and understand what's there?

If you discovered you must move to Macao to live the rest of your life, wouldn't you want to get a map and find out where it is? Wouldn't you want to start learning Portuguese, the official language? Even though it would no doubt take a lot of time and work, most people would devote themselves to learning the native language(s), customs, history, and such.

Similarly, your first approach to understanding the Bible can seem intimidating indeed. But be assured that this is something you can learn to do in small steps, as long as you keep going. As you progress through this book, you will see that Bible study is a valuable lifetime pursuit, so the time you spend now is by no means a waste—it is an investment in your future.

Don't be alarmed if you don't know anything about Jonah, John, James, Jeremiah, Joshua, Joseph, Jesse, Joel, or even Jesus. Don't go kicking yourself. And more importantly, don't go looking to kick your parents or schoolteachers. There are infinitely vast amounts of information that each of us is unaware of. (Just watch Jay Leno's person-on-the-street interviews or the contestants on any quiz show.) So don't waste time attempting to assign blame. If you want to fill in the gaps, and if you start now, you'll quickly get around to discovering what's so special about all these biblical people.

In fact, after reading, rereading, memorizing, and meditating on certain passages for years, some people tend to lose sight of how fresh and relevant the truths of Scripture are. If you are completely unfamiliar with the Bible, you are in for many thrills as you read it for the first time. Expect to meet several quirky new characters, visit new places, and (best of all) see for yourself what God thinks about you.

This book is intended to serve as a guide, to help you interact with Scripture personally. But first and foremost, listen for God's voice, not the author's. The Bible is God's Word. It speaks. And you hear what God has to say, not with your ears, but with your heart. You will be surprised at how quickly God's Spirit will go to work and help you understand the things you are reading. You are certain to have questions as you go along, but those should not impede your regular progress and growth as you begin to read.

The Next Step

If you just can't wait to get into the panoramic flow of Scripture, you could skip the next three chapters, turn to part 2, and start your journey through the Bible. Chapters 5 through 14 will help you zip from Genesis to Revelation, providing a broad overview of what's going on between the covers of your Bible. This quick overview is by no means intended to provide in-depth understanding, but it may be a helpful first step if the Bible is new or unfamiliar to you. It's like stepping up to a table where a jigsaw puzzle has been dumped out and assembling the frame first. You still don't have the puzzle all pieced together by any means, but when you begin to see the big picture, it becomes a bit easier to add a piece at a time until you have a clear vision of how all the pieces come together in a brilliant, unified whole.

BACKGROUND INFO

The more we know about the times and settings of any part of Scripture, the better we can understand what's being said. These short background bits of information will provide insight and help to clarify various portions of the Bible.

WHAT'S THE GOOD WORD?

These segments will be quotations from the Bible that are pertinent to the content of each chapter. Ambitious readers might want to select some of these to memorize and remember. We're using the *New International Version*.

SWORD DRILL

As other sections of this book provide answers to many of your questions, these Sword Drill sidebars will give you questions **without** answers—but you will be told where to look. ("Sword drill" is a classic Sunday school game that challenges participants to quickly locate various Bible verses or passages.) Have some fun with these as you familiarize yourself with the Bible.

Yet if you can hold off for just a bit, chapters 2 through 4 should be quite helpful as well. They will offer some of the details and reasoning for *why* the Bible is such a special Book.

Sadly, some people approach Bible reading as a chore or obligation. It's like uncovering a buried treasure chest filled with gold doubloons—and walking away because the writing on the coins isn't in English. But if we can come to realize exactly what we're holding as we turn the pages of Scripture, understanding the Bible takes on a whole new level of excitement. The next three chapters explain why it's definitely worth a bit of effort to learn to understand and apply Scripture.

Then, after going through the broad themes of the Bible at a cursory level, read part 3. Here you will learn how to start going a bit deeper, getting even more from the Bible. By then, you should understand a lot more about what was going on when the Bible was written, who the main contributors were, how various portions relate to one another, and more. At that point you will have sixty-six books to choose from, and a whole array of study options.

I truly believe you will be surprised how quickly the Bible begins to make sense—whether you've been at it for a while or are a brand spanking new first-timer.

Three recurring sidebars will be found throughout the rest of this book to use as additional aids. They are factual, and even fun, we hope. (At least they break up the text to provide some variety.) They begin with the next chapter, but you'll find some samples on pages 17 and 18 showing you what to expect.

Each chapter will conclude with a short review—usually a silly quiz just to be sure you were paying attention and got the point.

And speaking of concluding quizzes, let's see what you learned from this chapter.

 # Chapter Flashback

1. If you're ever playing *Pictionary* and need to draw Jonah, you can:
   a. Draw a blank.
   b. Draw a person eating fish.
   c. Draw a big fish with a person inside.
   d. Just ask the leader and maybe he'll cheat a little and help you out.

2. We should never forget that the Bible is:
   a. A lifeline
   b. A timeline
   c. A lifetime
   d. A Time-Life book

3. If you know less than you wish about the Bible, it's:
   a. Your fault
   b. Your parents' fault
   c. Time to get going
   d. Too late for someone *your* age

4. It can actually be quite exciting and advantageous to:
   a. Let others read the Bible and tell you what it says.
   b. Read Scripture for the first time.
   c. Recite Bible verses in your sleep.
   d. Keep asking yourself, "I wonder what the Bible would have to say about so-and-so if I ever bothered to read it?"

5. You will get the most out of the Bible if you listen for:
   a. The author's voice
   b. The voices of your kids screaming at each other downstairs
   c. The little voices in your head
   d. God's voice

Answers: (1) c, (2) a, (3) c, (4) b, (5) d

The Rites of Getting the Writing Right

THE UNIQUE CHARACTER AND DISTINCTIVES OF THE BIBLE

SNAPSHOT

If we didn't already have the Bible, do you suppose it could be written today? Let's find out.

Moderator: Everyone, please take a seat. We have forty chairs in here, so most of you should be able to sit. I think you know why we're here?

James: You want us to write the Bible, right?

Moderator: More accurately, we want to consider the feasibility of attempting such a work. For example, we're going to need several authors to record what God wants included.

Everyone: Me! Me! Me!

Moderator: Settle down. We'll get to that later. We also need to consider what style we want to use.

SNEAK PREVIEW

1. For many reasons, the Bible is unique among all books ever written.
2. The Bible is as relevant today as it has ever been.
3. Understanding the uniqueness of the Bible is a good beginning to understanding the Bible itself.

Moses: How about narrative?

David: Poetry!

Amos: Prophecy?

Luke: Historical documentary.

Paul: You know, a lot can be said in a well-written letter.

John: How about that new apocalyptic style that's all the rage?

Moderator: We'll probably be able to accommodate a bit of variety there. But there's also the issue of job assignment. Would everyone want to write the same amount?

Zephaniah: Well, it would hardly seem fair if people like, say, Obadiah and Jude only wrote a page or two while others, say, Isaiah and Ezekiel, just wrote page after page after page.

Peter: What if someone wants to write more than one section of this book?

Mark: What do you want: a First Peter and a Second Peter?

   [Everyone roars with laughter.]

Moderator: And something no one has mentioned yet—how do you expect to be paid for your contribution? Flat fee? Work for hire? Do you want royalties?

Hosea: None of us is in this for the money. I think we should simply write what God tells us, and we'll get whatever reward He assigns later.

Moderator: That's the right attitude. But I have to be honest with you, deadline for this project isn't for another 1,400 years. I doubt that any of you will still be around to collect, unless you're planning on beating Methuselah's record.

   [Much murmuring.]

Moderator: But what else should go on today's agenda?

Haggai: Who's our target market?

Matthew: Will we use focus groups to evaluate our work?

Daniel: How about the marketing plan? Projected first-year and five-year sales? International distribution?

Moses: If I were to write down all the laws, for instance, that section might come off as kind of dry in spots. So what kind of artwork and design should we consider to keep the reader turning pages?

Jonah: And endorsements! Who can we get to put their names on the cover to appeal to buyers?

Moderator: These are all great ideas, and we're off to a rousing start. But first let's take a short manna break and meet back here in fifteen minutes.

* * * * * * * * * * * * * *

Let's be thankful the Bible was written when it was and how it was. The authors sacrificed a lot (including royalties, book tours, and even their lives, in some cases) to contribute to what has become the Bible as we know it. Times sure have changed since then, and book publishing has become much less an art and much more a business. Yet a few things remain constant.

The One and Only

For example, one of the first lessons for all aspiring writers is, "Write what you know," which is what the human authors of the Bible did. But the crucial distinction that makes the Bible such a stand-alone Book is that those writers knew exactly what God wanted them to write. They had a degree of leeway in writing *style*, but the *substance* was all from God.

Peter made it clear that *he* was writing what he knew, and he spoke on behalf of the other Bible writers as

WHAT'S THE GOOD WORD?

We did not follow cleverly invented stories when we told you about the power and coming of our Lord Jesus Christ, but we were eyewitnesses of his majesty.

– 2 PETER 1:16

well: "Above all, you must understand that no prophecy of Scripture came about by the prophet's own interpretation. For prophecy never had its origin in the will of man, but men spoke from God as they were carried along by the Holy Spirit" (2 Peter 1:20–21).

So while some of the Bible is expressed in commandments, some in symbolism, some in poetry, some in parables, and so forth, it is *all* the Word of God. Forty or more authors wrote over a period of 1,400 or more years to compile an amazingly cohesive and comprehensive work. Such an inspired feat is never likely to happen again.

The Plot Thickens

The Bible begins with a narrative account of God creating an entirely new race of people and placing them in a wonderful paradise—only to have them quickly foul everything up. And it ends with an apocalyptic-style description of God eliminating the evil that has grown rampant throughout centuries of sin and inviting those who overcome to an even better paradise. In between is the story of the long anticipation of, the short life of, and the world-changing aftermath of the Savior of the world—a Savior who died but then rose from the dead to make possible the reunion of sinful humankind with a perfect heavenly Father.

BACKGROUND INFO

If you're new to the Bible, be prepared to encounter a few gory and horrendous segments. Certain portions will touch on issues many of us might rather avoid: incest, cannibalism, rape, cold-blooded murder, deceit and betrayal, and much more.

Along the way we are confronted with many basically good (though terribly flawed) individuals, some out-and-out villains, some events that can be backed up with history and archaeology, others that can't be proven, and hundreds of pages of names, genealogies, places, cross-references, prophecies, fulfillments, dreams, and visions. In its pages we read a panorama of great drama: personal and national struggles, heartless betrayals, tragic defeats, and miraculous victories.

You will quickly discover that some parts of the Bible are going to appeal to you more than others. As you read and learn more, your "favorite" sections will be subject to change, and they may not ever be the same favorites as your peers. That's another significant distinction of the Bible—God uses His Word to speak to different people in different ways.

Some people adore the Psalms; others prefer the action-oriented stories. Most people enjoy the come-from-behind victories and edge-of-your-seat narrow misses; few are as eager to scour the Mosaic Law for rules pertaining to infectious skin diseases and bodily discharges.

What to Leave in, What to Leave Out

One of the best reasons for believing the Bible is true is its inclusion of things we may be quick to ignore or downplay. Suppose, for example, you were writing your autobiography. Would you go out of your way to include every evil deed, lascivious thought, and dark secret of your life? Wouldn't you focus more on your positive accomplishments and contributions, painting a rather attractive verbal portrait of yourself?

The Bible is the story of humankind's encounter with the Lord of the universe, so think about how long God has been at work and how much He has done. Today we could pick any single second from the time line of history and write a Bible-length book about the miracles of God taking place. Someplace the sun will be rising to provide light and heat. Somewhere else the orange sunset will glow down on awestruck spectators. The rivers and oceans will be providing life-sustaining water. And we aren't even aware of most of the incomprehensible wonders taking place down in the ocean, deep in the forests and jungles, or high on the mountains where plants and animals live and die unseen by human eyes.

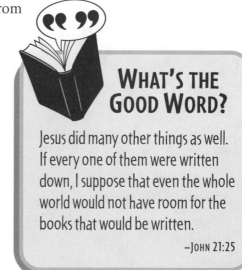

WHAT'S THE GOOD WORD?

Jesus did many other things as well. If every one of them were written down, I suppose that even the whole world would not have room for the books that would be written.

–John 21:25

In addition, in the brief span of that second, certain parents will be trembling as they hold a first child. Young men and women will be falling in love.

Relationships will be restored. Some people will be passing from the pains of death into the indescribable glory of eternal life. And numerous other men and women could testify of God's miracles taking place, quietly, in their hearts and minds.

But instead of a single second, the Bible covers many centuries of history. Logically, much more must be omitted than is included. For example, much is written about the life of Jesus, yet scholars tell us that the Gospels (Matthew, Mark, Luke, and John) cover only about forty days of His thirty-three-year life.

Most of us, if put in charge of "editing" the biblical panorama of history, would drop much of what is included in the Bible—perhaps some of the more mundane laws, vague prophecies, and especially some of the nastier stuff. We would very likely throw in some extra miracles of Jesus, some more Old Testament stories like Jonah's, and all the feel-good accounts we could pack into the determined length.

But no. While the Bible does indeed provide the highs of many people's lives and shows God acting time and time again to accomplish His will on earth, it is also meticulous in recording the darker side of human nature, especially among its heroes. We read of Noah's righteousness saving humankind from being wiped off the face of the earth . . . and then his getting drunk and naked, causing problems for his family members (Genesis 9:20–27). Abraham is upheld as a classic example of strong faith; yet he placed his wife in harm's way when his personal safety was at risk (Genesis 12:10–20). Lot is acknowledged as "a righteous man" (2 Peter 2:7); yet no sooner had he escaped Sodom and Gomorrah than his daughters took turns getting him drunk and sleeping with him in order to bear children (Genesis 19:30–38). Aaron, the first high priest personally appointed by God, was the ringleader in sculpting the golden calf (Exodus 32). Samson was a heroic legend, but his continual womanizing was his downfall (Judges 16).

SWORD DRILL

God miraculously protected Sarah after Abraham was quick to place his wife in a dreadful predicament to save his own hide (Genesis 12:10–20). What do you think Abraham did the next time a similar situation came along? (See Genesis 20.)

If someone were putting together a religious book only to manipulate and coerce the reader to lead a goody-goody life, would the authors take such a "warts and all" approach to the so-called heroes of the stories? Not likely! Yet the fact that the Bible reveals not only the shining moments of faith, but also the most shameful secrets of the major characters, lends credence to its believability. And it's surprising how few of the key figures escape without some kind of setback or major failure noted on their "permanent record" in Scripture. The first time we read the stories, we are usually inspired by the shows of faith and the rewards that result. Yet as we begin to understand the Bible better and better, we also learn to see the failures as valuable lessons as well.

As we have seen, Noah and Lot both got drunk and lived to regret it. Moses and David were guilty of cold-blooded murder. Abraham and Elijah had great moments of faith followed by bouts of despair and/or cowardice. Solomon, with seven hundred wives and three hundred concubines, might be labeled a sex addict by contemporary standards. The apostle Paul started out zealously attempting to have all Christians put to death. But if God can use such louts for His glory, maybe He can use us as well.

The Word on the Word

If the honest portrayal of its characters isn't enough to convince you that the Bible is indeed unique and is the Word of God, let's look at some other arguments from the Bible itself. The following passages represent only twenty-two of the total 31,173 verses in the Bible. Yet in these couple of dozen verses we will find enough to keep us thinking for a long while.

When Adding Is Subtracting

> Every word of God is flawless; he is a shield to those who take refuge in him.
> Do not add to his words, or he will rebuke you and prove you a liar.
> (Proverbs 30:5–6)

When God speaks, we need to be quick to hear and respond, not quick to add our own spin to what He is saying. That's why it's important to actually read the Bible—God's Word—instead of only reading books *about* the Bible. God's words are flawless. The words of most human authors tend to get confusing, boring, or otherwise flawed from time to time. As we learn to read the Bible for ourselves and trust the truth and accuracy of what we read, God becomes a shield and refuge instead of just a shadowy and mysterious figure.

God's Word: High and Outside

"For my thoughts are not your thoughts, neither are your ways my ways," declares the LORD. "As the heavens are higher than the earth, so are my ways higher than your ways and my thoughts than your thoughts. As the rain and the snow come down from heaven, and do not return to it without watering the earth and making it bud and flourish, so that it yields seed for the sower and bread for the eater, so is my word that goes out from my mouth: It will not return to me empty, but will accomplish what I desire and achieve the purpose for which I sent it." (Isaiah 55:8–11)

As we begin to approach the Bible, we need to keep one thing in mind: God is smarter than we are. We are incapable of fully comprehending His thoughts and purposes. Still, He provides His Word to steer us in the right directions. We will be able to understand much of what He has to say, but portions of the Bible are likely to remain mysterious, if not downright incomprehensible.

Yet in spite of any failure on our part to understand, we are also assured that God's words have a purpose that will be accomplished. We don't have to understand everything. (Thank goodness!) As long as we continue to read, listen, and ponder what is in the Bible, we will be enlightened by His truth at deeper and deeper levels. What seems outside our understanding at first reading, or second reading, or 618th reading, may suddenly become clear the next time we encounter the same passage.

The Bible isn't a book to read once and put back on the shelf. God continues to speak through His written Word, and we need to continue to listen.

If I Had a Hammer

"Is not my word like fire," declares the Lord, "and like a hammer that breaks a rock in pieces?" (Jeremiah 23:29)

Two of the major distinctions between savage tribes and civilized societies are the mastery of fire and use

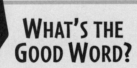

WHAT'S THE GOOD WORD?

"The LORD is my rock, my fortress and my deliverer; my God is my rock, in whom I take refuge, my shield and the horn of my salvation. He is my stronghold, my refuge and my savior—from violent men you save me."

–2 SAMUEL 22:2–3

of tools. In speaking to Jeremiah, God compares His Word to both fire and a hammer. These analogies come in the context of how they may also be misused.

Fire can be used for arson and a hammer for murder, neither of which is the intended purpose. Similarly, people can misuse God's Word for their own purposes or out of callous disregard.

SWORD DRILL

Who was reading God's Word in the wilderness, befuddled and confused, when God sent along an "interpreter" who made all the difference? (See Acts 8:26–35.)

But when used appropriately, fire can make raw meat taste much, much better or provide warmth and life during a long cold spell. A hammer can break apart obstacles or construct sturdy homes. Similarly, the Word of God, used appropriately, takes us beyond our secular caveman-level mentality. We walk uprightly, in a spiritual sense, and continue to mature spiritually as we apply the things we're learning.

The Right Comeback at the Right Time

> Then Jesus was led by the Spirit into the desert to be tempted by the devil. After fasting forty days and forty nights, he was hungry. The tempter came to him and said, "If you are the Son of God, tell these stones to become bread." Jesus answered, "It is written: 'Man does not live on bread alone, but on every word that comes from the mouth of God.'" (Matthew 4:1–4)

During Jesus' temptation, the devil made Him three offers. In each case, rather than succumb to the temptation or outperform Satan with miraculous feats, Jesus simply quoted an appropriate Scripture. And one of the very Scriptures He used was the reminder from Deuteronomy 8:3 that people don't live by bread alone, but "on every word that comes from the mouth of the LORD."

Just as people need food for physical sustenance, they need God's Word for spiritual life. Jesus promised His followers "abundant life" or "life . . . to the full" (John 10:10). This fullness of life is not simply a physical existence; through interaction with God, life becomes abundant and full. And just as we feed on bread at our meals, we need to feed on God's Word in order to keep living and growing in a spiritual sense.

An understanding of the Bible provides us not only with food for spiritual life, but also arms us with answers and understanding when *we're* facing temptation, or pain, or suffering, or persecution, or any other of life's little obstacles.

A Newer Format of "Word"

In the beginning was the Word, and the Word was with God, and the Word was God. He was with God in the beginning. The Word became flesh and made his dwelling among us. We have seen his glory, the glory of the One and Only, who came from the Father, full of grace and truth. (John 1:1–2, 14)

One of the Bible's titles for Jesus—and the one John uses to open his gospel—is "the Word." In our manic media-saturated society, words on the printed page don't tend to garner much attention. The electronic media tend to outshine their print forerunners.

But in terms of God's Word, the transformation is even more evident. From the time the Ten Commandments came down from Mount Sinai, God's people had access to His *printed* Word. In addition, God's Word was given to the prophets and then *spoken* to those who needed to hear. But in the incarnation (the becoming human) of Jesus, God's Word literally became flesh and blood—the *living* Word. Jesus came not just to read us God's Word . . . not just to speak the Word to us . . . but to model the reality of that Word in every way.

If we want to know what God has to say to us, we can read the Bible and find out. But if we want a better perspective that shows us how God's Word should be lived out in personal spiritual growth, human relationships, and numerous other practical applications, we need to pay special attention to the Gospels. Jesus not only taught with His words but with His every action.

Armored and Dangerous

Take the helmet of salvation and the sword of the Spirit, which is the word of God. (Ephesians 6:17)

WHAT'S THE GOOD WORD?

For God was pleased to have all his fullness dwell in [Jesus], and through him to reconcile to himself all things, whether things on earth or things in heaven, by making peace through his blood, shed on the cross.

– COLOSSIANS 1:19–20

We have already seen that God's Word is flawless, and that God acts as a shield for those who seek refuge in Him (Proverbs 30:5). Here we see God's Word compared to a sword. This comes at the end of a passage describing the "full armor of God" (see Ephesians 6:10–18). Most of the "armor" described is defensive: a belt of truth, a breastplate of righteousness, a shield of faith, a helmet of salvation, and so forth. But finally we are to take "the sword of the Spirit, which is the word of God."

Why do we need a sword? Because this armor is for battle, not dress up. God's Word arms us for conflict "against the rulers, against the authorities, against the powers of this dark world and against the spiritual forces of evil in the heavenly realms" (Ephesians 6:12). Our enemies are spiritual and invisible, but that doesn't make Satan and his forces any less real or threatening. The sword of God's Word is the primary weapon we're given to resist them.

The "duck and cover" strategy schoolchildren were taught in response to potential nuclear attack turned out to be quite naïve and ineffective and is no better for spiritual warfare. It's not enough to put on armor and take cover. We're to be soldiers, not armadillos. By understanding the Bible, we learn to wield a sword and fight back.

Turning the Sword on Oneself

> For the word of God is living and active. Sharper than any double-edged sword, it penetrates even to dividing soul and spirit, joints and marrow; it judges the thoughts and attitudes of the heart. (Hebrews 4:12)

This verse adds to the imagery of God's Word as a sword but puts it in a different context. This time, we are to consider applying the (s)word to ourselves. In this case, it serves less as a weapon of destruction and more as a doctor's scalpel. Just as a surgeon might delicately slice away a carcinogenic tumor to remove cancer and restore health to a body, God's Word can help us target the car-*sin*-ogens in our lives. As we eliminate each one, we grow spiritually stronger and healthier.

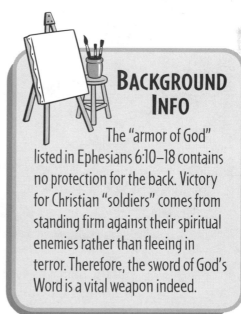

BACKGROUND INFO

The "armor of God" listed in Ephesians 6:10–18 contains no protection for the back. Victory for Christian "soldiers" comes from standing firm against their spiritual enemies rather than fleeing in terror. Therefore, the sword of God's Word is a vital weapon indeed.

Sin results in spiritual death (Romans 6:23). Conversely, God's Word is living and active. But before it can do us any good, we must allow it to penetrate our souls, spirits, thoughts, and attitudes.

A Breath of Fresh Life

All Scripture is God-breathed and is useful for teaching, rebuking, correcting and training in righteousness, so that the man of God may be thoroughly equipped for every good work. (2 Timothy 3:16–17)

Here we get a bit more clarity as to the source of Scripture. It is not only God's Word casually recorded by human stenographers. The content of the Bible is "God-breathed." God is the source of all life—physical and spiritual. Physically, at the creation of the world, God "breathed into [Adam's] nostrils the breath of life, and the man became a living being" (Genesis 2:7). Similarly, the God-breathed words of Scripture are infused with spiritual life and passed along from God's mouth to specially designated human beings. More than just words on a page, God's Word found in the Bible is inspired—without error and always trustworthy.

In addition, God's Word serves several specific purposes, among them teaching, rebuking, correcting, and training in righteousness. We'll look at these specific functions closer in chapter 4. For now, however, be assured that just as a paramedic might breathe into a victim's mouth to restore and sustain his life, the God-breathed Word of the Bible can "pink up" an otherwise gray and dying life for anyone who responds to it.

Through the Looking Glass

Do not merely listen to the word, and so deceive yourselves. Do what it says. Anyone who listens to the word but does not do what it says is like a man who looks at his face in a mirror and, after looking at himself, goes away and immediately forgets what he looks like. But the man who looks intently into the perfect law that gives freedom, and continues to do this, not forgetting what he has heard, but doing it—he will be blessed in what he does. (James 1:22–25)

SWORD DRILL

Who came back to life after four days in the grave, after hearing the words of Jesus tell him to do so? (See John 11:38-44.)

We have seen the Word of God compared to fire, a hammer, rain, bread, a sword, and more. But here we get new insight at a very basic level. The Bible should serve as a spiritual mirror of sorts. Suppose you were on your way to a big corporate meeting or anniversary dinner, stopped by the bathroom to check yourself out in the mirror, and discovered food between your teeth, dust bunnies in your hair, grease on your forehead, and some sort of mysterious nasal seepage. Would you give yourself a big thumbs-up and continue on your way just as you are? If so, you might not be invited to many more big corporate meetings or anniversary dinners (at least, not public ones).

Yet how many times do we zip past a Bible passage pointing out changes that need to be made in our lives, and close the covers without making the least little adjustment? The Bible serves as a mirror. We don't have to try very hard to see ourselves in its pages and realize it is speaking to us. Whether or not we respond, the mirror has done its job. If we walk away and do nothing, especially after seeing ourselves for who we truly are, we have only ourselves to blame.

The Real Dirt on God's Word

See how much good stuff we can discover in only 22 verses of Scripture? Just wait till you get to the other 31,151 verses!

Yet let's not get overly optimistic. We all know that merely picking up and reading the Bible doesn't have the same effect on everyone. Lots of people give it a try and give up after a while. Others read it regularly, yet it never quite stops being a chore for them. And some people are regularly excited about what they read and apply. What makes the difference?

Perhaps the best answer is found in the parable of the sower (Mark 4:1–20). Jesus told the story of a farmer who goes out to sow seed. As the farmer tosses the seed onto the ground, some land on the hard path where the birds quickly snatch it up. Some falls in rocky soil, where the plants readily sprout but cannot sink roots deep into the ground and are eventually withered by the sun. Some seed falls among thorns where the growing plants get choked out by the weeds. And some finds its way to the good soil, where it yields a productive crop.

Jesus explained that the seed represents the Word of God. Sometimes Satan intercepts or interferes with God's Word before it takes root in people's lives. Some people respond to God's Word at first and grow rapidly, yet never become rooted and crumble when "the heat is on." Others never divorce themselves from the negative influences in their lives and choke instead of growing as they should. But those who are open to receiving God's Word, who avoid the birds, the stones, and the thorns, are rewarded with "a crop—thirty, sixty or even a hundred times what was sown" (Mark 4:20).

WHAT'S THE GOOD WORD?

Do not be deceived: God cannot be mocked. A man reaps what he sows. The one who sows to please his sinful nature, from that nature will reap destruction; the one who sows to please the Spirit, from the Spirit will reap eternal life.

—GALATIANS 6:7–8

The ultimate effectiveness of God's Word in our lives depends largely on how willing and prepared we are to receive it. If we reject it outright, it's our choice to do so. If it is only one of thousands of other things vying for our attention, it's not likely to grow and flourish in our lives as it should. And if we attempt to grow too quickly, we're not likely to mature as we wish. But if we allow God's Word to take root in our lives and patiently wait for His growing season to arrive, we can count on a cornucopia of wonderful things that just keep coming and coming.

The seed of God's Word is the same for everyone, but the "soil" where it lands is up to you. Some people might need to do a bit of inner "cultivation" before they soften enough for God's Word to take root. Some may need to do some external weeding so that the desire to understand the Bible isn't choked out by the other pressures of life. And some may be expecting to read this single book to become biblically literate and spiritually mature, but spiritual growth is usually much more gradual.

So as you look ahead at the many pages yet to come in this book, consider a pace that will allow you to keep moving without feeling rushed. It's not simply a matter of whipping through the remaining chapters as quickly as possible. Slow down and give God the opportunity to speak to you.

Over the centuries, God has gone to great lengths to provide His Word so that we can read it, hear it, and understand it. He speaks clearly and intently. The big question as we begin is, Are we listening?

Chapter Flashback

1. The Bible was written by an estimated:
   a. Four authors over a four-year period
   b. Forty authors over a four-hundred-year period
   c. Forty authors over a 1,400-year period
   d. Fourteen authors over a case of Diet Mountain Dew

2. Which of the following is *not* such a good reason for believing the Bible?
   a. It describes not only the grand triumphs of God's people throughout history, but it also includes their vast failures and sins.
   b. It is "God-breathed" and therefore accurate and dependable.
   c. Despite its numerous human authors and the time period covered, it is amazingly coherent and applicable.
   d. The author of this guide says you should.

3. The Bible contains all of the following writing styles except:
   a. Haiku
   b. Narrative
   c. Apocalyptic
   d. Poetry and Song

4. The Word of God is compared to which of these lists of things?
   a. Raindrops on roses and whiskers on kittens
   b. Snips and snails and puppy-dog tails
   c. Mask, bracelet, flood, and freezing rain
   d. Fire, bread, rain, a hammer, a mirror, and a sword

5. If you're serious about understanding and applying what's in the Bible, the best results will occur if you are most like:
   a. A beaten path
   b. Rich, lush soil
   c. A thorny weed patch
   d. A rocky patch of land

Answers: (1) c, (2) d, (3) a, (4) d, (5) b

CHAPTER 3

Unshakable Truth Meets Movable Type

HOW GOD'S WORDS GOT ONTO OUR BOOKSHELVES

SNAPSHOT

"Okay, Peter, everything looks good and I think we're ready to proceed today."

"Uh, Mr. Gutenberg, are you still sure you want to begin with *this* project?"

"Peter, we've been planning this job for a long time. As my assistant, you know as well as I do that it has taken Gunther and Franz thirty-seven twelve-hour days just to prepare the characters of type to be used in this project."

"Yes sir, I know. And that's my concern. We're starting with such a . . . *monumental* task."

"Well, what would you suggest instead?"

"Something . . . *shorter*."

"Like what?"

"Perhaps a Top Ten List of, say, 'Ways to Tell You Have Bubonic Plague.' Or how about *Great Minds*

SNEAK PREVIEW

1. The Word of God has been preserved in many different forms throughout the centuries.
2. The accuracy of the Bible is above question by any current standards.
3. Great care has been taken to preserve the content and authenticity of Scripture in its various updates and translations into different languages.

of the Fifteenth Century? That should be a short book. Or you could draw from your personal experience and do *The World's Easiest Guide to Mirror Making.*"

"Those can come later. You know what we've planned for so long. It's 1452. Now is the time for this project."

"If you say so, Mr. Gutenberg. But the whole Bible? Printed on this wooden contraption with movable metal type? What crazy things are people going to attempt next . . . shortcuts to India?"

* * * * * * * * * * * * * * *

Yes, the Bible was the first book to be printed on Johann Gutenberg's innovative printing press with movable type. But even with that newfangled time-saver, it took over three years to produce the first 200 copies. Even the setup for this little task required much planning and preparation. Two pages were printed at a time, requiring more than 505,000 individual pieces of type. And as those two pages were being printed, the next two pages were being set, requiring another 505,000 characters.

Even though Gutenberg's movable-metal-type process required considerably more time than sitting down at a computer terminal and hitting "Print" when finished, still it was a vast improvement over the older ways of bookmaking. And the Bible was the first book to roll off his presses in 1455. Of course, the Bible was still in Latin at the time, so it didn't exactly become an instant best-seller among the masses of uneducated people.

Still, the Bible has long been special among other books. Long before Johannes Gensfleisch zur Laden Gutenberg was born, the Bible already had a lengthy history of being unique among all the other books ever written. We'll get back to Gutenberg and some

BACKGROUND INFO

Before Gutenberg, books were produced by wood engraving. A skilled worker would take a block of wood and cut away everything except what he wished to be printed—either text or illustration. Consequently, books were quite costly because of the intensive time required to produce them. And the wooden plates were fragile, subject to cracking, wearing down, fire, and maybe even hungry termites.

of the distinctions of how the Bible came to be, but first we want to see how it started and what made it distinctive in the first place.

Who Came Up with This Method of Writing a Book?

These days, most books come about as a result of an author or authors who convince a publisher of the validity of a particular topic. The publisher agrees to fund the writer's efforts and put the finished product into print. In return, the author may be expected to provide an outline of what he is going to write and perhaps a sample chapter or two to prove his or her ability to write. Almost always, a contract is provided that spells out the details incumbent on both writer and publisher. Foremost among the details is usually the deadline, at which time the author is expected to be finished and hand over a manuscript to the publisher for the next phase of bookmaking.

When more than one author is involved in a project, the process is further complicated. It becomes a matter of who is going to write what portion of the book and avoiding gaps or unnecessary duplication.

The Bible, however, defies current logic in how it came to be written. We saw in the previous chapter that the Bible has in the neighborhood of forty "authors," none of whom were ever "on deadline" to hurry something along just so it could get published. In fact, a time span of about 1,400 years went by as the Bible was written. If such a project were attempted today, the end result would very likely lead the reader in forty different directions, no two of which would overlap.

BACKGROUND INFO

Consider the difficulty of beginning a writing project today and not having a finished product before the early 3400s! Would anything written today be remotely relevant then?

Yet the Bible stands as not a collection of assorted works, but a coherent, singular work that tells an ongoing story. And millions of people worldwide will bear witness that it is still just as true, accurate, relevant, and applicable as it ever was.

What we want to examine in this chapter is how the Word of God, given to these more than three dozen "writers," went from God's mouth to your eyes. How did the things they received from God end up written in English and bound so nicely in your Bible for easy reference?

"N TH BGNNNG"

What we know as the Old Testament was originally written almost entirely in Hebrew, with a few portions in Aramaic, a similar language that was spoken throughout southwest Asia at the time. Vowels wouldn't be added to the language for several centuries, so the original Hebrew words were all consonants.

Tr rdng ths prgrph wtht vwls. T's nt s sy, s t?

Now try reading *this* paragraph *with* vowels. It's so easy, isn't it?

So even when scribes were able to find reliable documents, the long strings of consonants in the original language were a challenge to interpret and reproduce. Even though the New Testament was written in Greek (again, with just a spattering of Aramaic), the writing style was all capital letters with little punctuation, word separation, or even division into paragraphs.

SONOWTRYREADINGTHISSENTENCEINSUCHASTYLE. When you consider the lengths of some of the names and places throughout the Bible that would be tucked away in these long strings of letters, it doesn't make you want to quit your day job to become a Bible scribe, does it?

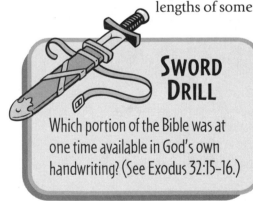

SWORD DRILL

Which portion of the Bible was at one time available in God's own handwriting? (See Exodus 32:15–16.)

But before interpreters could even get to the process of translation, they had to be able to find and read the manuscripts. The nature of early writing made this an additional challenge in many cases. We can sit down with a good reliable Cross ballpoint pen and a stack of durable cotton-based paper, and what we write will last a good long time. Some of the later New Testament Bible manuscripts were on paper, but most of the earlier ones were on either papyrus or parchment.

Papyrus came from a common plant that was cut into strips, layered, dried, and used for writing purposes. But not surprisingly, papyrus became quite fragile with time. Parchment came from animal skins, which made it considerably more durable. First the skin was treated, dried, and specially prepared, which included hair removal. You might think it would be more natural to write on the side of the skin that hadn't been so hairy, and most of the writers did indeed choose that side. However, it turns out that the side of the skin which had the hair removed was better at absorbing and retaining the ink. So while the parchment held up much better than papyrus, the *writing* on it still tended to fade over time.

The Significance of "Holy"

The Greek word for papyrus was *byblos*, and the word for "books" became *biblia*. So all the God-breathed books *(biblia)* that were faithfully written down, preserved, reproduced, and handed down throughout time, eventually became *the* Book *(Bible)*. Although *biblia* was a plural word, our variation, *Bible*, has always been singular.

Of course, these days publishing companies would have long and intense committee meetings to come up with a title a bit more intriguing and attention-getting—perhaps *The Big Thick Book About How to Live*, or *Answers, Promises, and Wonders*, or some other overblown and ineffective title. God's name as author would be large on the front cover, with a long list of His credits and accomplishments on the back. And if that weren't enough, a number of other people would be solicited to say nice things about His work to help convince you to buy His Book.

WHAT'S THE GOOD WORD?

As obedient children, do not conform to the evil desires you had when you lived in ignorance. But just as he who called you is holy, so be holy in all you do; for it is written: "Be holy, because I am holy."

–1 PETER 1:14–16; SEE ALSO LEVITICUS 11:44–45

But the addition of the word "Holy" has always been enough to distinguish the significance of the Bible from any other book. Indeed, *holy* implies something that has been set apart. God is holy, far removed from the sinfulness of humankind. The Holy Place and Most Holy Place in the Israelite tabernacle and temples were places symbolic of God's presence, set apart for only the priests.

To enter the Most Holy Place uninvited or inappropriately, even if you *were* a priest, could result in death.

Just as God's person is holy—set high above that of anyone or anything else in the universe—so is His Word to be elevated above all other self-help books, advice columns, how-to manuals, or any other print resources at our disposal today. It is upheld as an unquestionable source of truth by Christians, and will remain the standard by which to live. That's what the "Holy" means as an adjective to "Bible."

SWORD DRILL

What hard lesson did a guy named Uzzah learn about holy things? (See 2 Samuel 6:1–7 and Numbers 4:15.)

People who disregarded holy things were put to death during Old Testament times. People who disregard God's Word today clearly don't drop dead immediately (which is a good thing for all of us). But we do miss out on much of the "abundant life" that Jesus promises is possible, and if we dare disregard certain portions of God's Word, we miss out on eternity with Him when this life is over.

Problems, Concerns, and Arguments

Yet some people find numerous reasons to dispute the authority of the Bible. They say it was written by men, and men make mistakes. They say it was written so long ago that it is no longer relevant to our lives in the twenty-first century. They say that even if it started out as the authoritative Word of God, all the translators throughout the centuries have "edited" it to serve their own purposes. And, actually, these are all valid concerns for anyone not brought up with a respect for or understanding of the Bible.

The Matter of Authorship

As we saw in the previous chapter, God chose to use human beings to record His Word. But they were specially selected, spiritually enlightened individuals who recorded just what God told them. And isn't it somewhat comforting to know that those "authors" shared the same questions, sufferings, joys, and other common experiences that all people have?

We can also enjoy the variety of styles of writing. Some readers are drawn to the emotional, poetic expressions of David's psalms. Others prefer straightforward historical narratives, such as Exodus or Acts. People are different, but there's something there for everyone.

For example, each of the Gospels (Matthew, Mark, Luke, and John) is a description of the life of Jesus, yet we benefit greatly from being able to read all four accounts, because we may find truths in one that the other authors chose not to include. Matthew seems to focus primarily on Jewish readers, while Luke's message appears more Gentile-oriented. This difference, however, doesn't make one Gospel any more or less important than the others.

Just because God selected certain people to record His inspired Word doesn't mean the writers were all clones of one another. His chosen writers pass along His message with different styles, but with equally reliable authenticity.

If God had completely bypassed human messengers, we might be inclined to ignore what He was saying simply because He is at a level so superior to our own. Our struggles wouldn't even faze Him. But by communicating through people who empathize with us, His Word takes on a greater sense of reality and relevance.

The Matter of Relevance

And speaking of relevance, how about the argument that the Bible was written too long ago to speak to people today? Certainly, much of it seems like ancient history, because it is. Lots of the prophecies, for example, predict that both Israel and Judah would be defeated and taken into captivity, which they were. Others promise they would be delivered from captivity, which they were. So what's the point for us?

Certainly, much of the Bible might be perceived as just another lesson in history. But its lessons should be seen as *spiritual* ones, not merely *historical* ones. The Bible, as we have seen, is essentially an ongoing story of a powerful yet loving God and how He relates to His people. And while people change and we see ourselves as far more informed and sophisticated than a bunch of nomadic tribes wandering through the deserts of Sinai, God doesn't change. He has always existed and will always continue to exist as a perfect, complete Being. People can improve, but God never can. So the God who related with Adam and Eve, with

Moses and the Israelites, with David and the kings, with the prophets, and with the first-century church is exactly the same God we worship today.

What God declared as truth 4,000 years before Christ came is still true. We may no longer be tempted to drift from God to worship Baal or set up Asherah poles in our yards, but we are still tempted to drift from God to pursue other priorities. We no longer are asked to bring perfect cattle as sacrifices to God, but we are commanded to place ourselves on the altar, figuratively, as living sacrifices (Romans 12:1). You may not covet your neighbor's ox or donkey, but don't tell me you weren't a bit covetous when he brought home that new Jaguar. (Different "animal," same basic feeling of envy.)

WHAT'S THE GOOD WORD?

He who is the Glory of Israel does not lie or change his mind; for he is not a man, that he should change his mind.

—1 Samuel 15:29

So while various specifics have changed over the centuries, the underlying truths remain. The Bible is still as relevant at steering us through the difficulties of life as it ever was.

Some take offense that the Bible gets so specific about how slaves are to relate to masters, or women to men. These were hot issues when it was written, and the people of God went on record saying there was a right and wrong way to handle things. But is it really too much a stretch to apply those master/slave passages to boss/employee relationships? And if we dare to look closely, we start to see that voluntary submission to others is supposed to be a universal practice among all Christians—not just a mandate for slaves, women, and other selected groups (see, for example, Romans 13:1; Ephesians 5:21).

The Matter of Possible Errors by Translators

But how about that other question: How do we know that the Bible we read today is actually what God dictated to His designated writers centuries ago? That's where we get back to the importance of the papyrus and parchment manuscripts. And it is surprising how much evidence is available to show that the copying and recopying throughout the centuries has maintained an accuracy and authenticity that is beyond question.

Archaeologists simply don't find copies of the *Odyssey* in Homer's handwriting, or Leviticus in Moses' own penmanship. Our acceptance of ancient literature is not based on original manuscripts, because none exists. So one key indication to how trustworthy documents are is how little time has lapsed between the original writing and the earliest copy we can find. The suspicion is that with each successive copy, the likelihood of crucial mistakes can increase.

The average gap for much ancient literature is about 1,000 years. For example, Aristotle lived and wrote from 364 to 322 B.C. Five copies of his work exist, the earliest dating to around 1100 A.D.—a gap of 1,400 years. Similar gaps are found in the writings of Caesar, Euripides, Herodotus, Tacitus, and other old-timers. And in most cases, relatively few copies of the work exist at all. Next to the Bible, Homer's *Iliad* holds the record with almost 650 copies. So it's not unusual for us to trust old writings based on these criteria.

For much of our contemporary history, we were working with copies of Old Testament documents that dated back to about 900 A.D. The final portion of the Old Testament had been written in about 400 B.C., so the lapse was a bit higher than the average, yet not unreasonable. But when a shepherd stumbled onto the caves containing the Dead Sea Scrolls in 1947, he uncovered much older copies of the Old Testament. All the books were represented except the Book of Esther, and the scrolls dated back to about 150 B.C.—more than a thousand years earlier than those we already had! And when the scholars finished comparing the 150 B.C. version with the 900 A.D. version, more than 95 percent of the work was word-for-word identical. The other 5 percent consisted almost entirely of spelling variations or updates of archaic words or grammar. No significant alterations were found.

BACKGROUND INFO

Even if every single copy of the New Testament had been destroyed, it was so frequently quoted that we could examine the works of the early church fathers and retrieve all but eleven verses!

Clearly, the people who copied the Scriptures did so with the greatest care and accuracy. They held themselves to the highest standards involving not only the meticulous work they did, but even the quality of the animal skins and ink used in the process. The scribes literally counted every letter and every word to verify that a copy was exactly like its predecessor. And they would count to verify the middle letter of each scroll. If a single mistake was found, the new copy was immediately destroyed.

In the case of the New Testament, copies of portions have been found that date to within a generation of the original, with whole books within 100 (rather than 1,000) years and its entirety within 250 years of the original writing.

In addition to the short time lapses and minimal variations, the copies of biblical manuscripts far outnumber those of any other ancient work. And new discoveries of old manuscripts are being made on a regular basis. (It is amazing how much new discoveries have tended to verify what Christians already believe rather than create any crises of faith.)

Most recent counts of Greek New Testament documents fall between 5,300 and 5,500, with almost twice that many copies of the Latin Vulgate. In total, when we add other older versions, there are more than 24,000 manuscript portions of the New Testament. Some people estimate that the number of Bible manuscripts available is more than thirty times that for any other book, and that the Bible has more manuscript evidence than any ten other works of ancient literature combined.

BACKGROUND INFO

A **jot** (or iota) was the smallest Greek letter, much like our letter **i,** and the **tittle** was the equivalent of the dot above the **i**. To be sure to include every jot and tittle was like saying to dot all the i's and cross all the t's. The phrase is used in the King James Version of Matthew 5:18.

A Few Exceptions to the Rule

Of course, none of this matters much if we don't believe what was written in the first place. But such statistics should remove any suspicion that shady scribes throughout the ages may have altered the original content of the Bible. In terms of time references, accuracy in translation, and sheer numbers of available manuscripts, the Bible sets an unparalleled standard.

This is not to say that it is impossible for people to get things wrong. God doesn't magically ensure that every single person who translates His Word from one form to another will avoid mistakes. Perhaps some of our fears arise based on what we've seen come off the presses *after* Mr. Gutenberg's use of movable type. Apparently, the later we get in history, the harder it is to find conscientious scribes with the same determination to get every "jot and tittle" just right.

In the past few centuries, we have seen a number of glitches from the original that were quickly corrected, yet still tend to raise concern from time to time. For example:

➤ A Bible printed in Oxford in 1792 noted that it was Philip (rather than Peter) who would deny Christ (Luke 22:34).

➤ A Bible in the mid-1600s misprinted Psalm 14:1 to read, "The fool hath said in his heart there is a God" (instead of "there is no God"). The printers were fined and all copies quickly confiscated.

➤ A Bible version in 1611 erroneously printed that it was Judas (rather than Jesus) who went with his disciples to Gethsemane (Matthew 26:36).

➤ A 1562 edition read, "Blessed are the placemakers" (Matthew 5:9).

➤ In the first Bible printed in Ireland (1716), Jesus tells a man to "sin on more" rather than "sin no more" (John 5:14).

➤ Somehow, a heading in a 1717 Bible became the Parable of the Vinegar instead of the Parable of the Vineyard (Luke 20:9–16).

➤ A 1572 edition included a woodcut of the Roman myth of Jupiter seducing Leda disguised as a swan, quite out of place at the beginning of the Book of Hebrews.

➤ And in perhaps the worst offense of all, a 1631 Bible missed a key word in Exodus 20:14 and changed one of the Ten Commandments to "Thou shalt commit adultery."

There are other similar instances of flubs and misprints throughout the centuries, yet considering the number of Bible versions that have been published and the significant length of each one, the mistakes have been surprisingly few. Still, it's enough to make some people wonder how much they can trust what they read after all the translations and language adaptations have taken place. But we have such an abundance of old and authentic manuscripts that any such mistakes can be easily identified and corrected.

Why the Bible Is No Longer Greek to Us

And with these few clunkers aside, different dependable versions of the Bible have continued to be produced until today. Several of the changes have been due to shifts in language. When Greek became the universal tongue, the Hebrew Old Testament was translated into the more widely recognized Greek (about 250 B.C. to 150 B.C.). When Latin replaced Greek, a version of the Bible was produced known as the Vulgate, translated by Jerome between 383 and 405 A.D.

But with the fall of the Roman Empire, the European continent became a war-torn mix of languages and cultures. Along came the bubonic plague and the Middle Ages. Few people could read and write, much less in Latin. A number of English-speaking countries were eventually established, yet the Bible was still in Latin and could be read only by clergy and monks.

It seemed a logical idea to translate the Bible into English, which is exactly what John Wycliffe decided to do in the mid-fourteenth century. He finished the New Testament in 1380 and the Old Testament two years later, in spite of opposition from the church. (At the time, it was possible to purchase positions in the church's highly structured hierarchy, which was an effective church fund-raiser. Wycliffe and others felt all the layers of church leadership were interfering with common people receiving and genuinely understanding the Bible.)

Wycliffe's version was a translation of the Latin Bible—not of the original languages. Wycliffe and his team went about reading what they had translated to those who would listen, finding many eager audiences along the way. Wycliffe died in 1384, but in 1396 the church dug him up and burned his bones, tossing the remains into a local river.

By 1408 the church had issued a decree forbidding any further translations of the Bible without church approval. And six years later the restrictions were tightened so that anyone even reading Scripture in English would be required to "forfeit land, catel, life, and goods from their heyres for ever."

But the times, they were a-changing. The fifteenth century was a period of curiosity and enlightenment. Columbus sailed the seas to discover a new world, and Galileo peered into the heavens. Numerous others turned their attention to science and other fields of learning. And after Gutenberg started mass-producing Bibles in Latin, it was just a matter of time until the Word of God found its way into more and more languages.

William Tyndale picked up in the sixteenth century where Wycliffe had left off. After failing to get the church's endorsement, Tyndale went ahead with a New Testament translation of his own and found a printer to publish it (but he had to leave England and go to Germany to do so).

> ## SWORD DRILL
>
> Human language originally became "confused" at the tower of Babel (Genesis 11:1-9). But where in the Bible did a large group of people of various nationalities all hear about Jesus, unexpectedly, in their own native languages? (See Acts 2:1-12.)

Tyndale worked from the original New Testament Greek, and he made corrections and improvements with each new printing. Copies were smuggled into England, hidden in cotton bales, bundles of flax, sacks of flour, and such. He started a translation of the Old Testament and completed several books, but for his efforts he was eventually convicted of heresy, strangled, and burned at the stake. Shortly after his death, however, the church saw that the demand for an English Bible was too great to ignore.

Who Authorized the Authorized Version?

A number of other Bible translations popped up in the 1500s, many based largely on the work of Wycliffe or Tyndale. But the groundbreaking work was the Authorized King James Version of the Bible. In 1603, James VI of Scotland took the throne as James I of England. Henry VIII had rejected the pope's authority (because the pope wouldn't grant his request for a divorce), and Protestantism was established in England. Later rulers switched back to Catholicism, and then back to Protestantism. Each new ruler would have his or her favorite version of the Bible and tended to cast aspersions on other translations.

One of the first things James I did was call a conference of bishops and Puritan leaders to try to settle many of the differences that had arisen within the church.

One leader suggested a new translation of the Bible to do away with the "dueling Bibles" problems of the past. James was no big fan of the current Bible and quickly resolved to move ahead with a new one.

BACKGROUND INFO

Even though the King James Version was based largely on one of the existing Bibles (with help from some of the other versions), it took about fifty years before it became a popular, then the favorite, version. But after it did, it remained the most widespread Bible of English-speaking Protestants throughout most of the twentieth century.

He selected fifty-four of the top Hebrew and Greek scholars available (of which forty-seven eventually participated when the project began four years later). After two years of intensive work (without pay) and nine months of reexamination and revision, the team was finished. The King James Version (or Authorized Version) of the Bible was first published in 1611.

The King James Version eventually became so identified as the official Word of God that later attempts to further modify the language of the Bible were met with stringent opposition. Even though the English language changed significantly over four centuries, and even though many older (and most would say, more reliable) manuscripts were uncovered during that time, some people clung to the King James Version as the only trustworthy Bible.

Various levels of intensity have arisen in this ongoing debate, with an outspoken few claiming the King James Version of 1611 is inspired by God to the point of becoming more authoritative than even the original manuscripts, and that any other version is inaccurate, heretical, and clearly of the devil. (Such people have been labeled "onlyites.")

Certainly, there were advantages to having a single version of Scripture. Many enjoyed (and still do) the poetry and phrasing of the Early Modern English language. People could memorize and recite Scripture together without various translations making it awkward. And the words and phrases that brought a person to God were treasured, so the person might naturally want others to hear and believe those same words as well.

Others find such arguments unconvincing, shortsighted, and naïve. Why possibly overlook older, more trustworthy manuscripts? Why continue to read and teach from an archaic language that new generations of seekers find foreign and awkward? Besides, the 1611 King James Version spoke of unicorns and used other odd terminology that created potential suspicion and/or confusion.

Many were convinced it was time for an updated translation of Scripture based on the older Hebrew and Greek manuscripts that were being discovered. Besides, linguists had developed a better understanding of the old Hebrew language than was available to those on the King James team, leading to more accurate translations of certain words. So the English Revised Version came out in the late 1800s, followed by the American Standard Version in the early 1900s.

WHAT'S THE GOOD WORD?

The grass withers and the flowers fall, but the word of our God stands forever.

–Isaiah 40:8

At about the same time, many thousands of Greek papyri were uncovered in Egypt, revealing that the New Testament had been written in "everyday" Greek (the colloquial language of the people) rather than classical Greek. This discovery encouraged a number of interpreters to create fresh translations in contemporary English, and the trend continues until today.

We've seen *The New Testament in Modern English*, *The Amplified Bible*, *The Revised Standard Version*, *The New Revised Standard Bible*, *The New English Bible*, *The New American Standard Version*, *The New International Version*, *The New King James Version*, and more. One of the newest translations currently being released is *Today's New International Version* which, among other things, is attempting to use more gender-inclusive language in places where the original versions don't specify a gender preference.

In addition to these literal translations of Scripture, paraphrased versions (restatements of translations using contemporary idioms to make the text clearer) have also become quite popular and widespread. Among the earliest and most popular is *The Living Bible* (TLB), which began as one man's attempt to make the Bible more understandable for his own children. Another popular paraphrase still in the works (at this writing) is *The Message,* with the New Testament already published and the first portions of the Old Testament just being released.

So in a nutshell, that's how the Word of God has gone from being heard by faithful people, recorded on papyrus or animal skin, translated from Greek or Hebrew or Aramaic, and ending up on your bookstore shelf or in your hotel room drawer. If you investigate its history for yourself, any doubts as to its reliability and authenticity should be put to rest. We can trust what the Bible has to say because we can trust that God originally said it.

Enough said?

Chapter Flashback

1. The Bible was originally written in:
   a. Hebrew, Latin, and Greek
   b. Hebrew, Greek, and Aramaic
   c. Latin, Greek, and Aramaic
   d. King James English

2. Early versions of the Bible did not include:
   a. Old Testament prophecies on scrolls
   b. New Testament sections on paper
   c. The Psalms in MP3 format
   d. Various portions on papyrus and parchment

3. The adjective "holy" means the Bible:
   a. Is set apart from all other books and writings
   b. Should never be touched
   c. Is an official religious document
   d. Needs some Spackle

4. John Wycliffe and William Tyndale are:
   a. Members of the King James translating team
   b. Two people primarily responsible for your being able to read the Bible in English

    c. Original members of Fleetwood Mac

    d. Two college professors

5. The printer first responsible for mass-producing the Bible was:

    a. King James I

    b. Steve Guttenberg

    c. Johann Gutenberg

    d. Garth Brooksenberg

Answers: (1) b, (2) c, (3) a, (4) b, (5) c

My Word!

THE IMPORTANCE OF PERSONALLY KNOWING AND APPLYING WHAT'S IN THE BIBLE

SNAPSHOT

A young man, far away from his beloved fiancée, receives a letter from her. He finds a place where he can be alone to read her words and think about each precious one.

The Letter: *My dearest love, I miss you so much.*

The Guy: *[Thinking to himself:]* Speaking of missing, Kobe Bryant was throwing bricks last night. That basketball game was a lot closer than it should have been.

The Letter: *It's been such a long time since I've heard from you. How have you been?*

The Guy: *[Sniffing the air:]* As soon as I finish this letter, I need to remember to buy some Odor Eaters. These shoes are starting to smell like beached bass in the hot sun.

The Letter: *I keep hoping to hear from you, you handsome guy.*

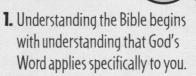

SNEAK PREVIEW

1. Understanding the Bible begins with understanding that God's Word applies specifically to you.
2. If you find Bible reading too difficult, perhaps you need to consider a different translation.
3. The primary goal of reading the Bible shouldn't be to understand the Bible better but to understand God better.

The Guy:	*[Scratching hip:]* Then I need to get some antiseptic. This boil I've been sitting on could blow any day now.
The Letter:	*You are very special to me. My love for you is perfect and complete. When we're together, I feel tremendous joy.*
The Guy:	Rats! I forgot to take out the garbage today—and the kitchen already could pass for a toxic waste dump.
The Letter:	*I recall all the special times we've spent together—every second of every minute. Words cannot express the passion I feel for you.*
The Guy:	*[Massive yawn]* I've got to start getting more sleep.
The Letter:	*I only hope you feel the same way about me. I'll be yours forever. I promise that the next time we meet . . .*
The Guy:	*[Another yawn]* Maybe I'll read the rest of this later. If I remember. *[Folds letter, sticks in back pocket, and lies down to nap.]*

* * * * * * * * * * * * * *

Perhaps the behavior of the young man in this scenario seems inordinately callous, bizarre, or even deranged. After all, if you've made a commitment to someone, and that person has gone all out to express his or her love and devotion to you, shouldn't such an expression be regarded with utmost excitement and joy?

God's Word as recorded in the Bible is such an expression of love, devotion, sacrifice, passion, total acceptance, and much more. Yet how many of us can honestly say we haven't at times allowed our minds to wander while Bible reading—much as the self-absorbed guy in the previous scenario? If we treated other people's communications to us the same way we treat God's, those people would want nothing more to do with us. Thankfully, God is more forgiving.

Still, God was quite intentional in providing us with His Word. When we yawn or whine our way through regular Bible reading, we dishonor many of His faithful people who have gone to a lot of trouble over the centuries to ensure God's message was recorded. Just because a slacker high school student doesn't see the purpose in learning the periodic table or quadratic equations doesn't mean they aren't important. He had better learn them anyway—until the exam, at least. Similarly, great biblical truths await discovery whether or not we ever choose to absorb them.

Doesn't the Bible Say ...?

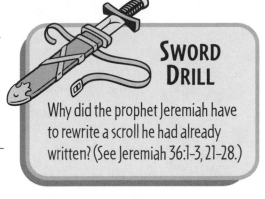

SWORD DRILL

Why did the prophet Jeremiah have to rewrite a scroll he had already written? (See Jeremiah 36:1–3, 21–28.)

Many of us grow up not with a personal regimen of Bible reading and comprehensive study but rather with a host of assumptions—many based on what other people have *told* us the Bible says. And armed only with those assumptions (which may or may not be correct), many people are willing to get into intense discussions on what they think concerning heavy theological topics: What is God like? What happens when we die? Is hell a reality? Would a loving God really condemn anyone to eternal punishment? And so forth.

The trouble is, their assumptions may be based on sources other than God's Word. Some of those sources may indeed be things they trust—parents, church, Christian friends, and others. Yet if they never pursue biblical truth for themselves, they are unable to cite specific references, and they begin to ask vague questions that frequently start with, "Doesn't the Bible say somewhere that . . . ?" Perhaps you've been confronted with such questions:

➤ Doesn't the Bible say women aren't as important as men?

➤ Doesn't the Bible say that Christians should never associate with nonbelievers?

➤ Doesn't the Bible say that whites are superior to blacks?

➤ Doesn't the Bible say we should handle poisonous snakes to prove our faith in God?

Indeed, the Bible has been used to defend each of these suppositions, but that has little to do with what the Bible actually says. For example, Christian wives *are* asked to submit to their husbands (Ephesians 5:22), but there are clear expectations on the part of the husband as well (Ephesians 5:25–33). And the

Bible adds that from God's perspective, He sees no distinction at all among people who place their faith in Him.

Yes, the Bible says Christians should not be "yoked together" or "teamed up" with those who are unbelievers (2 Corinthians 6:14). So are the Amish correct in their attempt to withdraw from secular society? Perhaps. But the Bible also shows instance after instance of Jesus reaching out to unbelievers and making eternal differences in their lives—and tells us to imitate His example (John 4:1–26; Ephesians 5:1–2; Philippians 2:5; etc.).

WHAT'S THE GOOD WORD?

There is neither Jew nor [Gentile], slave nor free, male nor female, for you are all one in Christ Jesus. If you belong to Christ, then you are Abraham's seed, and heirs according to the promise.

– GALATIANS 3:28–29

One must significantly contort the clear truths of Scripture to support white supremacy, yet you can find white supremacists able to quote certain portions of Scripture like a pastor. They dwell on a curse Noah placed on one of his sons who supposedly fathered the dark-skinned races . . . or some such line of thinking. But again, the clear truths of New Testament Scripture indicate that God does not show favoritism (Acts 10:34–35; Romans 2:11; Ephesians 6:9; Colossians 3:25; James 2:9; etc.). Nor should we.

SWORD DRILL

What happened after Paul was bitten by a poisonous viper and nothing bad happened to him? (See Acts 28:1-6.)

As for the handling of poisonous snakes, some rural churches make this a regular practice, although the Bible never actually tells us to test our faith in such ways. A primary reference is found in the final verses of the gospel of Mark (16:9–20), which also refers to drinking deadly poison without harm. In crisis situations, God may indeed see fit to deliver His people in miraculous ways. But that doesn't mean we're given a guarantee of His safety if we choose to go around doing foolish things.

Becoming More Head Strong
(Adding Context to Content)

So it's not always wise to make broad, ironclad rules based on just a verse or two of a Bible passage. We are challenged to love God with not only our whole hearts and souls, but with our whole minds as well (Mark 12:30). And how can we love God with a sound mind if we're dealing in half-truths about what He has told us?

For example, a peculiar couple of verses are found in the Book of Proverbs: "Do not answer a fool according to his folly or you will be like him yourself. Answer a fool according to his folly, or he will be wise in his own eyes" (Proverbs 26:4–5). So which is it? Are we to answer a fool according to his folly or not? Isn't this a clear contradiction in the Bible?

Then again, can't a case be made that each of these approaches might be the correct tactic, depending on the situation? For example, have you ever seen a television talk show where one person on a panel expresses an outrageous opinion and all the other (usually reasonable) members end up spending the entire time arguing with him? The ramblings of the "fool" are all that get covered, and usually the other people wind up looking just as foolish as he is. So there are times when it is more prudent to ignore such foolishness for the common good.

But now suppose that you're in a setting where the topic moves to religion and someone is passing himself off as an expert. It's clear the person is quite misinformed, yet his personality makes everything he says sound like gospel truth. Eventually, you hear him summarize his beliefs with the statement that, "I understand that Jesus never personally made the claim to be God, so I don't put much stock in Christianity." It seems he has convinced the entire group that he is correct.

Do you simply walk away from him? Perhaps. Or maybe you find a nearby Bible, point to John 10:30, and ask, "What do you suppose Jesus meant when He said, 'I and the Father are one'?" If a silence ensues, flip over a few pages to John 14:9 and add, "Jesus said here that anyone who had seen Him had seen God the Father. How do you explain that?"

You may not change the person's mind with any amount of reason or proof. But you at least have answered the foolish statements, and those listening are not so easily deceived by such foolishness.

WHAT'S THE GOOD WORD?

Always be prepared to give an answer to everyone who asks you to give the reason for the hope that you have. But do this with gentleness and respect, keeping a clear conscience, so that those who speak maliciously against your good behavior in Christ may be ashamed of their slander.

−1 PETER 3:15-16

This is just one example of using our heads when it comes to biblical mandates. If we make it a hard and fast rule to share every bit of truth we know at every opportunity in an attempt to single-handedly eliminate foolishness from the face of the earth, we quickly become as annoying as those cult members who attempt to thrust pamphlets on us as we're hurrying through the airport. But if we never rebut the false things we hear, we miss opportunities for meaningful conversation about God, faith, and spiritual things. You never know when you may be the person God intends to use to make an eternal difference in someone else's life.

It is always wise to seek the larger context of Scripture for any portion we read. If you are focusing too heavily on one particular verse or passage, and some other believer is focusing too heavily on some other verse or passage, you may find yourselves at odds and arguing about something trivial, when in fact Scripture contains so much more you should be agreeing on.

A Better Grip on Scripture

As you personally begin to read and comprehend what's in the Bible, you'll quickly see how frequently it is misquoted or misrepresented. In fact, one reason many people are so reluctant to approach Bible reading is because they fear what they've heard from other people about how difficult it is to absorb, how harsh it is toward certain groups of people, and other things that are not necessarily true.

It is imperative to see for yourself what God has to say. Yes, you should probably expect a certain degree of confusion when you are first hit with all the history, geography, genealogy, funny names, and other fascinating portions of Scripture.

(After all, you wouldn't expect to give the works of Shakespeare a quick read through and feel you really understood the Bard.) But with time, repetition, and piecing together what you're learning, you're likely to be surprised at how much you never knew and how you can now make sense of things that previously perplexed you.

If a young child has a father who works long hours and is not home as much as he wishes, the mother might frequently say, "Your father is working for you, and he loves you very much." But unless the child also hears affirmation from the father's own lips, he is likely to begin to question the reality of the father's love. Similarly, we've all been told that God loves people. But until we personally hear from Him—from His Word—we don't comprehend the depths of His love and the extent of what He has already done for us and has in store for our futures. Hearing a pastor or TV evangelist say the words is nowhere close to reading them yourself and sensing that God is speaking directly to you.

As people first begin to read the Bible for themselves, a common experience is that all the biblical promises begin to jump out at them—life to the full, eternity with God in heaven, unexplainable peace in the midst of troubles, and much more. Hundreds of promises are tucked away within the passages of Scripture, and some people pursue Bible reading like a treasure hunt.

Then, with time, some of the other passages begin to sink in. After seeing "what's in it for me," we begin to notice what's expected *from* us. Are we *really* supposed to love our enemies . . . and strive for

BACKGROUND INFO

Here's some helpful advice from Richard Baxter, an English Puritan who lived and wrote in the seventeenth century: "In necessary things, unity; in doubtful things, liberty; in all things, charity."

WHAT'S THE GOOD WORD?

And I pray that you, being rooted and established in love, may have power, together with all the saints, to grasp how wide and long and high and deep is the love of Christ, and to know this love that surpasses knowledge–that you may be filled to the measure of all the fullness of God.

–Ephesians 3:17-19

perfection (Matthew 5:43–48)? Are we really expected to let someone cheat us without taking the cheater to court (1 Corinthians 6:7)? Are we really going to be held accountable on Judgment Day for every careless word we speak (Matthew 12:36)?

When new Bible readers start absorbing some of these more weighty passages, one of two things usually happens. One group of readers pretty much stops looking so hard. Their Bible Promise Treasure Hunt may continue, but once the knowledge of these more challenging passages kicks in, the promises don't even seem as encouraging. Therefore, Bible reading and understanding slows considerably or stops altogether.

Devoted seekers, however, become just as attentive to the harder challenges as they are to the promises, and they begin to see how obedience to the commands is interconnected with the fulfillment of the promises. The promises fix their attention on God and keep them motivated as they begin the challenge of practicing their faith in practical ways. As the next part of this guide propels us from Genesis through Revelation, we're going to look at the totality of Scripture—both promises and challenges. To focus too heavily on either one at the exclusion of the other can lead to a terribly unbalanced understanding of the Bible.

God's Good Breath

WHAT'S THE GOOD WORD?

Do your best to present yourself to God as one approved, a workman who does not need to be ashamed and who correctly handles the word of truth.

– 2 TIMOTHY 2:15

A number of good reasons to read the Bible are found in 2 Timothy 3:16–17: "All Scripture is God-breathed and is useful for teaching, rebuking, correcting and training in righteousness, so that the man of God may be thoroughly equipped for every good work."

To begin with, Paul is reminding Timothy (and us) that *all* the Bible is "God-breathed." With this confirmation in mind, we then see some specific ways the Bible is intended to speak to us: teaching, rebuking, correcting, and training in righteousness.

Teaching

The Bible teaches us about God, Jesus, angels, heaven and hell, and the unseen spiritual world all around us. But the Bible also teaches us about ourselves. It gives us God's perspective on humankind, which is quite different than many of the other philosophies we hear promoted. In some cases, we will see that God places a much higher value on us than we would ever place on ourselves. In other cases, we may discover that a misguided, overblown sense of self-worth will deflate with the slightest heavenly pinprick. But most of the lessons of Scripture will be positive ones as we learn to distinguish truth from error.

Rebuking

So as we move into the second function of Scripture that Paul lists, we should not be offended if we find ourselves rebuked by some of what we read in the Bible. That's what it's there for. We act in defiance of God, and His Word calls us on it. Salvation doesn't put an end to our sin; neither does Bible reading. We will struggle with temptation and sin until we die and God replaces our temporary, sin-stained bodies with perfect eternal ones (1 Corinthians 15:42–44).

SWORD DRILL

Who did Jesus once rebuke with the phrase "Get behind me, Satan!"? (See Matthew 16:23.)

But unfortunately, one of the prevailing sins among Christians is pride. We get excited about Bible reading, we develop a bit of understanding, and before long we think we've learned all we need to know about God. But as we continue reading, we are reminded of the importance of genuine, hard-to-come-by Christian traits: humility, service, sacrifice, and more. For those of us fostering sin (whether intentionally or unintentionally), sometimes the simple truth of Scripture stings like a slap of rebuke.

Correcting

Other times we simply need a nudge of correction. Isaiah the prophet reminds us, "We all, like sheep, have gone astray, each of us has turned to his own way" (Isaiah 53:6). This is true of believers and nonbelievers, new Christians and mature ones. But as a good shepherd uses his rod to gently tap the shoulder of an errant lamb

about to wander down a dangerous road or over a steep cliff, so the Good Shepherd uses Scripture to keep us on track—if we're willing to respond.

Few of us like to be corrected, much less rebuked. We may resist such things—even if the source is the Bible itself. But we shouldn't, because no one is exempt. No one can read the Bible cover to cover and think, *Yep, I'm doing everything it says to do, all day every day.*

Training in Righteousness

If we want to minimize the correcting and rebuking, we can devote ourselves more intently to the teaching portions and the final of the four specifics named by Paul: training in righteousness. Literally, this word meant "child-training." New believers who are "born again" find themselves in a state of spiritual infancy. Just as we might train our children in music with piano lessons or in baseball with Little League, we need to train ourselves in righteousness by reading and applying what the Bible has to say. The better we learn those lessons in righteousness, the less we will need to be corrected and/or rebuked.

But whether we're growing as spiritual children, learning hard lessons as mature spiritual adults, or being rebuked and corrected in between, we dare not lose sight that all Scripture is indeed God-breathed and directed at us. It's tempting (and rather easy) to subconsciously come to believe that the promises are for me and the tough challenges are for other people. So that's exactly why we need to get personally involved with Scripture. Not only do we see the whole picture, but we see it from a clear perspective.

WHAT'S THE GOOD WORD?

Like newborn babies, crave pure spiritual milk, so that by it you may grow up in your salvation, now that you have tasted that the Lord is good.

–1 PETER 2:2-3

Avoiding Version Aversion

In the previous chapter, it was mentioned that numerous translations and paraphrases of the Bible have been published throughout the centuries, with no small slew of them in recent years. If you're looking to go into (or get back into) a regimen of personal Bible reading, you may find yourself shopping for a Bible and befuddled by the vast number of options you find on the shelves of your local bookstore.

Perhaps you have a King James Version you were given as a child, or one that has been handed down as a family heirloom. The KJV was the Bible of choice for centuries, and it may be your preference as well. If so, just be aware that you may need help with some of the 400-year-old words and contexts that no longer make sense and need explanation. Your challenge will be greater than that of someone who uses a more contemporary translation, but God still speaks clearly through His Word.

Another concern is how accurate you want your version to be. Do you just want a simple read through without devoting much time for study or contemplation? If so, you might choose a paraphrase instead of a literal translation. You'll get the basic gist of every aspect of Scripture in familiar language. Just be aware that even though these paraphrases are usually quite accurate, they aren't literal translations. You probably don't want to establish dogma or doctrines based on any paraphrase of Scripture. If you want something more precise and literal, yet still not as foreboding to read as the King James Version, you might want to look into *The New American Standard Version, the New International Version,* or some similar modern English translation. And if the elegant-sounding King James Version is still tops on your list, be aware that *The New King James Version* has dealt with many of the most difficult to understand passages, yet retains the style that many people prefer.

Below are a couple of familiar passages as they are found in three different translations (the King James Version, *The New American Standard,* and *The New International Version)* and two paraphrases *(The Living Bible* and *The Message).*

Ephesians 2:8–9
KJV: "For by grace are ye saved through faith; and that not of yourselves: it is the gift of God: not of works, lest any man should boast."

NASB: "For by grace you have been saved through faith; and that not of yourselves, it is the gift of God; not as a result of works, so that no one may boast."

NIV: "For it is by grace you have been saved, through faith—and this not from yourselves, it is the gift of God—not by works, so that no one can boast."

TLB: "Because of his kindness you have been saved through trusting Christ. And even trusting is not of yourselves; it too is a gift from God. Salvation is not a reward for the good we have done, so none of us can take any credit for it."

The Message: "Saving is all his idea, and all his work. All we do is trust him enough to let him do it. It's God's gift from start to finish! We don't play the major role. If we did, we'd probably go around bragging that we'd done the whole thing! No, we neither make nor save ourselves."

The Lord's Prayer (Matthew 6:9–13)

KJV: "Our Father which art in heaven, hallowed be thy name. Thy kingdom come. Thy will be done in earth, as it is in heaven. Give us this day our daily bread. And forgive us our debts, as we forgive our debtors. And lead us not into temptation, but deliver us from evil: For thine is the kingdom, and the power, and the glory, for ever. Amen."

NASB: "Our Father who is in heaven, hallowed be Your name. Your kingdom come. Your will be done, on earth as it is in heaven. Give us this day our daily bread. And forgive us our debts, as we also have forgiven our debtors. And do not lead us into temptation, but deliver us from evil. [For Yours is the kingdom and the power and the glory forever. Amen.]"

SWORD DRILL

What prompted Jesus to provide "the Lord's Prayer" as a model? (See Luke 11:1-4.)

NIV: "Our Father in heaven, hallowed be your name, your kingdom come, your will be done on earth as it is in heaven. Give us today our daily bread. Forgive us our debts, as we also have forgiven our debtors. And lead us not into temptation, but deliver us from the evil one."

TLB: "Our Father in heaven, we honor your holy name. We ask that your kingdom will come now. May your will be done here on earth, just as it is in heaven. Give us our food again today, as usual, and forgive us our sins, just as we have forgiven those who have sinned against us. Don't bring us into temptation, but deliver us from the Evil One. Amen."

The Message: "Our Father in heaven, reveal who you are. Set the world right; do what's best—as above, so below. Keep us alive with three square meals. Keep us forgiven with you and forgiving others. Keep us safe from ourselves and the Devil. You're in charge! You can do anything you want! You're ablaze in beauty! Yes. Yes. Yes."

As you can see from just these few verses, some translations are quite similar, and others provide vast variety.

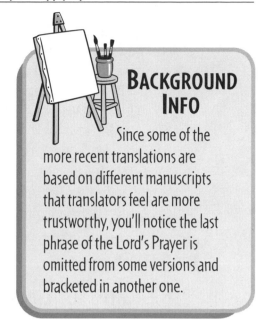

BACKGROUND INFO

Since some of the more recent translations are based on different manuscripts that translators feel are more trustworthy, you'll notice the last phrase of the Lord's Prayer is omitted from some versions and bracketed in another one.

Just Out: The NIV Study Bible for Left-Handed, Red-Haired, Teenage, Bulimic Lumberjacks!

Whichever translation or paraphrase you prefer, you can probably find a number of Bible options using that specific text. Most will have footnotes, maps, indexes, and other aids to Bible study, but many address specific user interests: women's issues, men's issues, small groups, students, kids, recovery, soul care, prophecy, new believers, and so forth. While the Bible text will be exactly the same in an NIV Study Bible, an NIV Student Bible, and an NIV Kid's Bible, the notes and study aids will be quite different.

So if you're planning on picking out a new Bible for more intensive personal use, ask around to see what other people like. Go to a good-sized bookstore and do some comparison shopping. Decide what translation or paraphrase you want, and then see what your options are for a study Bible using that particular version.

However, try not to fall into the trap of becoming overly dependent on the footnotes and study helps. God's Word, in most places throughout the Bible, is plain and clear. Even when you get to a portion that's a bit difficult to comprehend, read and reread the passage, meditate on it for a while, and come back to it later. Determine what you think it means before consulting the notes. If you find you just can't help but refer to the notes prematurely, you may first want to use a pew Bible or some other inexpensive Bible with no "bells and whistles." Let God speak to you through His Word. Later you can reread the same passages in a study Bible and see what the commentators have to add to your comprehension of the verses.

In the final chapters of this guide, we will examine some other resources you may want to use to amplify your understanding of God's Word after you've read it on your own.

Reading for the Right Reasons

A final word of warning needs to be said. Reading the Bible for a half hour each day is not an automatic, easy-does-it way to find yourself in God's good graces. The purpose of understanding the Bible is not primarily to master the names, places, facts, and other trivia bits. A solid comprehension of the Bible is not enough in itself, even if you are able to impress your pastor and dazzle your friends with your vast knowledge.

Look at it this way. Suppose you are in a dating relationship, quickly approaching marriage. You are forced to be apart from your beloved for reasons beyond your control, but you correspond with heartfelt romantic, colorful, scented letters back and forth, supplemented with more immediate E-mails. Those written expressions of love get you through a lot of hard times and lonely days.

On an occasional weekend, however, you're able to get together. When you do, is your top priority to sit in your respective corners of the room and keep reading the letters you have written to each other? If so, the author and publisher encourage you to seek immediate professional help.

When you're in the presence of someone who loves you unconditionally, the written correspondence you've had becomes secondary. So we should read the Bible not merely to know the Bible, but to know God. Understanding God's Word should definitely be a priority for us, but primarily because such understanding leads us closer to God Himself.

It may sound a bit simplistic, yet the religious leaders of Jesus' day missed this point. Many of them had studied and even memorized the written Scriptures, which foretold the coming of the Messiah in many clear and descriptive passages. But when Jesus showed up with numerous clues and more than enough outright statements that He was indeed the person whom the Scriptures had predicted, the Jewish leaders weren't convinced. His claims almost got Him killed early in His ministry (Luke 4:14–30) and did indeed lead to His crucifixion three years later. The main charge against Him was blasphemy, for equating Himself with God.

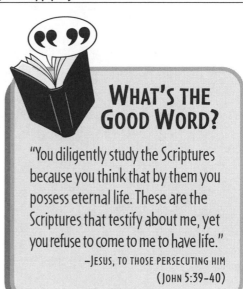

WHAT'S THE GOOD WORD?

"You diligently study the Scriptures because you think that by them you possess eternal life. These are the Scriptures that testify about me, yet you refuse to come to me to have life."

–JESUS, TO THOSE PERSECUTING HIM
(JOHN 5:39–40)

As we begin our intentional pursuit of better understanding the Bible, let us not make the same mistake. Knowing what's in the Bible is great, but truly understanding the Bible means we treasure God's Word because it leads us closer to God.

Chapter Flashback

1. You'll get the most out of Bible study if you:
a. Let your pastor interpret Scripture for you.
b. Read commentaries first.
c. Read it for yourself and let God speak to you.
d. Let someone else read it and tell you all the good parts.

2. We are commanded to love God with our hearts, souls, and:
    a. Minds
    b. Tithes
    c. Songs
    d. Elbows

3. All Scripture is God-breathed and useful for:
   a. Other people, so they'll treat you better
   b. Teaching, rebuking, correcting, and training in righteousness
   c. Teacher training and correcting rebuke
   d. Correct teaching and rebuking righteousness

4. If you're having a lot of trouble understanding your current Bible version, you might want to:
   a. Get a tutor.
   b. Audit a Bible class.
   c. Find a different translation or paraphrase.
   d. Curl up in the fetal position until someone helps you.

5. The best reason for studying God's Word is:
   a. It just might cause God to like you better.
   b. It helps you increase your Bible knowledge.
   c. It can bring you financial rewards if you're ever on *Jeopardy!* and the Final Jeopardy category is "Bible."
   d. It helps you focus on God's presence in your life.

Answers: (1) c, (2) a, (3) b, (4) c, (5) d

PART TWO

Through the Bible

Lots of us are brought up with some—and perhaps a lot of—Bible knowledge. We know the basic stories of Samson, Jonah, Joseph, Paul, Moses, and so forth. But to be honest, we're lost in knowing exactly where these individual stories fit into the unified whole of biblical history. If asked to give a reasonable overview of the Bible from start to finish, we would be hard-pressed to do so.

So the goal of this section is to start in Genesis and end in Revelation, passing through all of the Bible books on the way and getting a good feel for the "plot" of the Bible. We won't stop anywhere long enough to learn all the facts and all the lessons the characters may offer us. (You can get to that later.) But what we miss in details, we should gain in seeing a unified whole of what the Bible is all about.

You'll see, for instance, that Samson was one of the judges—and just what that means. Jonah was a prophet but probably not the best example. We'll move from patriarchs, to judges, to kings and prophets, to the New Testament. And even though it may not seem like it as you're reading the next ten chapters, we'll go quickly enough so that when you finish you should have a concise understanding of the whole Bible.

The rest of your life can then be spent going back and filling in the innumerable details and applications. You'll be reminded again later that going *through* the Bible is by no means the same as being *through with* the Bible. But it's a good start.

From Eden to Egypt

GENESIS

SNAPSHOT

Eve: It's another beautiful day here in Paradise.

Adam: It certainly is. So what are your plans for today?

Eve: Well, I've just finished watching yet another gorgeous sunrise. I thought I'd lie here in my hammock for a while, go take a dip in the Tigris River, have a spot of lunch, come lie down some more, take a couple of laps in the Euphrates, walk with God again this afternoon, watch yet another gorgeous sunset, and then a late dinner. How about you?

Adam: I thought I'd weed the Garden. *[Both Adam and Eve laugh heartily at the joke, knowing there are no such thing as weeds.]* What's for breakfast?

SNEAK PREVIEW

1. This chapter will cover the accounts of Creation; Adam and Eve; Cain and Abel, Noah and the Flood; the Tower of Babel; and the early leaders of Israel: Abraham, Isaac, Jacob, and Joseph.
2. In addition to the important biographies in Genesis, the geographic movement of the main characters is also noteworthy.
3. The Book of Genesis covers a time period of many centuries.

Eve: What do you want?

Adam: Today I think I'll have a mango-raspberry-banana smoothie.

Eve: You didn't like what I fixed yesterday?

Adam: The pineapple-guava-kumquat blend was excellent, my dear, but with all these great trees I thought I'd go for a bit of variety.

Eve: Here you go. Try this.

Adam: Delicious! Life just doesn't get any better than this, does it?

Eve: Well . . . I was just thinking about that. If only someone would invent a way to freeze water, maybe we could put some little chunks of it in our smoothies and make them . . . what's the word? . . . *cold.*

Adam: Oh, Eve! You and your desire to improve on perfection! You're going to get us both in trouble someday!

* * * * * * * * * * * * * *

Human beings can hardly help but think in terms of starting points. We establish annual celebrations for birthdays, anniversaries, historical events, and other important "firsts," and well we should. We can *kind of* wrap our minds around a concept like eternity that stretches forever into the future, even though we're dazzled by the enormity of such a thought. Yet even for those who have put a lot of thought into the possibility of living forever, it's still quite the challenge to look eternally *backward* and discover no beginning point to time. While our world and universe certainly had a beginning, we cannot say the same about God. He never had a beginning. He will never have an end. He is *eternal.*

The Way the World Begins: Not with a Bang, but a Creator

So the Bible begins with four simple, yet vastly complex, words: "In the beginning God." As for everything else, "the earth was formless and empty, darkness was over the surface of the deep" (Genesis 1:2). But in a succession of spoken pronouncements, God created day and night, heavens and earth, land and sea, vegetation, the entire animal population, and finally, human beings. Apparently, He was saving the best for last, because we are told that people were made in His own image. In addition, the humans were designated to "rule over" the other animals (Genesis 1:26).

This chapter's opening snapshot reflects a common misperception among those who have never actually read the biblical story of Creation, that Adam and Eve—the first man and woman—sat around all day, every day, with little or nothing to do. But according to Genesis, God created them with a distinct purpose and immediately gave them some specific responsibilities.

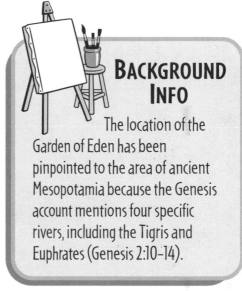

BACKGROUND INFO

The location of the Garden of Eden has been pinpointed to the area of ancient Mesopotamia because the Genesis account mentions four specific rivers, including the Tigris and Euphrates (Genesis 2:10–14).

We don't know exactly what their job descriptions were, but we know that Adam and Eve had assignments in the Garden of Eden. Among other things, Adam was to work the garden and take care of it (2:15), and was to name the animals (2:19). In addition, the man and woman were expected to spend time with each other (2:20–25) and with God (3:8).

Some people attempt to find common ground between the Creation story and the theory of evolution. Certainly, the progression from plants to animals to humans is an element of both viewpoints. Some even speculate that God may have overseen evolution up to the point where He created Adam. Others resist such thinking because the Creation account describes not only an intentional act of God but also an intensely personal one. God wasn't just creating a better variety of animal that could run on two legs, but rather He was purposefully creating soul-possessing beings in His own image with whom He could walk and talk (Genesis 3:8–9).

SWORD DRILL

How did the creation of Adam differ from the creation of Eve? (See Genesis 2:7, 21–22.)

Besides, the biblical account frustrates any serious attempt to juxtapose evolution with Creation. Without getting into all the debate issues here, consider that even if we make certain allowances that Adam might have been simultaneously created/evolved, the account of Eve's subsequent creation defies any scientific theory. God used different methods to bring about Adam and Eve, yet both cases are clearly intentional efforts on the part of a loving and omnipotent Creator.

Eden: The Wrong Fruit Is Bad for You

In fact, God created a perfectly functioning world. Adam and Eve had all they could ask for—jobs to keep them busy and fulfilled, regular walks with God, a magnificent setting surrounded by beauty, and each other. Who could ask for anything more?

As we know too well, usually we *all* can ask for more. No matter how good our lives are going, our wish lists aren't ever empty. In the case of Adam and Eve, the single thing denied them was the fruit of one particular tree in the garden—the Tree of the Knowledge of Good and Evil. God had made it clear that eating from that one tree would cause them to "surely die" (Genesis 2:17).

This tree is all Satan had to work with to tempt Adam and Eve to disobey God's clear command, but it was more than enough. First the devil, in the form of the serpent, caused Eve to question God's words (3:1). After getting her attention, he caused her to question God's motives (3:4). In spite of everything God had given them, and everything God had told them, they wanted more. This desire is present, in some form, in essentially every sin.

So Adam and Eve ate the fruit and, sure enough, they discovered the difference between good and evil. No longer comfortable with their nakedness, they made a feeble attempt to "cover up" their sin and hide from God (3:7–9); but He isn't so easily deceived.

God banished them from the garden. Otherwise, they ran the risk of eating from the Tree of Life and living forever in a sinful state, apart from God (3:22). Theirs was a death sentence, so to speak, because once out of the garden, they would eventually die. Yet even though Adam and Eve weren't aware of it—nor are many of us—physical death was mild punishment compared to eternal life without God.

Along with their eviction from Eden, God pronounced a series of curses. The woman would be subject to her husband, and would have greatly increased pains during childbirth (3:16). The man would have to endure "painful toil" and sweat to make a living from now on (3:17–19). And the serpent was doomed to crawl and "eat dust." In addition, a prophecy was added that the offspring of the woman and the offspring of the serpent would be in constant conflict, and that one future day the woman's offspring would "crush the head" of the serpent's offspring (3:14–15).

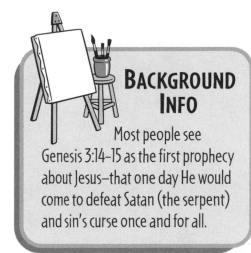

BACKGROUND INFO

Most people see Genesis 3:14-15 as the first prophecy about Jesus–that one day He would come to defeat Satan (the serpent) and sin's curse once and for all.

Know Cain, Know Pain

To provide more adequate covering for Adam's and Eve's newly discovered nakedness, God replaced their fig leaves with animal skins (3:21), requiring a shedding of blood to cover their sin. This is the first hint of death in the Bible. Unfortunately, we don't have to wait long for the second mention.

Adam and Eve had children. Abel tended flocks and Cain grew crops. Both sons offered a sampling of their work to God, who was pleased with Abel's offering but not with Cain's. Cain felt frustration and envy, so God issued a personal warning to Cain about his attitude (4:4–7). Despite the warning, Cain killed Abel.

God passed judgment on Cain's crime, sentencing him to become a "restless wanderer on the earth" rather than settling down. Yet just as God didn't immediately kill Adam and Eve after their sin, in another act of mercy He spared Cain's life and even placed a mark of protection on him (Genesis 4:10–16).

The fact that Cain feared death from strangers as a "restless wanderer on the earth" (4:14) indicates a rapidly growing population. Some people speculate that Adam and Eve may have had a great many children in the Garden of Eden, and

BACKGROUND INFO

God's response to Cain and Abel's offerings wasn't a matter of fruits versus animals on the altar. Later, the Israelites would be encouraged to make offerings of not only animals but grain and oil as well. The reason God wasn't pleased with Cain was more a matter of the older brother's attitude. (See Hebrews 11:4 and 1 John 3:12.)

they may have been there for a long time prior to being cast out. Since Eve's punishment was "greatly increased" pains in childbearing, perhaps she first experienced a relatively painless process. In addition, if the long life spans of the first humans are taken to be literal, it would account for several generations of children, grandchildren, great-grandchildren, and so forth in the person's lifetime.

The next portion of Genesis introduces us to the world's first bigamist, Lamech (4:19); the father of all musicians, Jubal (4:21); the first metalworker, Tubal-Cain (4:22); and others. What we see are civilizations springing up. And what we see next is that things are going downhill quickly.

Rain, Rain, Noah Way

People were living long, long lives but not very good ones. Sin finally became so rampant throughout the world that "the LORD was grieved that he had made man on the earth, and his heart was filled with pain" (6:6). He determined to destroy what He had created and start over again with the only righteous man remaining on earth—Noah.

The story of Noah's building an ark (Genesis 6–9) is one of the most familiar in the Bible. In addition to Noah were his wife, his three sons, and their wives—making a total of eight sailors in all. And while most people know a version of the story, many are unaware of all the details. For example, everyone knows that two of each animal were on the ark, but there were seven of each kind of clean animal—those that would be suitable for offerings (and later, for food)—and *seven* of each kind of bird (Genesis 7:2–3). We know it rained forty days and forty nights, but are we aware that it took so long for the water to recede that Noah and his family were enclosed in the ark for over a year (7:11; 8:13–14)?

We know a dove returned with an olive branch, but that was the third of four times Noah sent birds out of the ark (8:6–12). We know that God gave Noah the sign of the rainbow but may not have heard that sometime after de-arking Noah raised grapes, got drunk and naked, and created problems for his kids (Genesis 9).

Noah was a one-of-a-kind righteous man in his generation, yet the Bible doesn't hide the facts of his later life from us. If we read carefully, we could let Noah teach us the dangers of drunkenness, yet many people insist on finding out for themselves.

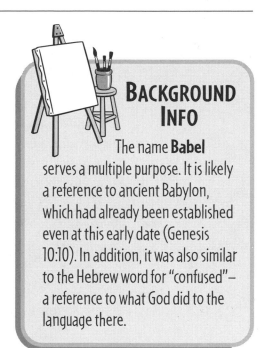

BACKGROUND INFO

The name **Babel** serves a multiple purpose. It is likely a reference to ancient Babylon, which had already been established even at this early date (Genesis 10:10). In addition, it was also similar to the Hebrew word for "confused"– a reference to what God did to the language there.

The Power of Babble

Even though God restarted humankind with Noah and his family, it was a short matter of time until the population grew, and again people went their own way instead of God's. The Lord's clear instructions had been to "be fruitful and increase in number; multiply on the earth and increase upon it" (9:7). But the people didn't want to spread out as God had intended. They chose instead to build a tower into the heavens "so that we may make a name for ourselves and not be scattered over the face of the whole earth" (Genesis 11:4).

Yet while the people were naïvely attempting to build a tower into God's domain, we read that "the Lord came down to see the city and the tower" (11:5). For the Creator of the earth, this tower of pride was no accomplishment at all. Still, God realized that the stubborn will of sinful humans needed to be checked. And this time, He used a much simpler solution: He "confused their language" so they couldn't understand each other. The common language enjoyed by mankind suddenly became a mélange of various languages, and the like-speaking groups scattered to different geographic locations. Instead of a proud human monument, the Tower of Babel became a testimony to a God who could use the power of babble to get people to do as He had instructed.

Abraham: My Home Is No Longer Ur Home

One of the most revered Old Testament figures to this day is Abraham. He lived in "Ur of the Chaldeans" (Genesis 11:31), a highly civilized area of Mesopotamia that was in the same general location as modern Iraq. God spoke to Abraham, whose name at the time was Abram, and told him to leave his home. Abram's destination at the time was unclear. All he knew was that it was a land God would show him. However, God had also promised to bless Abram, make his name great, and make him "into a great nation" (12:1–3).

I Learned the Truth at Seventy-Five

Abram was already seventy-five years old and was no doubt past his years of youthful adventure. Still, he obeyed and left behind civilization, routine, and everything else to follow God.

His dad died along the way, but Abram was still looking out for his wife Sarah (then called Sarai) and nephew Lot, and Abram had a number of people to care for his herds and flocks. After trekking all the way to Canaanite territory, in what is modern-day Israel, God again appeared to Abram and said, "To your offspring I will give this land" (Genesis 12:7). The promise of offspring was probably more thrilling to Abram than the real estate, because Sarah had been unable to have children.

For a Wife and a Nephew, Sarah Lot of Trouble

However, Sarah was quite a beauty. When a famine drove Abraham's group to Egypt, the pharaoh put the moves on her. Abraham had anticipated this problem. His solution? Tell the authorities Sarah was his sister and allow her to join Pharaoh's harem! God miraculously got them out of this little problem and a similar one years later (12:10–20; 20:1–18).

Lot was getting into trouble of his own. After an argument with Abram, Lot separated from him (amicably, thanks to Abram's graciousness), but soon found himself kidnapped by a coalition of invading kings. Abram quickly put together a rescue party and reclaimed his nephew (14:13–16). Of course, Lot returned to his new home in Sodom, which would soon cause other problems for him.

Kidding Around

Abram, with God's help, was dealing adequately with the external problems. It was the problems within his own home that were creating even greater tension, however. He had been promised an heir. God had even formalized this promise into a covenant—a solemn, official, unbreakable agreement (Genesis 15).

But Abram was getting on in years. And even though Sarah was ten years younger, she was still no spring chicken, even by Old Testament standards. When Sarah saw she was still having no success in bearing children, she encouraged Abram to pursue one of the customs of the day—sleep with one of her handmaids and have a child who would count as his. (It doesn't appear that Abraham put up much resistance to this suggestion.)

> **SWORD DRILL**
>
> God and Abraham didn't merely shake hands to "seal the deal" after making this covenant. How did God commemorate what had taken place? (See Genesis 15:8–21.)

The conflict between Sarah and Hagar the handmaid began as soon as Hagar became pregnant. Before the baby was even born, Hagar got snippy with Sarah, so Sarah kicked her out (with Abram's permission). But an angel met Hagar in the desert and told her to return and submit to Sarah. He promised Hagar that her son would have descendants "too numerous to count" (16:10). The baby was born and named Ishmael. Abraham was eighty-six at the time.

But this was not what God had intended for Abram. God waited until Abram was ninety-nine and promised him a child that he and Sarah would have. Both Abram and Sarah responded to this news with laughter (17:17; 18:10–12). At this point God instituted the ritual of circumcision as a sign of the covenant between Himself and Abram. All the males in Abraham's household and employment were circumcised. In addition, this was when Abram ("exalted father") had his name officially changed to Abraham ("father of many"). Sarai became Sarah, though both names can be interpreted as "princess."

Sodom and Gomorrah Get Fired

While waiting for God to act, Abraham was also told of God's plan to obliterate Sodom and Gomorrah, two cities with an international reputation for wickedness. Abraham was naturally alarmed because Lot and his family were living in Sodom. Abraham went through a bartering process with God, and God eventually agreed to spare the city if even ten righteous people could be found (18:16–33). But it was not to be.

Two angels (in the guise of men) went to Sodom, and what they found there confirmed the sad state of the townsmen. Lot implored them not to spend the night in the square, but instead to be his houseguests. They finally agreed, but before long the house was surrounded by "all the men from every part of the city of Sodom—both young and old." They demanded Lot send out his two guests "so that we can have sex with them" (19:4–5).

BACKGROUND INFO

Hospitality was a big deal in ancient times. An offer to visit was good for three days, and the host became responsible for his guests. Therefore, when the two men visited him in Sodom, Lot was willing to sacrifice his own family members to prevent the stigma of having something happen to visitors in his home.

Unable to reason with the mob, Lot even offered them his two virgin daughters, but the crowd wanted the men and were about to break through the door to get them—or so they thought. Since these "men" happened to be angels, they inflicted blindness on the crowd. Then the angels had to physically pull Lot and family out of the city before God destroyed it. They warned everyone not to look back. But as burning sulfur rained down on Sodom and Gomorrah, Lot's wife turned around—and turned into a pillar of salt (19:24–26).

Lot and his daughters escaped, but his daughters' desperation to preserve the family line drove them to take turns getting their father drunk and sleeping with him. Both had children by Lot, leading to the formation of the Moabites and Ammonites, who would cause all sorts of grief for the Israelites for centuries to come.

God Gave Them Something to Laugh About

Meanwhile, back on the Abraham plantation, Sarah indeed became pregnant as God had promised. She eventually gave birth—at age ninety—to a son. The joke was on them, so Abraham named the child Isaac ("he laughs").

The birth of Isaac was such a joy for Sarah, but it was the last straw in the tension between Hagar and her. The handmaid and her young teenager, Ishmael, were sent packing, but God again protected them. The descendants of Isaac became the Jews. The descendants of Ishmael became the Arabs. Both groups trace their history all the way back to Abraham, but that's just about where the similarities end.

Isaac: From Offering to Offspring

Isaac's birth to Sarah when she should have been far beyond her childbearing years was a tremendous miracle that fulfilled God's promise to Abraham. No less impressive was the next miracle, involving Abraham and his now teenage son. God gave Abraham a startling, strange command: "Take your son, your only son, Isaac, whom you love, and go to the region of Moriah. Sacrifice him there as a burnt offering on one of the mountains I will tell you about" (22:2).

> ## WHAT'S THE GOOD WORD?
>
> And God is faithful; he will not let you be tempted beyond what you can bear. But when you are tempted, he will also provide a way out so that you can stand up under it.
>
> –1 CORINTHIANS 10:13

This is a perplexing passage that is difficult to understand and explain. We read that God "tested" Abraham (22:1), even though He never "tempts" people (James 1:13) and even limits the degree of our temptations from other sources. It may sound like a fine line, but schoolteachers don't give tests to their students attempting to trick them in any way. Rather, the tests serve as tools to reflect how much the student has learned. It is an immensely satisfying feeling to be asked, "How'd you do on the big test?" and respond, "I aced it!" (Or so I am told.)

I've Seen Fire and I've Seen Wood

The bigger question in this case is why Abraham's test involved such a bizarre and cold-blooded assignment. After twenty-five years of faithfulness to God and waiting for a son, and another few years watching that miracle son learn to walk and talk, Abraham is told to sacrifice Isaac. To make things worse, along the way up the mountain, Isaac pointed out that he'd seen fire and wood but the sacrificial lamb seemed to be missing (22:1–8).

Still, Abraham followed God's instructions to the letter. He built the altar, stacked the wood, and tied Isaac to the top. He picked up the knife and was fully prepared to plunge it into his son. But having shown his willingness to obey even God's most difficult commands, Abraham "aced" his test. An angel prevented him from completing the dreaded act, and God provided a ram to take Isaac's place atop the altar (vv. 9–13).

WHAT'S THE GOOD WORD?

Abraham reasoned that God could raise the dead, and figuratively speaking, he did receive Isaac back from death.

–HEBREWS 11:19

Some consider this story a model for the surrounding "religious" people who included regular child sacrifice among their worship habits—proof that Abraham's God would deliver. Or perhaps God was simply allowing Abraham to experience (to a small degree) the divine pain of sacrificing a precious and beloved son (see 22:2). Either way, Abraham displayed so much faith that he believed God would resurrect Isaac from the dead if that's what it took.

We are told that "Abraham believed the LORD, and he credited it to him as righteousness" (15:6). The New Testament emphasizes this point to demonstrate that salvation is a matter of faith, not merely adhering to a bunch of laws that didn't come along until *after* Abraham (Romans 4:3, 22–25).

SWORD DRILL

If you practice random acts of kindness such as watering a stranger's camels, what might be in it for you? (See Genesis 24:10–23, 61.)

And despite the potential trauma for Isaac, his last-minute deliverance from death must have been a valuable lesson about God to boost his own faith at a young age.

The Quiet Patriarch

We don't know nearly as much about Isaac as we do Abraham. We know Abraham went to great lengths to find him a godly woman as a wife (Genesis 24). We know God appeared to him to confirm the promises previously made to Abraham (26:24–25). We know he used Abraham's pass-your-wife-off-as-your-sister-to-keep-from-being-killed trick, yet God protected Rebekah as He had Sarah (26:1–22).

But perhaps Isaac is best remembered as the father of twin boys who happened to be as different as two kids can be.

Here Comes Jacob (Someone Call the Bunco Squad)

Isaac and Rebekah had twin sons, Jacob and Esau. Not only weren't these twins identical, they were barely fraternal. Even before they were born, they "jostled each other within [Rebekah]" (Genesis 25:22). And during their delivery, Esau was born first, but Jacob's hand came out grasping Esau's heel.

Esau was his father's pride and joy—a son who loved hunting and the outdoor life. Jacob was Mom's favorite, and spent his time "among the tents." Esau was bold and boisterous; Jacob was quiet. Esau was impulsive while Jacob was a planner and a schemer.

Esau, as the older of the two, was entitled to the birthright—including his father's blessing and a hefty share of the inheritance. But he came home famished after hunting one day, and Jacob wafted a steaming bowl of stew under his nose. Without even considering the significance of what he was doing, Esau agreed to trade his birthright to Jacob in exchange for the food (Genesis 25:29–34).

Pulling the Wool over Isaac's Eyes—and Jacob's Arms

Later, however, Isaac was planning on officially bestowing his blessing on Esau. He sent his older son out to gather some wild game for his favorite dish. But since Isaac was blind by this time, Rebekah and Jacob quickly put together a plan to trick him. Rebekah fixed his requested meal using goat meat. And since Esau had been an extraordinarily hairy person from birth (Genesis 25:25), she used the goatskins to make arm toupees for Jacob and dressed him in Esau's clothes.

In a clear case of premeditated deceit, Jacob took the food to Isaac, who was immediately suspicious. Why was "Esau" back so quickly? Because, replied Jacob, "The LORD your God gave me success" (Genesis 27:20). But Isaac wasn't convinced the voice was Esau's. He summoned "Esau" to come closer, feeling the arms and becoming satisfied only after smelling the scent that was exclusively *Eau de Esau*. The deceit worked. Isaac pronounced the family blessing on Jacob, thinking all the time he was Esau. And no sooner had Jacob made a quick exit than the real Esau came in. Both Isaac and Esau regretted the mistake, but the giving of the birthright was irrevocable.

Easily duped, but not easily appeased, Esau threatened to kill Jacob as soon as Dad had passed on. Rebekah, not willing to let that happen, convinced Isaac to send Jacob away, back to her family, where he could find a wife. (They were none too thrilled with the local women Esau had chosen as wives.)

A Stronger and Smarter Opponent

Along the way, God introduced Himself to Jacob in a dream. Even before he was born, Jacob had been designated as God's choice to receive the blessings handed down from Abraham and Isaac (Genesis 25:23), but it seems Jacob had done little to familiarize himself with the God of his father Isaac and grandfather Abraham. Through a long and seemingly convoluted path of acquiring flocks, wives, and children, Jacob came to discover that as good as he was at outwitting other people, he was no match for God.

He learned this first in a dream he had while on the run from Esau (Genesis 28:10–22). The lesson was reinforced years later as he was preparing to return home. For all he knew, Esau still had an arrow with Jacob's name on it. But in addition to doing everything he knew to do to protect his new family, Jacob also prayed (Genesis 32:1–12). While he was alone, a man showed up and wrestled with him all night. Jacob realized this was God and refused to let go until he received a blessing. The Lord changed his name from Jacob to Israel ("he struggles with God") and did indeed bless him. But He also "touched the socket of Jacob's hip" and wrenched it, leaving Jacob with a limp and a reminder of who was ultimately in control (32:22–32).

BACKGROUND INFO

We refer to "Jacob's ladder," which is how Jacob's dream was described in the King James translation. More accurately, Jacob probably dreamed of a large staircase with angels ascending and descending (Genesis 28:10–17).

As it turned out, Esau was ready to forgive, and Jacob went home. Apparently, Rebekah had died by that time, and Jacob never got to see her again. But in a few years, Jacob and Esau together buried their father.

Jacob had returned with two wives and their two handmaids, all of whom had borne him children. His favorite, Rachel, had been childless the longest but had finally given him his eleventh son, Joseph. (He also had a daughter.) Upon their return home, Rachel again became pregnant, but she died giving birth to Jacob's twelfth son, Benjamin.

Jacob's (Israel's) twelve sons became, essentially, the twelve tribes of Israel, or, collectively, the Israelites. But one of them almost didn't make it to adulthood.

O Brother, Who Art Thou?

Portions of the story of Joseph, Jacob's eleventh son, are familiar to most people —if not from Scripture, from the productions of Dream Works or Andrew Lloyd-Webber. Since he was Rachel's only son (for a while), Joseph was Jacob's favorite. Jacob showed his favoritism in different ways, including the not-so-subtle gift of a fancy robe. Joseph didn't help himself either, as he described his strange dreams of other family members all bowing down to him (Genesis 37:1–11).

When an ideal opportunity presented itself, the ten older brothers plotted to get rid of Joseph. Most wanted to kill him; only one was planning to rescue him. But when the situation presented itself, they sold him, and he found himself in Egypt. God was with him, even as a servant. When he was falsely accused of attempted rape, God was with him in prison. And between the years of seventeen and thirty, Joseph went from favored son, to Egyptian flunkey, to prison felon . . . to Pharaoh's number two man over all of Egypt!

> **SWORD DRILL**
>
> How did Joseph manage to make the jump from prison to prominence? (See Genesis 40–41.)

Before long, a famine sent his brothers to Egypt seeking food, and they did indeed bow before Joseph, not even knowing who he was. He made very sure they had changed for the better and that they would do nothing similar to the little brother he discovered he had, Benjamin. And after he was convinced of their sincere repentance, they had a tearful reunion (42–45:15). Pharaoh was so impressed with Joseph that he financed the move of Joseph's entire family to one of the prime real estate sites in Egypt—an area called

Goshen. Joseph eventually died in Egypt, but he first made sure his remains would be carried back someday to the land God had promised Abraham, Isaac, and Jacob.

A (Bio- and Geo-) Graphic Beginning

So the Book of Genesis, in one respect, is a series of biographies: Adam and Eve, Noah, Abraham and Sarah, Isaac, Jacob, Joseph, and others. These might seem to be far-above-average holy men and women. But as you look closer, you discover a gamut of sinful actions that involved essentially everyone in Genesis. From shortly after the Fall, the world began seeing rampant sin in the form of murder, incest, promiscuous sex, drunkenness, homosexuality, rape, jealousy, violence, and more—and the "patriarchs" were no exception. Yet in spite of their problems, they persevered due to their underlying faith in God.

From a geographic standpoint, the Book of Genesis begins in Mesopotamia with Adam and Eve, transfers to Israel with Abraham, takes a few side trips into Egypt to avoid famines, and ends there where it seems that everyone might live happily ever after. But as we'll see in the next chapter, that's about to change.

Chapter Flashback

Here's a different kind of flashback. Rather than multiple choice this time, match the character in Genesis with the events from his or her life.

(1) Adam   A. At times, could have just killed a handmaiden.

(2) Cain   B. At one time, one of only eight people not killed.

(3) Noah   C. His twin brother wanted to kill him.

(4) Abraham   D. His ten brothers wanted to kill him.

(5) Sarah   E. His father almost killed him.

(6) Isaac   F. He killed his younger brother.

(7) Jacob   G. Was banished and allowed to die to prevent a worse fate.

(8) Joseph   H. Died far from original home in a land God had promised him.

Answers: (1) G, (2) F, (3) B, (4) H, (5) A, (6) E, (7) C, (8) D

The Wander Years

EXODUS, LEVITICUS, NUMBERS, DEUTERONOMY

SNAPSHOT

"Hurry and get in the car, kids. Where's your mom? If we don't get out of this church parking lot *right now,* there's going to be a horrendous line at the Sizzler."

"Sorry. I got caught," Mom said, panting just a bit. "Marge Bensen wanted to tell me about her rebellious son again. I know her husband is dead and she has a problem teenager, but what am I supposed to do to help her? She's a nice person, but she can really bring you down."

"Dad! Speed up!" Junior said. "Mr. Baldry is about to back out. If we get behind him, we'll never get any lunch. He's a nice person, but he drives like Great-Grandma."

"Janie, how was Sunday school this morning?" Mom asked.

SNEAK PREVIEW

1. This chapter will take a look at the life and leadership of Moses, from his miraculous delivery as a child to his leading the Israelites out of Egypt to the Promised Land.

2. Under Moses' leadership, God provided His people with a number of laws to govern their lifestyles and relationships.

3. Although all the people were well aware of God's presence and direction, their response to Him is not a particularly pretty picture of spiritual growth and maturity.

"*Bor*-ing. The opening music was great, and the games were fun. When we told each other about our challenges last week, it was really helpful. But then Mr. Taylor went off on this Bible lesson about Samson that must have lasted five or ten whole minutes. He's a nice person, but sometimes he can really ramble on."

"How about your class, Junior?" Dad asked.

"Okay, I guess. Way better than church, that's for sure. What was the deal with Reverend Waldorf harping about all the suffering people in other parts of the world? We have our own problems, you know."

And as if it had been the morning's responsive reading, Mom, Dad, Junior, and Janie all spoke in unison: "He's a nice person, but . . . "

* * * * * * * * * * * * * * *

Have you ever noticed how nice most other people seem . . . until they do something that conflicts with your own personal plans, wishes, or opinions? If not, you probably won't understand much in this chapter, because we're going to see a large group of people become extraordinarily whiny and inconsolable. God was performing miracle after miracle to spring the people of Israel from the slavery of Egypt and personally lead them to a place—a promised land—of their own. Yet they rebelled time after time and made life miserable for their leader, Moses. They never would have thought of themselves as bad people, but . . .

A Million Israelites Later . . .

The previous chapter ended with Jacob (Israel) relocating to Egypt where his long-lost son, Joseph, was second-in-command. Thanks to his God-given interpretation of Pharaoh's mysterious and prophetic dreams of cows and grain, Joseph had been alerted to prepare for a coming famine; so Egypt was the place to go for food.

At that time, Jacob's family had consisted of only a few dozen people who moved to Egypt (Genesis 46:26–27). But fast-forward about four centuries. The families had grown into an impressive force of hundreds of thousands of people. As the numbers of Jacob's children (known as the Israelites) were growing, all fond memories of Joseph by the Egyptians were being forgotten. As a matter of fact, one day a new Pharaoh realized how much damage that group of Israelites could do if they ever decided to join ranks with an enemy of Egypt.

So Egypt decided to enslave the Israelites and keep them occupied building cities and doing other grunt work. However, "the more they were oppressed, the more they multiplied and spread; so the Egyptians came to dread the Israelites and worked them ruthlessly" (Exodus 1:12–13).

It got to the point where Pharaoh ordered the Hebrew midwives to immediately kill any male children born. The midwives discreetly refused to comply, but Pharaoh didn't back down either. It was during this dangerous and turbulent time that Moses was born.

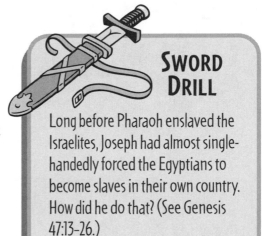

SWORD DRILL

Long before Pharaoh enslaved the Israelites, Joseph had almost single-handedly forced the Egyptians to become slaves in their own country. How did he do that? (See Genesis 47:13–26.)

Moses to Pharaoh: "Nile Be Back"

Moses' mother kept him a secret for three months until she could hide him no longer. At that time she took a papyrus basket, waterproofed it with tar and pitch, put the child inside, and placed the homemade boat among the reeds. Moses' sister watched from a distance. After all, this was the Nile River. One errant drift into the current and the next stop would be the middle of the Mediterranean Sea—and that's if he managed to dodge all the crocodiles.

But God was watching over Moses. Otherwise, it was just a coincidence that Pharaoh's daughter went down to the reeds for bath time, and it was just a coincidence that the baby started crying at just that moment, and it was just a coincidence that she was more than willing to adopt him—and (biggest coincidence of all) she needed a wet nurse, so she ended up *paying* Moses' mother to raise the child. It was Pharaoh's daughter who named the baby *Moses* ("draw out") because she drew him out of the water.

So Moses spent the first forty years of his life as Egyptian royalty. The Bible says essentially nothing about this portion of his life, but he must have had some

BACKGROUND INFO

The same word that is used for Moses' "papyrus basket" is also used for Noah's "ark." So in a sense, Moses was rescued with an ark just like Noah, although Noah's was considerably larger.

degree of knowledge about his roots. One day he saw an Egyptian beating a Hebrew slave. He looked around, didn't detect any witnesses, killed the Egyptian, and buried the body in the sand. The perfect crime? Hardly. The very next day he broke up a fight between two Israelites, and one of them asked, "Are you thinking of killing me as you killed the Egyptian?" (Exodus 2:11–14).

Realizing his crime was no secret, Moses fled to a wilderness area called Midian. Good thing, too, because Pharaoh would have had him killed. The next forty years of Moses' life were spent on the lam in the desert. He married the daughter of a local priest and had a couple of kids. And surely his sudden transition from an urban, wealthy lifestyle to remote shepherd was difficult, but God was preparing him for yet another phase of his life.

One day Moses' shepherding duties took him to "the far side of the desert" where he noticed a bush that seemed to be on fire yet didn't burn up (3:1–3). He went closer to check it out, and God spoke to him from the burning bush. God explained that He was aware of His people's suffering in Egypt, and that Moses would be the one to lead them to freedom. Here was Moses, hiding from the Egyptian authorities but being asked to not only return but to stand before Pharaoh himself and demand the release of close to a million people.

Moses had a number of good excuses, but God answered every one. (You can read about their encounter in Exodus 3:11–4:17.) God not only sent Aaron (Moses' older brother) to help him but also gave Moses a number of miraculous signs to use if needed (4:1–9).

Today's Forecast: Hail, Darkness, and Scattered Frogs

Moses did exactly as God instructed—and was emphatically rejected. Pharaoh scoffed at his request to have the Israelites released, and the Egyptian was determined to show everyone who was boss. He instructed the slave masters to stop providing straw for the manufacture of bricks, yet refused to reduce the daily quotas. Consequently, the Israelites had to work much harder to get their work done. And they directed the full blame not at Pharaoh, but at Moses.

God continued to encourage Moses, but the people refused to be consoled. Moses wanted to know (as most of us would) how he could ever sway Pharaoh if he couldn't even gain the respect of the Israelites. But God was way ahead of him and said, "See, I have made you like God to Pharaoh, and your brother Aaron will be your prophet" (Exodus 7:1). It was God's plan to harden Pharaoh's heart, making the eventual exodus of all His people all the more spectacular.

SWORD DRILL

No sooner had God sent Moses to Egypt than we read that, "the LORD met Moses and was about to kill him." What was the problem, and how was it resolved? (See Exodus 4:24-26.)

And indeed, Pharaoh's heart was hardened. At God's instruction, Moses initiated a series of plagues on the Egyptians. There were ten in all, the first nine being:

1. The water of the Nile was turned to blood, polluting the primary source of drinking water.

2. A plague of frogs rose up throughout Egypt—in beds, ovens, and everywhere. Dead frogs were piled in large heaps, creating not the most pleasant nasal sensation.

3. Aaron struck the ground with his staff, and instead of dust rising, gnats swarmed throughout the land of Egypt.

4. Flies followed the gnats, appearing in dark storms.

5. A plague struck the Egyptian livestock, killing them all. By now people were

BACKGROUND INFO

Pharaoh's magicians, using "secret arts," were able to simulate the same effects of the first two plagues (though apparently not able to **undo** them). But by the third plague and onward, they cowered along with the rest of the Egyptians (other than Pharaoh) because they recognized such power was "the finger of God" (Exodus 8:19).

noticing that only the Egyptians were being tormented by these plagues. In contrast, "not even one of the animals of the Israelites had died" (Exodus 9:7).

6. After the animals were struck, Moses tossed soot from a furnace into the air, resulting in a plague of boils settling on the people of Egypt.

Pharaoh's magicians weren't even able to stand before Moses because of their own sores.

7. Next came the worst hailstorm in the history of Egypt. Moses had forecast it ahead of time and warned the Egyptians to stay indoors. Those who disregarded his advice found themselves and their possessions pounded with hail that "stripped every tree" (9:25). The hail hit everywhere—except in Goshen, where the Israelites lived.

8. Although the crops were severely beaten down by the hail, a few of them survived—until a plague of locusts blew in during an all-day east wind and settled on Egypt until the ground was black. It didn't take long until "nothing green remained on tree or plant in all the land of Egypt" (10:15).

9. Then it got dark—spooky, scary dark. For three days it was impossible for Egyptians to see or travel, although the weather in Goshen was sunny and bright.

WHAT'S THE GOOD WORD?

"For by now I could have stretched out my hand and struck you and your people with a plague that would have wiped you off the earth. But I have raised you up for this very purpose, that I might show you my power and that my name might be proclaimed in all the earth."

–GOD'S MESSAGE TO PHARAOH THROUGH MOSES
(EXODUS 9:15-16)

Between plagues, Pharaoh showed various levels of repentance and tentatively agreed to grant Moses' request to take his people away. But without fail, after each crisis was over, Pharaoh's heart was again hardened, and he refused to comply with what he had promised. After the plague of darkness, however, when he again reneged on his word, Moses told him, "I will never appear before you again" (Exodus 10:29).

What a Difference a Marked Door Makes

God had prepared Moses for one more plague—the worst of them all. By this time, even though Pharaoh stubbornly refused to back down, many other Egyptians were eager to hear what Moses had to say. He had been quite successful in forewarning them of the previous disasters, and this time he was saying the oldest son of each and every family (and even the firstborn cattle) would die.

However, Moses told the Israelites that their families could avoid this tragedy by sacrificing a year-old sheep or goat, a male with no defects. The blood of the animal was to be applied to the top and both sides of the doorframe of the home. And the meat was to be used for a final meal in Egypt before the Israelites left for a new destination where they would be free again.

At midnight, God was true to his word. He struck down "all the firstborn in Egypt, from the firstborn of Pharaoh, who sat on the throne, to the firstborn of the prisoner, who was in the dungeon, and the firstborn of all the livestock as well" (12:29). The only exceptions were the homes where God saw the blood on the doorframes.

After this plague, Pharaoh not only allowed the Israelites to leave—he insisted on it. He even asked Moses to bless him before leaving. And he sent away the entire group of Hebrews with all their flocks and herds, and all the silver, gold, and clothing they had received from their neighbors.(12:35–36). The Israelites ate their last quick meal with unleavened bread and left Egypt to journey to the Promised Land —the place that had been promised to Abraham and was now held out as a promise to them as well. They had spent 430 years in Egypt "to the very day" (12:41).

BACKGROUND INFO

Some people read about the death of firstborn sons and accuse God of being overly harsh. However, God's final plague on Egypt was no more severe than Pharaoh's own judgment when he had ordered the death of all newborn Hebrew males. God's plague limited the deaths to one per family, which is more than Pharaoh had done. And had Pharaoh not been so stubborn, the Israelites would have left with no plagues hitting Egypt–much less this final one.

Water, Water, Everywhere, But Not a Place to Wade

But it didn't take long for Pharaoh to have second thoughts. When his initial grief wore off, he realized he had turned loose a workforce of 600,000 men and decided to get them all back. He sent his army after them, with no less than "six hundred of the best chariots, along with all the other chariots of Egypt" (14:7).

The Israelites had just pitched camp beside the Red Sea. When they looked up and saw the entire Egyptian army bearing down on them, they were trapped between a rock and a wet place.

SWORD DRILL

When the people left Egypt for the Promised Land, why did God plan an indirect route for them rather than a beeline? And what unusual cargo were they carrying? (See Exodus 13:17–19.)

It should have been a moment for courage and faith. After all, God was continually before them in the form of a pillar of cloud by day and pillar of fire by night. He had just led them away from one of the most powerful empires on earth. He had done so by performing a long series of impressive miracles. So how did the people respond? "They said to Moses, 'Was it because there were no graves in Egypt that you brought us to the desert to die? What have you done to us by bringing us out of Egypt? Didn't we say to you in Egypt, 'Leave us alone; let us serve the Egyptians'? It would have been better for us to serve the Egyptians than to die in the desert!'" (14:11–12).

By now Moses had a bit of experience in responding to the fear and criticism of the people. He patiently told them not to be afraid—to just watch what was about to happen. At that point, the pillar of cloud—God's presence—moved from before the people to a position between the Israelites and the Egyptians. The cloud cast light on the Israelites, but the Egyptian forces were in total darkness. Then Moses stretched his staff over the sea, and the waters parted, forming two walls between which the Israelites marched through on dry land (Exodus 14:21–22).

When the Egyptians attempted to follow, they descended successfully to the sea's bed. They were in wild pursuit when God caused their chariot wheels to jam "so that they had difficulty driving" (14:25). They were stranded between the walls of water as Moses, from the far side of the sea, again stretched out his hand and the passage was closed. The entire army of Egypt, to a person, drowned.

Addicted to Whine

So the Israelites had witnessed spectacular plagues that prompted their escape from Egypt; their successful escape included walking between liquid cliffs that didn't come down on them. Yet as they continued their journey to the Promised Land, no sooner would they encounter the least little problem than they would again start to gripe to Moses (as they had at the Red Sea) about turning around and going back to Egypt. It became a pattern repeated over and over as they went along their way.

When they couldn't find water immediately, they complained. God provided it for them, often in miraculous ways. When they worried about food, they complained. God sent manna, day by day, to keep them fed. When they complained about manna, He sent quail. Yet the people never learned to stop grumbling. They were being temporarily inconvenienced, to be sure, but there were no direct flights to the Promised Land. They were getting there the only way possible. And after all that had been done for them, their whining was like a slap in the face to Moses' leadership, not to mention God's.

Don't Have a (Golden) Cow

Among the worst of their offenses was completely giving up on Moses and God at the foot of Mount Sinai. The people had assembled for a holy ceremony, and they knew Moses was going up on the mountain to speak with God. While Moses was away

WHAT'S THE GOOD WORD?

When our fathers were in Egypt, they gave no thought to your miracles; they did not remember your many kindnesses, and they rebelled by the sea, the Red Sea. Yet he saved them for his name's sake, to make his mighty power known. He rebuked the Red Sea and it dried up; he led them through the depths as through a desert.

–PSALM 106:7-9

receiving the Ten Commandments and numerous other specific guidelines for living, the people (no surprise by now) grew impatient. This time they petitioned Aaron to design "gods who will go before us" (32:1). To appease them, Aaron collected their Egyptian earrings and used the gold to fashion a calf, crediting the idol with leading them out of Egypt.

God knew exactly what was going on, of course, and suggested that He and Moses postpone their meeting. By this time, God even suggested that He destroy all the whiny Israelites and provide Moses a better bunch of people to lead. Moses interceded for the Israelites, however, and God spared them. But their blatant idolatry was not to be tolerated. Moses came down the mountain, carrying the Ten Commandments in God's own handwriting (32:9–16). When he saw for himself what was going on, he smashed them to the ground, destroying them.

BACKGROUND INFO

The "worship" practices of other nations frequently included sexual activity. Perhaps the Israelites' acceptance of the golden calf as a "god" also sparked a sexual frenzy similar to what they had witnessed among other religions.

When confronted, Aaron attempted lame excuses. Meanwhile, the people were frenzied and out of control. Moses called for volunteers who were "for the LORD," and a number of Levites rallied around him. At God's instruction, they strapped on swords and then went throughout the camp slaying their fellow Israelites consumed with pagan celebration.

About three thousand people were killed by the Levites. Those who survived were chastised by Moses, who ground the golden calf into powder, mixed it with water, and made the people drink it. In addition, God sent a plague among them (Exodus 32:19–20, 27–28, 35).

One Decent Moment

All things considered, Israel got off light for this great offense. Moses rejoined God on Sinai again to make another copy of the Ten Commandments—this time with Moses doing the carving. It was clear to all that Moses was spending time in God's presence, because when he descended the mountain his own head was radiant with light, and he had to place a veil on his face before people would come near him. In addition to the Ten Commandments, God provided Moses with a number of other laws and some very specific instructions on building a mobile tabernacle, establishing priests, and other essentials.

When they took up a collection for supplies to construct the tabernacle, the people eagerly brought so much that Moses issued a command to stop giving (Exodus 35:2–36:7). But it was one decent moment in a long series of whining and griping.

I Spy Someone Yellow

The ultimate failure of the people came just a while later when they reached their destination—perched right on the edge of the Promised Land. Moses sent spies ahead to scout out the land and report back. One representative from each tribe was chosen.

SWORD DRILL

What was impressive about the grapes the spies found in the Promised Land? (See Numbers 13:23.)

After forty days, the twelve spies returned with their report and with some produce from the land. Two of the twelve, Joshua and Caleb, were eager to move forward into this wonderful land that "does flow with milk and honey" (Numbers 13:27). But the other ten were too concerned with the obstacles they had seen. The people there were "of great size"—so much so that the spies thought of themselves as grasshoppers in comparison.

This was another opportunity for the people to step out in faith. Not only was Moses still with them, but now other leaders were boldly joining him with the faith to move forward. And God had continued to perform miracle after miracle, repeatedly showing His ability and willingness to see them through their journey to the end. But the people, for the most part, hadn't learned a thing.

It should have been a golden moment; instead, it was a cowardly shade of yellow. After the negative report of the ten spies, the people loudly bemoaned this latest challenge and actually prepared to stone Moses and the leaders who were advising moving ahead (Numbers 14:1–10).

WHAT'S THE GOOD WORD?

"The LORD, the LORD, the compassionate and gracious God, slow to anger, abounding in love and faithfulness, maintaining love to thousands, and forgiving wickedness, rebellion and sin. Yet he does not leave the guilty unpunished; he punishes the children and their children for the sin of the fathers to the third and fourth generation."

–GOD TO MOSES (EXODUS 34:6-7)

Suddenly the presence of God appeared in their midst, which brought their rebellion to a rapid end. Once again, God suggested the option of obliterating the sinful, whining people and letting Moses start over with a new and faithful bunch. But again, Moses pointed out that the other nations were observing them and learning about their God. Moses didn't want anyone to think God had failed in His mission, and God again spared the nation.

Still, God showed His displeasure in a number of ways. The ten pessimistic spies died immediately in a plague (Numbers 14:36–38). And all the people who grumbled were sentenced to wander in the wilderness for another forty years before God would bring them back to the Promised Land. They would die during that time, but their children would be allowed to enter.

This harsh sentence seemed to shock some of the Israelites. They didn't want to accept what God had decreed, so they reconsidered and decided to enter the land regardless of what God and Moses had said. More accurately, they *tried* to enter the land but were routed and driven away by the inhabitants (Numbers 14:39–45).

For Decadence, Four Decades

During the next forty years, the people had all the laws God had given them, but no permanent residence. As they moved from place to place, they would transport the tabernacle where the priests would offer their sacrifices. But worship didn't come easy for these people with their nomadic lifestyle. For one thing, they failed to maintain the annual observance of the Passover—the new holiday to commemorate their escape from Egypt. For another, at times they showed a blatant disregard for God's laws and Moses' leadership. In each instance, God had to respond.

➤ A man caught gathering wood on the Sabbath was stoned to death (Numbers 15:32–36). In another instance, someone who blasphemed God received the same sentence (Leviticus 24:10–23).

➤ A rebel group of 250 men led by a man named Korah attempted to wrest power away from Moses and Aaron. God took care of the problem with a well-directed earthquake and fire from heaven (Numbers 16).

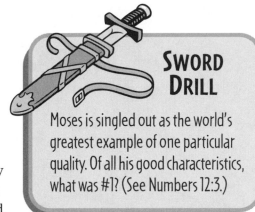

SWORD DRILL

Moses is singled out as the world's greatest example of one particular quality. Of all his good characteristics, what was #1? (See Numbers 12:3.)

➤ When the people as a whole *still* grumbled about food and water shortages (other than the manna, which they were quite tired of by now), God at one point sent poisonous snakes into the camp. Many were dying, and the others quickly begged Moses to set things right with God. At God's instructions, Moses erected a bronze serpent on a tall pole. Anyone who looked at the bronze snake would live (Numbers 21:4–9).

➤ In addition to having to fight other nations from time to time, once the Israelites faced an enemy who hired a "prophet" specifically to curse them. The prophet's name was Balaam, but God would not allow him to curse Israel. At one point, God even stationed an angel in Balaam's path, which Balaam could not see, though his donkey could. When he started beating the animal, God allowed the donkey to speak to Balaam—and in a somewhat comic scene, Balaam continued the conversation and began to *argue* with the donkey! (Numbers 22:21–35).

SWORD DRILL

What amazing sign did God use to indicate that Aaron (and the Levites) were for sure His choice as spiritual leaders? (See Numbers 17.)

➤ The men of Israel, when given the opportunity, were quick to have sex with Moabite woman and worship their gods. A plague from God (and some immediate executions by leaders still faithful to God) killed 24,000 people (Numbers 25:1–9).

Rock, Tantrum, Schism

After seeing a lot of your peers die in earthquakes, firestorms, and other various plagues because they had defied God, you might think it was time to straighten up and fly right. Yet again and again, when faced with any obstacle, the first response of the people was to grumble and accuse Moses. God was still faithfully providing for them, in spite of their lousy attitudes. But at one point Moses got fed up.

BACKGROUND INFO

God's refusal to let Moses at least set foot in the Promised Land is one of those cases (as in the instance when God accepted Abel's offering but not Cain's) where we assume God's knowledge of the person's inner thoughts was a primary reason for His decision. Perhaps Moses had been motivated by pride or lacked faith to simply speak to a rock rather than treating it as a piñata. We can't be sure.

The people were grousing about lack of water (no big surprise), and God had a plan to provide it for them. Previously He had instructed Moses to strike a rock, which he did, and ample water came gushing out (Exodus 17:1–7). This time, God told Moses to *speak* to the rock. But in a weak moment, Moses shouted at the people and whacked the rock twice with his staff. Water came out and the people were satisfied, but God was displeased with Moses' disobedience. In contrast to all the horrible things the people had been doing, Moses' little snit doesn't seem like a very significant offense. Yet God said Moses would not be allowed to enter the Promised Land (Numbers 20:1–13).

Just before Moses died, God allowed him to look down from Mount Nebo into the land where his people would be going. Then God personally buried Moses in a place no one knows. He died at age 120, "yet his eyes were not weak nor his strength gone." And even though the people had scorned his leadership time and time again, they grieved Moses' death for thirty days (Deuteronomy 34:1–8).

Coming Up: The Choice of a New Generation

Most of the story of Moses is scattered throughout the biblical books of Exodus, Leviticus, Numbers, and Deuteronomy. You'll also find a bunch of laws (all important to doing God's will), explanations of Jewish festivals and celebrations, genealogies, and numerous other mundane and fascinating bits of information.

The Book of Genesis, we have seen, spanned centuries of time. The next four books, however, covered a mere 120 years—the events connected with the life of Moses from birth to death. And essentially all of that information pertains to only the final third of his life.

WHAT'S THE GOOD WORD?

"The LORD said, 'I have indeed seen the misery of my people in Egypt. I have heard them crying out because of their slave drivers, and I am concerned about their suffering. So I have come down to rescue them from the hand of the Egyptians and to bring them up out of that land into a good and spacious land, a land flowing with milk and honey.'"

—EXODUS 3:7–8

But Moses got the job done. He took the Israelites to the edge of the Promised Land not once, but twice. The first time the people weren't even close to having the faith necessary to enter, defeat the imposing tribes established there, and claim what God said was theirs. How about this new generation? We'll see how they did in the next chapter.

Chapter Flashback

1. If Moses' parents had fully obeyed Pharaoh's commands, Moses would have been:
   a. Prince of Egypt
   b. Israel's greatest leader
   c. A normal Egyptian citizen
   d. Just another infant mortality statistic of the ancient world

2. During his forty years of hiding in the wilderness, Moses acquired:
   a. Flocks and herds too numerous to count
   b. A wife, a kid or two, and a call from God
   c. A bad attitude
   d. An odor like you wouldn't believe

3. Which of the following are all among the ten plagues on Egypt?
   a. The Nile turning to blood, body boils, rats
   b. Frogs, flies, the return of the Mummy
   c. Darkness, hail, death of livestock
   d. Gnats, locusts, cooties

4. God fed his people in the wilderness with:
   a. Manna
   b. Aaron's magic rod
   c. Five loaves and two fish
   d. A Starbucks at every stop

5. Moses was allowed to look into the Promised Land but not to set foot there, because:
   a. He spoke to a rock instead of hitting it.
   b. He didn't obey God.
   c. He was becoming old and weak.
   d. He was voted out of the tribe.

Answers: (1) d, (2) b, (3) c, (4) a, (5) b

Broken Promises in the Promised Land

JOSHUA, JUDGES, RUTH

SNEAK PREVIEW

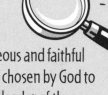

1. Joshua, a courageous and faithful commander, was chosen by God to replace Moses as leader of the Israelites.
2. After Joshua led the people into the Promised Land, they were governed by a series of judges during a time when "everyone did as he saw fit."
3. In contrast to numerous stories of Israel's self-centered and spiritually decadent condition is the selfless and inspiring story of Naomi, Ruth, and Boaz.

SNAPSHOT

"Hello, and welcome to Driver's Ed. My name is Mr. Wildman, and I think you'll find I give you a lot more freedom than other instructors. I'll take the passenger seat. Go ahead and drive . . . what's your name?"

"I'm Andrea, but this is my first class. I haven't even read the manual."

"Manual, shmanual. Forget those confining rules! There are thousands of miles of open road out there. You turn the key. You put it in drive. You stomp the pedal on the right. Nothing to it!"

"Don't you want me to put on my seat belt?"

"Seat belt?! What are you, a baby? Get going!"

"Here comes a stop sign, sir. What do I do? What do I do?"

"Stay calm. As you can clearly see, nothing is coming from either direction, so just keep going. That big red sign is there as a *suggestion* to stop if you need to. Since you don't need to stop, hit it!"

"Hit the sign?"

"No. The gas. Hit the gas!"

"Okay. But we're coming up on a grammar school. *Now* what do I do?"

"Good question. Here's what you need to know about school zones: People drive really slow . . . so you can pass a lot of cars at once. Go for it!"

"But there's a bunch of little kids crossing the street."

"Do what I say!" (Mr. Wildman's voice was rising in pitch and volume.) "Pass these six cars and two buses or I'll flunk you right now."

"If you say so," Andrea said as she winced and gunned the motor.

"See how those kids dove out of your way? That's why they teach 'em to look both ways before crossing the street. If they're going to stop for you, why do you need to stop for *them?*"

"I, uh, think I'm going to be sick."

"Not in my car you're not. Quick! Take a right."

"You mean where the sign says, 'Airport. No Entrance'?"

"Are you still obsessed with signs? Those signs are there for other people. Here I am trying to show you how fast this baby can go, and all you can do is whine about signs!"

"Y . . . you're the teacher."

"Now take a left onto runway 27. It's the longest one and you can really pick up some speed."

"Should I really be doing 90?"

"No. You *should* be doing 110."

"I hate to be a *whiner,* but there's a plane heading straight for us."

"I suppose now is a good time for me to give you the one rule I do live by. If you come up against something that's way bigger than you are, *get out of the way. [Takes control of wheel as car lurches to the side and skids to a stop.]* Are you okay?"

"Uh . . . I guess," said Andrea, "but I'm not paying for the car antenna that the plane clipped off."

Mr. Wildman ignored the comment and spoke while raising the hood. "The car stalled out, but I think I can get it started again."

"Don't bother. I'll walk!"

* * * * * * * * * * * * * *

There's a tendency among some in our society to flaunt established rules. People in business who do "whatever it takes" to win the big accounts and make money for the company are those who get bonuses and promotions. We acknowledge and perhaps even envy those who are perceived as rebels and those who "think outside the box."

Yet most rules exist for good reason. Traffic laws are just one example. In addition, recent current events have made us aware of the importance of airport security checks and procedures. And the Bible is clear about the importance of lifestyle and moral "laws"—even though many such rules are blatantly disregarded by contemporary culture.

During the journey from Egypt to the Promised Land, the Israelites had been given a number of specific rules to live by. While the rules came to be known as the Mosaic Law, the *source* of the rules was God Himself as He addressed diet, sexual guidelines, relationship problems, worship habits, and more. The God-given laws were quite specific, as were the penalties for those who disobeyed.

God had done as He had promised. He brought His people out from under the grip of one of the most powerful forces on earth, releasing them from slavery and personally escorting them to the Promised Land. And after a few mistakes and shortcomings, the people had promised to follow Him after they got there. Yet, as we will see in this chapter, it won't take long for the Israelites to become an entire nation of rebels and mavericks—or, in other words, disobedient children. And on such a widespread level, it won't be a pretty sight.

But first let's give them a bit of credit and see what they did *right*. (It won't take long.)

Joshua: A New Landlord in Town

The Book of Deuteronomy ended with the death of Moses. The next book picks right up with God's call of Joshua. Forty years previously, the Israelites had camped on the brink of the Promised Land, but their fear and grumbling had prevented them from entering. That generation had died while wandering in the wilderness. This time, the people were ready.

SWORD DRILL

In the noise and confusion of battle, how would the invading Israelites know which home was Rahab's so they could spare the inhabitants? (See Joshua 2:17–21.)

Rahab's Hideaway

As Moses had done, Joshua first sent spies into the land. This time two men sneaked into the walled and well-defended city of Jericho, where they hid out at the home of Rahab, a prostitute. They discovered that the people of Jericho had heard of how God traveled with the Israelites and protected them. Even though Jericho seemed impenetrable, Rahab told her guests, "All who live in this country are melting in fear because of you" (Joshua 2:9).

Men from Jericho came to Rahab's home looking for the spies, but she hid them beneath piles of flax drying on her roof; then she sent their pursuers on a wild-goose chase. What she asked in exchange for her help was safety for her family and herself when Jericho was destroyed. The spies readily agreed.

No Bridge over the River Jordan

Meanwhile, the Israelites were rallying together, realizing their long wanderings were almost over. First, however, they needed to get across the Jordan River at flood stage. No problem: Joshua sent ahead some priests carrying the ark of the covenant—and as soon as their feet got to the water's edge, the river stopped flowing. It "piled up in a heap" at a distance upstream (Joshua 3:16). The priests with the ark stood in the riverbed while the Israelites crossed the Jordan River as they had the Red Sea—on dry land.

With the water still receded, Joshua summoned one person from each tribe to go to the center of the riverbed and grab a stone, which Joshua used to build an altar as a remembrance of what God had done that day. Twelve stones for the twelve tribes of Israel. After everyone was across and the stones were gathered, the priests carried the ark to the other side. Immediately, the waters came rushing downstream and resumed their flood-stage levels.

Takin' Care of (Old) Business

News of this event quickly spread throughout the land, creating even more fear among the peoples. But the nation of Israel was not yet ready to fight. First the people needed to attend to some long-overlooked business. Many of the males born during the wilderness wanderings had never been circumcised, so the ceremony was performed and everyone stayed put until they had time to heal.

WHAT'S THE GOOD WORD?

"I will give you every place where you set your foot, as I promised Moses. . . . No one will be able to stand up against you all the days of your life. . . . I will never leave you nor forsake you."

—GOD TO JOSHUA (JOSHUA 1:3, 5)

In addition, the Passover was celebrated for the first time in a long while. It had been instituted the night of the exodus from Egypt, but neglected while in the wilderness. Now that the Israelites were at their final destination, they celebrated Passover again. At that point they gathered some food from the local area, and never saw manna again. God was expecting them to move ahead and provide for themselves.

Yet there would be no easy admittance into the Promised Land. Just because the Israelites had arrived didn't mean the inhabitants would simply leave. Joshua had been designated by God to be the new landlord, and as such he would have to conduct some evictions.

These Jericho Boots Are Made for Marching

God's first assignment for the Israelites was to take the massive walled city of Jericho. To make this assignment perfectly clear, God sent a heavenly figure to converse with Joshua before moving ahead. This messenger of God gave Joshua a simple, yet very detailed, battle plan for taking Jericho (Joshua 6:2–5).

Joshua and the Israelites followed this plan to the letter. For six straight days, they simply marched once around the walled city of Jericho. On the seventh day, they made seven laps. To show that this was no mere hike, the priests led the way with the ark of the covenant and played horns to signify God's arrival (much as trumpets might be played today to announce the presence of a visiting dignitary).

On the seventh day, after the seventh lap, after the sound of the rams' horns, as the people gave a unified shout, the great wall of Jericho suddenly collapsed into a pile of rubble (Joshua 6:15–20). The Israelites stormed in, took over, and burned the city. The only survivors from Jericho were Rahab and her family, who from then on took their residence with the people of Israel.

Ai-Yi-Yi-Yi-Yi!

The next city was called Ai, and should have been a breeze to conquer compared to Jericho. However, the forces that attacked Ai were quickly forced to retreat, and thirty-six Israelites died.

> ## BACKGROUND INFO
>
> Identified only as "commander of the army of the LORD," Joshua's visitor (Joshua 5:13–6:5) could have been: (1) an angel; (2) God in human form; or, (3) Jesus in a pre-incarnate appearance. This is one of several places in the Old Testament where the distinctions between God and God's messengers aren't as clear as we might like.

Upon investigation, Joshua discovered that God was angry because someone in Israel had committed a major sin. When attacking Jericho, the people had been instructed to keep no spoils because the city and all that was in it was devoted to God (Joshua 6:18–19). A man named Achan, however, had swiped a pretty robe and a bit of silver and gold. It didn't seem like much, but under the circumstances it was as if he had stolen not from Jericho but from God. Consequently, Achan was held responsible for the humiliating defeat at Ai, and he and his entire family were stoned to death (7:19–26). The next attack on Ai was successful. (If Achan had only waited, the Israelites were allowed to keep the spoils from Ai [8:2, 27].)

Are We in Alaska, or What?

After exposing and addressing the sin of Achan, Joshua and the Israelites were unstoppable. Even when a coalition of five local kings combined their armies to confront Israel, God told Joshua not to worry about it—he could be assured of victory.

Indeed, as the Israelites attacked, God provided air support with a barrage of large hailstones. The enemies turned and fled, and it looked as if many would escape under cover of darkness. But Joshua prayed to God for the sun and moon to "stand still over Gibeon" and received in response "about a full day" of additional light (Joshua 10:1–15, especially v. 13). A day without a sunset is an unheard-of event for anyone who hadn't summered in or near the Arctic Circle. But whatever happened, and however it occurred, the Bible tells us, "There has never been a day like it before or since" (Joshua 10:14).

Stopping Short

Joshua and the Israelites kept pushing forward until they had established themselves in the new land. But Joshua was getting older, and much land remained to be conquered, so assignments were made by tribe to effect a division of labor—a simple task, since Moses had previously determined which tribes should get which plots of land.

> ## BACKGROUND INFO
>
> Much speculation takes place about exactly what happened the day "the sun stood still." Some people feel the terminology is a bit strange, but that nothing actually happened out of the ordinary. Others feel that God miraculously slowed the turning of the earth so that we had one, singular, forty-eight-hour day in the midst of all the other twenty-four-hour ones. Still others hold out the possibility of peculiar eclipses or refracted light that illuminated the area without actually altering the physics of the universe.

Once the land was divided, it would be the responsibility of each tribe to keep moving, keep fighting, and dispose of all the enemies located in the assigned territories. God was specific about this. Otherwise, the only option was to ally with the natives, which would surely lead to intermarriage and involvement in the various pagan religions.

God had foreseen that this was exactly what was going to happen. He had told Moses: "You are going to rest with your fathers, and these people will soon prostitute themselves to the foreign gods of the land they are entering. They will forsake me and break the covenant I made with them. On that day I will become angry with them and forsake them; I will hide my face from them, and they will be destroyed" (Deuteronomy 31:16–17).

The leadership of Joshua, from beginning to end, was a bright spot in the history of Israel. The tribes went ambling into their territories charged with faith and determination, but it didn't last very long. With Moses and Joshua no longer in charge, we find very few decent leaders who had learned anything from them. This would be a time when "Israel had no king; everyone did as he saw fit" (Judges 21:25).

Scuzzy People's Court with Judge Whoppers

Although the Book of Joshua ends on a spiritual high, the following Book of Judges describes a repeated cycle of defeat. The people never did as God instructed; they failed to evict all the other nations in their territories. It wasn't long, therefore, before the tribes found themselves enslaved again—not by a mighty power like Egypt, but by local bullies they could and should have run out when they had the chance. Those local nations grew into problems that would last throughout Israel's history.

God didn't give up on His people, but His deliverance never lasted long because the people simply refused to respond to Him and change their ways. The cycle that developed from this attitude is summed up early in the book: "Then the LORD raised up judges, who saved them out of the hands of these raiders. . . . Whenever the LORD raised up a judge for them, he was with the judge and saved them out of the hands of their enemies as long as the judge lived; for the LORD had compassion on them as they groaned under those who oppressed and afflicted them." But the Scripture then adds: "When the judge died, the people returned to ways even more corrupt than those of their fathers, following other gods and serving and worshiping them. They refused to give up their evil practices and stubborn ways" (Judges 2:16, 18–19).

Over and over again God bailed out His wayward people, and over and over again they went right back to idolatrous ways as soon as they were free of their enemies.

Below are the people who served as judges over Israel. Some you may have never heard of. Others have quite a reputation.

Othniel (Judges 3:7–11)

Not long after they had arrived in the Promised Land, the Israelites "did evil in the eyes of the LORD" by forgetting who got them there and worshiping other gods instead. Consequently, God allowed them to be overtaken by their enemies. After eight years of suffering, they "cried out to the LORD" and He provided a deliverer. The first "judge" was a nephew of Caleb (one of the two faithful spies) named Othniel. He went to war, freed the Israelites, and they had peace for a few decades until they again forgot God and reverted to worship of idols.

Ehud (Judges 3:12–30)

After the Israelites endured eighteen years of subjection to Moab, God designated Ehud as the next judge. His is a rather gory and graphic story. The king of Moab demanded monetary tribute from Israel, and Ehud was chosen to deliver it. When he arrived, he told the king he had a secret message, and they retired to a private room. When the two of them were alone, Ehud pulled a small sword (unexpectedly, with his left hand) and plunged it into the obese body of the king—so obese, as a matter of fact, that his stomach fat closed over the handle of the sword. Ehud made his escape as the king's servants stood around assuming he was taking a particularly long bathroom break. With the king dead, Ehud led a military charge against Moab and was victorious.

Shamgar (Judges 3:31)

The next threat to Israel was the Philistines. We know very little about the judge Shamgar, because only one verse is devoted to him. We know, however, that he killed 600 Philistines with an "oxgoad"—basically a pointy stick used to herd

BACKGROUND INFO

The biblical concept of "judges" is quite different from the formal, robe-wearing, legal experts we are familiar with. Far from being cultured and refined, the judges that followed Joshua were frequently raw and rowdy. This was seldom a problem, however, because God didn't call on them to settle mild disputes. It was their mission to rid the land of the powers that had imposed themselves on God's people. Doing so usually required courage, strength, and bloodshed—not a neutral courtroom demeanor.

large animals. And if you think that's some small feat, try to imagine how you would respond if it were your assignment.

Deborah/Barak (Judges 4–5)

Deborah was a prophetess who summoned Barak and told him to lead the resistance against the latest Canaanite king who had subdued the Israelites. But Barak was reluctant because the commander of the army was a nasty man named Sisera, who had 900 iron chariots at his disposal. Barak said he would take the job only if Deborah went with him. She agreed but told him that because of his hesitance, the "honor" of the Israelite victory would not go to him, but to a woman.

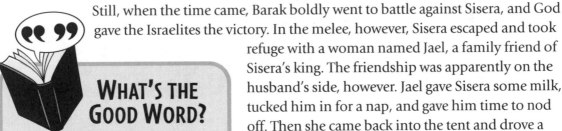

Still, when the time came, Barak boldly went to battle against Sisera, and God gave the Israelites the victory. In the melee, however, Sisera escaped and took refuge with a woman named Jael, a family friend of Sisera's king. The friendship was apparently on the husband's side, however. Jael gave Sisera some milk, tucked him in for a nap, and gave him time to nod off. Then she came back into the tent and drove a tent peg through his head.

WHAT'S THE GOOD WORD?

No king is saved by the size of his army; no warrior escapes by his great strength. . . . But the eyes of the LORD are on those who fear him, on those whose hope is in his unfailing love, to deliver them from death and keep them alive in famine.

—PSALM 33:16, 18–19

We tend to remember Jael's willingness to act on behalf of her people more than Barak's, and we also tend to give more credit to Deborah for the victory than to Barak. However, it is Barak who is mentioned in the list of faithful people in Hebrews 11 (v. 32).

Gideon (Judges 6–8)

The next enemies to subdue Israel were the Midianites. They were cruel people who would swoop in, take whatever they wanted, and destroy the rest. God sent an angel to instruct a man named Gideon to deliver Israel this time, the irony being that Gideon was found threshing wheat in a winepress, hoping not to be discovered by the Midianites. But after an encounter with the angel and a number of initial steps of faith, Gideon eventually took the job.

God instructed Gideon to shrink his army from an initial 32,000-soldier force to a group of 300. And even then they didn't need swords. One night Gideon formed three groups of 100 men each and positioned them in the hills around the Midianite camp. Each man carried a trumpet and a torch covered by a pitcher. At Gideon's signal, they all smashed the jars, grabbed the torches with one hand and the trumpets in the other, and started shouting and blowing the horns. The noise initiated a God-sent confusion throughout the Midianite army. The Midianites started killing each other, and those still alive fled.

Yet in spite of Gideon's faith and devotion in a time of crisis, late in his life he built a little idol for his town. We read that, "All Israel prostituted themselves by worshiping it there, and it became a snare to Gideon and his family" (Judges 8:27). It was a sad closing note on the life of an otherwise outstanding hero.

Abimelech (Judges 9)

Gideon had many wives who provided him with seventy sons. He also had a concubine who gave him a son. This offspring, named Abimelech, went to his own kinfolk and tried to raise grassroots support to become the next judge over Israel. And to increase his standing, he murdered all of Gideon's other sons except for the youngest one, who escaped.

> ## SWORD DRILL
>
> Many people know that Gideon "put out a fleece" to ensure that God would indeed work through him (Judges 6:36-40). But do you know what Gideon's first assignment was, and what nickname he received as a result of doing it? (See Judges 6:25-32.)

His scheme worked for a while, but after three years of Abimelech's leadership, God sent a spirit of discord between the self-designated judge and the people of Israel. A series of skirmishes ensued. In one, Abimelech killed about a thousand people by burning down a tower into which they had fled. But when he tried the same strategy a second time, a woman heaved a millstone over the side and cracked his skull. Not wanting to die at the hand of a woman, he had his armor-bearer finish him off first. (Of course, the Bible records the actual reason for his death—another act by a brave woman during this period of Israel's history.)

BACKGROUND INFO

Concubines were not little "hotties" that Israelite husbands had on the side. A concubine relationship was a legal marriage, and children by the relationship were considered legitimate. However, the rights of a concubine were not as complete as those of a regular wife. A concubine could be sent away anytime with just a small gift, and her children weren't entitled to an equal share of the inheritance (if any at all).

Tola, Jair, Ibzan, Elon, and Abdon (Judges 10:1–5; 12:8–15)

This series of judges led Israel for a total of seventy years, though few details are provided for their reigns. In between Jair and Ibzan was the judgeship of Jephthah.

Jephthah (Judges 10:6–12:7)

Jephthah served as judge only six years, though much more is said about him than the previously mentioned seventy-years-worth of judges combined. He faced off against the Ammonites after Israel had been subjected to their mistreatment for eighteen years. Jephthah was the black sheep of his family because his mother was a prostitute. In fact, he had run away from home and had formed a "group of adventurers"—perhaps his own version of merry men centuries before Robin Hood came up with the idea.

But when Ammonite persecution intensified, Jephthah's other family members tracked him down and convinced him to be Israel's leader. He started by attempting a diplomatic and peaceful settlement with the king of the Ammonites, but the king ignored him. So Jephthah followed up with a military attack and was victorious.

His personal victory party was cut short, however. Before going into battle, Jephthah had vowed to sacrifice to God the first thing that came out of his door when he returned home. After the victory, as he rode up, the first thing he saw was his only child—a virgin daughter—joyfully dancing to tambourines in celebration of his victory. Vows to God were unbreakable, so "he did to her as he had vowed" (Judges 11:34–40).

Samson (Judges 13–16)

Most people know some of the stories about Samson, though not so many can identify him as one of Israel's judges. He wasn't exactly a paragon of virtue whom parents would want their kids to follow. He was impulsive, self-centered, and his mind seemed to be on sex much more often than it was on God. He had a penchant for Philistine women, even though the Philistines had been in control of the Israelites for forty years.

His engagement to a Philistine woman not only didn't work out—it resulted in the deaths of thirty men (for their clothing), the capture of 300 foxes used to torch Philistine crops, the death of his fiancée and her father, and the start of a long-standing feud between Samson and the Philistines. Later Samson killed 1,000 Philistines in a single fight, armed only with a donkey's jawbone. And still he slept with Philistine prostitutes.

Eventually, he fell for a Philistine woman named Delilah, whom the other Philistines paid to discover the secret of Samson's strength. God had instructed Samson's parents to raise him under the terms of a Nazirite vow, which included a prohibition against cutting his hair. After lying to Delilah three times, Samson finally gave in and told her his strength was in his hair. In no time she had betrayed him. He awoke with a crew cut and surrounded by enemies. With no strength to fight back, he was captured, blinded, imprisoned, and forced to work for the Philistines.

But his prison sentence gave him time to think about God and repent. Meanwhile, his hair was growing back. At a big Philistine celebration honoring their god Dagon, someone thought it would be a kick to bring Samson out and publicly humiliate him. Samson prayed for one final dose of strength and asked his handlers to place him where he could feel

BACKGROUND INFO

The sacrifice of Jephthah's daughter is a difficult passage to understand. Human sacrifice was not intended to be part of worship for the Israelites. But the law was also clear: "Whatever your lips utter you must be sure to do, because you made your vow freely to the LORD your God with your own mouth" (Deuteronomy 23:23). Some interpreters attempt to reconcile these harsh options with the belief that Jephthah's daughter was "sacrificed" to God in that she was never allowed to marry—which was indeed a harsh sentence for a woman during that era. Others feel the text clearly indicates a literal, traditional sacrifice—which would require a burnt offering (Judges 11:30-31).

BACKGROUND INFO

Dagon, a popular Philistine god, appears numerous places in the Bible. He may have been a fish god ("Dag" meant **fish**) or a god of agriculture ("Dagan" meant **grain**).

the columns of the Philistine temple. The temple was packed with spectators, and 3,000 more were crowded onto the roof. Samson pushed against the columns, and the temple collapsed. So Samson killed more Philistines in his death than he had killed during his lifetime (Judges 16:30).

The rest of the Book of Judges (chapters 17–21) contains a number of tragic stories that reflect just how bad the spiritual state of Israel had become during the era of the judges. But in stark contrast is the narrative of the following book—the story of Ruth— which took place during the same era.

Ruth: Sometimes You Reap More Than You Sow

Ruth was a Moabite woman, which, if you've been paying attention, might not sound like something to be proud of. The Moabites went back to Lot's older daughter, who escaped from Sodom with him. She got him drunk and had a son by him, naming the child Moab (Genesis 19:36–37). It was a Moabite king who tried to pay Balaam to curse Israel, and when that didn't work, the Moabites seduced the Israelites instead, resulting in thousands of deaths (Numbers 22:1–7; 25:1–9). Now the Moabites were among the nations that had recently subjected Israel (Judges 3:12).

WHAT'S THE GOOD WORD?

"Where you go I will go, and where you stay I will stay. Your people will be my people and your God my God."

– RUTH TO HER MOTHER-IN-LAW, NAOMI

(RUTH 1:16)

Yet a famine drove a number of Israelites to Moab, where some of them married Moabite women. Ruth and her sister both married Israelite men, but both men soon died, as did the husband of Naomi, Ruth's new mother-in-law. Naomi decided to return to Israel, and her daughters-in-law planned to accompany her. She told them to stay, and one did. But Ruth had apparently seen something in Naomi that impressed her, and she insisted on going wherever Naomi went.

After this downer of a beginning, the rest of the Book of Ruth is a spectacular love story. One of Naomi's relatives was a wealthy bachelor, and Ruth just happened to go to his fields to pick up grain. (The kind thing to do for the poor during this time was for harvesters to leave whatever grain fell to the ground for them to pick up.)

When Naomi discovered that Ruth had stumbled into Boaz, a relative, on her own, Naomi stepped into the role of matchmaker. She devised a plan for the welfare of her widowed daughter-in law. (You can read Ruth 3 for the details.) And Boaz, honored to be noticed by Ruth, went through all the proper legal and social channels to ensure everything was done properly.

Ruth and Boaz were eventually married. One of their great-grandsons would become King David (Ruth 4:13, 16–17), and from the same lineage would eventually come Jesus Christ. Not bad for a Moabite girl.

But the lesson many people miss from this account has little to do with love and romance. In a bleak and depressing time when "everyone did as he saw fit," the Book of Ruth shows that those who saw fit to do good—to display love, commitment, and devotion—could flourish and receive God's blessing just as in any other time. God doesn't grade nations on a curve. He did, and does, recognize and reward the faith of individuals.

The era of judges is fast coming to a close. The next chapter will take a look at the kings of Israel, and we'll see if they could do any better. (Don't get your hopes up.)

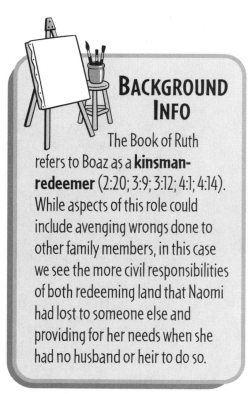

BACKGROUND INFO

The Book of Ruth refers to Boaz as a **kinsman-redeemer** (2:20; 3:9; 3:12; 4:1; 4:14). While aspects of this role could include avenging wrongs done to other family members, in this case we see the more civil responsibilities of both redeeming land that Naomi had lost to someone else and providing for her needs when she had no husband or heir to do so.

Chapter Flashback

It's time for another matching exercise. Match each of the following accomplishments with the person responsible. (There are more people listed than accomplishments, so choose carefully.)

A. Abimelech	E. Ehud	I. Naomi
B. Achan	F. Gideon	J. Rahab
C. Boaz	G. Jael	K. Ruth
D. Deborah	H. Joshua	L. Samson

(1) God-fearing prostitute who helped the Israelites and survived after the walls of Jericho came down

(2) Prostitute-loving judge who learned his lesson too late and didn't survive a temple coming down

(3) Rogue judge who didn't want to survive after a millstone conked him on the head

(4) Courageous woman who ensured an enemy commander didn't survive (by inserting a tent peg through his head)

(5) Moabite woman who, after numerous bad examples, brought honor to being a Moabite

(6) Israelite woman who brought honor to the title of "mother-in-law"

(7) Judge who won a decisive victory with an "army" of only 300 men

(8) Israelite leader who paved the way into the Promised Land—and commanded the sun to stand still as he did

(9) Disobedient fellow whose offense cost the lives of thirty-six people—before those of himself and his family

(10) Terrific female judge long before Sandra Day O'Connor and Ruth Bader Ginsberg

Answers: (1) J, (2) L, (3) A, (4) G, (5) K, (6) I, (7) F, (8) H, (9) B, (10) D

CHAPTER 8

It's Just One King After Another!

1 Samuel Through 2 Chronicles

SNAPSHOT

Samuel: I'm telling you, you don't want a king.

People: Oh, yes, we do!

Samuel: Why, exactly?

People: Because we want to be like all the other nations.

Samuel: Oh, *that's* a good reason. Wasn't that the reasoning behind the golden calf? How'd that work out for you?

People: Well, this system of judges hasn't been a rousing success, that's for sure.

Samuel: Whose fault is that? God keeps choosing people to lead you out of trouble, but then you start worshiping other gods again. One person can't keep all the rest of you in line. I should know!

SNEAK PREVIEW

1. After the series of judges, the people of Israel were led by a long series of kings.

2. After the first three kings, the Israelites were divided into two kingdoms–"Israel" and "Judah," each with its own ruler–and all but a scant few of those kings "did evil in the sight of the LORD."

3. In contrast to the rampant wickedness of many of the kings, God's prophets Elijah and Elisha were powerful and positive examples of faith.

People: Hey, Sam, we have no complaint with you. You've done an outstanding job. But you're getting up in years and those sons of yours are . . . not so outstanding. In fact they're dishonest and self-seeking. No offense, but we don't want them. We want a king.

Samuel: A king will draft your children into his armies.

People: Okay by us.

Samuel: He will force some of you to work in his fields and palaces.

People: It will lower the unemployment rate.

Samuel: He will tax your grain, wine, olives, and flocks for himself and his cronies. And I promise you won't like it.

People: [Chant] We want a king! We want a king! We want a king!

Samuel: God says okay. But just remember: You asked for it.

* * * * * * * * * * * * * * *

A conversation very much like the one in our "Snapshot" is recorded in 1 Samuel 8. The people had grown weary of the recurring, dysfunctional cycle of idolatry, enslavement, repentance, heroic judge, freedom, idolatry, enslavement, repentance, . . . you get the idea. Even though the people were at fault for choosing to return to idolatry each time God set them free, the blame (as usual) was placed on the leadership. They felt that if they had a king "like all the other nations," everything in their lives would be peachy.

SWORD DRILL

How did Samuel come to be so special to God in the first place? (See 1 Samuel 1, 3.)

They took their plea to Samuel, a prophet/judge who from childhood had faithfully represented God during a time when "the word of the LORD was rare; there were not many visions" (1 Samuel 3:1). As an old man hearing the demands of a spiritually fickle people, Samuel took it personally. But God made it clear to Samuel: "It is not you they have rejected, but they have rejected me as their king" (1 Samuel 8:7).

Actually, the Mosaic Law provided guidelines for human kings to rule over Israel (Deuteronomy 17:14–20). Yet it seems clear the people simply wanted to blend in among their idolatrous neighbors rather than stand out as a theocracy led by the unseen King of the universe. Like their ancestors at the foot of Mount Sinai who fashioned the golden calf, they wanted a tangible symbol to stand in front of them like all the other cultures seemed to have. Having an omnipotent (albeit invisible) God wasn't good enough.

Saul's Fair in War–But Downright Poor in Obedience

Still, God granted their request and chose a striking individual to be the first king over Israel. Saul was "an impressive young man without equal among the Israelites—a head taller than any of the others" (1 Samuel 9:2). In addition, Samuel promised Saul: "The Spirit of the LORD will come upon you in power . . . and you will be changed into a different person" (1 Samuel 10:6).

Saul had some initial successes, proving himself a competent military leader. However, he never quite mastered the faith and obedience portions of his life. He had been given specific instructions to wait for Samuel to make an offering at an assigned time. But when Saul's men saw what they were up against—an immense Philistine army with 3,000 chariots—they began to desert. Saul hastily made the offering himself (probably to rally the troops as much as to honor God), after which Samuel immediately showed up and rebuked him (1 Samuel 13:1–15).

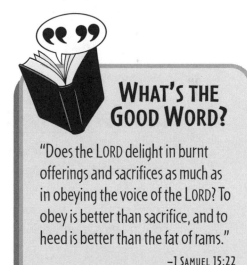

WHAT'S THE GOOD WORD?

"Does the LORD delight in burnt offerings and sacrifices as much as in obeying the voice of the LORD? To obey is better than sacrifice, and to heed is better than the fat of rams."

–1 SAMUEL 15:22

Later Saul was given clear directions to completely conquer and obliterate an enemy, sparing neither people nor animals. He won a decisive victory, yet refused to kill the opposing king and several of the best animals. Again chastised by Samuel, Saul tried to defend his actions (1 Samuel 15). But by this time, God had determined to replace Saul with "a man after his own heart" (1 Samuel 13:14). In addition, Samuel was never again sent to assist King Saul (15:35).

Instead, Samuel was immediately sent to anoint the person who would become the next king. All Samuel knew was that the candidate would be one of the sons of a man named Jesse (the grandson of Ruth and Boaz). Jesse had seven strong, strapping sons to show Samuel that day, and Samuel would have gladly endorsed several of them. But as each came forward, God vetoed one son after another. After seven passes and no one else around, Samuel asked Jesse if he had any other sons. David, the youngest, was tending the sheep and was called in. God confirmed that this was indeed His next choice as king over Israel, and Samuel anointed the youngster.

WHAT'S THE GOOD WORD?

"The LORD does not look at the things man looks at. Man looks at the outward appearance, but the LORD looks at the heart."

–GOD TO SAMUEL (1 SAMUEL 16:7)

Saul would remain king for a number of years, however, making things rather dicey for David from time to time. Initially, Saul and David got along fine. As God's Spirit departed from Saul, the king was beset with an evil spirit. The only thing that seemed to alleviate his misery was for David to play the harp for him. And when David discovered the over-nine-feet-tall Goliath harassing Saul's soldiers, Saul was ecstatic when David disposed of the giant. But that was a turning point.

Dave's Rave Reviews

The David and Goliath story is probably the best-known event in David's life, but it was only his debut. From that point onward, more is written about the life of David than any other Old Testament figure. The first time we see David, he is being anointed. Then, almost immediately, he is drafted to help King Saul and volunteers to fight Goliath.

David's great victory, however, ignited a flame of jealousy in King Saul that could not be extinguished. The king was troubled to hear David's praises sung in the same breath as his own. Twice he tried to spear David with a javelin while David was playing for him, eventually forcing David to flee. While on the run, David accumulated a fighting force of his own and would routinely fight the enemies of Israel.

Twice David had ideal opportunities to kill or capture King Saul, whose pursuit was relentless. But both times he declined to do so, realizing that as long as Saul was also "God's anointed," David had no right to interfere. Soon enough, Saul's spiritual decline led to his defeat and death. Sadly, Saul's sons died in the same battle. While it paved the way for David's rise as king, David also lost his best friend—Saul's son, Jonathan.

The (Reluctantly) United Tribes of Israel

The people of Judah endorsed David as their king right away. However, many of King Saul's family members, officers, and supporters sought a different successor. A prolonged conflict ensued during which David's forces got stronger and stronger as Saul's support dwindled. Key officers switched loyalties and ranking figures were assassinated—much like what we have witnessed in modern-age Middle-East disagreements. But during this entire transition period, David showed nothing but the highest respect for King Saul and his family. On occasion, he even avenged the dirty deeds that had been committed by others. (See, for example, 2 Samuel 1:1–6 and 4:1–12.)

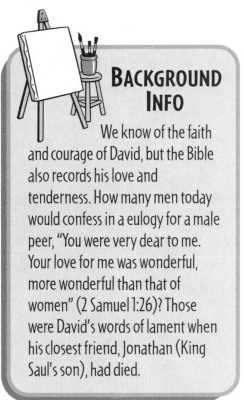

BACKGROUND INFO

We know of the faith and courage of David, but the Bible also records his love and tenderness. How many men today would confess in a eulogy for a male peer, "You were very dear to me. Your love for me was wonderful, more wonderful than that of women" (2 Samuel 1:26)? Those were David's words of lament when his closest friend, Jonathan (King Saul's son), had died.

David became king of Judah at age thirty. The tensions between Judah and Israel lasted seven and a half years, after which David became king over both Israel and Judah. And when it came time to establish a capital city, David wisely avoided choosing one in either of the existing competitive territories. Instead, he set his sights on Jerusalem (also known as Zion, Salem, and Jebus), an old and established city *between* Israel and Judah. Though the Jebusites who inhabited the well-fortified city were confident no one could run them out, David had little trouble taking over the city and beginning a building project to erect a palace for himself and his growing family.

He Should Have Taken a Cold Shower Instead of That Bathsheba

David's rise to power is an inspiring success story. But later, after he had established himself, he committed an act that created dissension in his family for the rest of his life. He saw a woman taking a bath, lusted after her, and sent for her. The woman was Bathsheba, and her husband Uriah was off at war. She became pregnant by David, who then brought Uriah home on furlough so he would sleep with his wife, go back to the battle, and then think nothing of it when his wife announced her pregnancy.

But Uriah refused to see his wife, staying "on duty" at the palace instead. When none of David's subtle plans worked, he arranged a more direct scheme to have Uriah killed in battle. After hearing of Uriah's death, David married Bathsheba and she had their child. (See 2 Samuel 11.) However, God refused to allow the baby to live, sending a prophet named Nathan to confront David. The king was repentant, and Bathsheba's next son by David was Solomon. But a consequence of David's sin with Bathsheba was God's mandate that, "The sword will never depart from your house" (2 Samuel 12:10).

BACKGROUND INFO

Hardly had the tribes settled into the Promised Land than they began to have problems and misunderstandings. Part of the problem was geographic, with nine and a half tribes on one side of the Jordan River and two and a half on the other. Eventually, the northern tribes—the majority—became known as "Israel," with the southern section collectively called "Judah" (even though Judah was at first only one of the original twelve tribes). As separate entities, sometimes Israel and Judah would fight against each other, and other times would unite against common enemies.

Sibling Rivalry Leads to Civil War

And sure enough, it wasn't long before one of David's sons (Amnon) began to lust after his half sister (Tamar). When other seductive ploys failed, he raped her. Perhaps David still felt pangs of conscience over his own indiscretions and didn't feel justified in taking action against Amnon. But another of David's sons (and Tamar's full brother), Absalom, was unwilling to stand by and do nothing. He waited long enough for Amnon to let down his guard and then murdered him.

David dearly loved Absalom, and during Absalom's three-year self-imposed exile, David mourned every day (2 Samuel 13:37–39). After a bit of conniving and negotiation, Absalom was allowed to return. But again he broke David's heart by attempting to overthrow his father. This time it was David who fled Jerusalem. In the battle that followed, Absalom eventually was killed and David and his forces returned to rule again.

But after all David's hard work to unite Israel and Judah, the tensions within the kingdom continued as the citizens who supported Absalom clashed with David's loyal followers. The Philistines and others remained external threats. And in David's old age, yet another of his sons, Adonijah, attempted to set himself up as the next king. When David heard what was happening, this time he took immediate action.

> **SWORD DRILL**
>
> Absalom lost five pounds every time he got a haircut (2 Samuel 14:25–26). But how did his fine head of hair eventually lead to his death? (See 2 Samuel 18:9–15.)

David wasted no time in publicly declaring Solomon the next king, effectively short-circuiting Adonijah's plans to usurp power. In addition, David targeted specific individuals whom he knew would create problems for Solomon and told the new king to take extreme measures to remedy the problems, even specifying in some cases to "bring his gray head down to the grave in blood" (1 Kings 2:6, 9). David had been merciful throughout his reign, but the potential threats to his son motivated him to action. Before long, "the kingdom was now firmly established in Solomon's hands" (1 Kings 2:46).

Solomon: Head Wise and Heart Foolish

In spite of David's sins—as flagrant and significant as they were—he was still a man after God's own heart. His choice of Solomon to follow him was God's plan as well. One of the first things we hear about Solomon was that God appeared to him in a dream and told him, "Ask for whatever you want me to give you" (1 Kings 3:5). Solomon asked for wisdom to rule his people well. God was pleased and granted him not only great wisdom but also riches and honor. However, God

BACKGROUND INFO

The contents of 1 and 2 Chronicles revisit much of the material already covered in the books of Samuel and the Kings. Written as a kind of historical retrospective during a difficult time in Jewish history, the unidentified author challenges and encourages his readers. Most of the less-than-flattering accounts of David and Solomon are omitted or downplayed in Chronicles. In the Hebrew Scriptures, Chronicles (originally a single book) concludes the Old Testament.

also warned Solomon to "walk in my ways and obey my statutes and commands as David your father did" (1 Kings 3:14).

David the warrior had done most of the dirty work, subduing Israel's enemies and pulling together a fickle nation. With the bloodshed behind him, Solomon was able to turn his attention to building on what David had already done. This was a golden age when "the people of Judah and Israel were as numerous as the sand on the seashore; they ate, they drank and they were happy" (1 Kings 4:20).

Conquered enemies paid tribute to Solomon, and the king established an international trading empire, bringing in high-quality cedar lumber, ivory, spices, precious stones, horses and chariots, baboons, and lots of other things you wouldn't normally expect to see in the Middle East. After a while, nothing of importance in the empire was made of silver because "the king made silver as common in Jerusalem as stones" (1 Kings 10:27).

Solomon's first big project was to construct a permanent temple to replace the portable tabernacle the priests had repeatedly set up and taken down

SWORD DRILL

In an early ruling as king over his people, how did Solomon show his great wisdom by ordering the death of a baby? (See 1 Kings 3:16–28.)

through their wanderings in Egypt and entry into the Promised Land. David had desperately wanted this assignment, but God refused his offer because of the wars he had fought and blood he had shed. It would be David's son, "a man of peace and rest," who would build the temple. David, however, did much of the planning and preparation (1 Chronicles 22:2–10).

A common belief was that Solomon's temple was built on the very spot where Abraham had attempted to sacrifice Isaac centuries earlier. The temple was built in seven years, at which time the ark of the covenant was positioned in its special location in the Most Holy Place. As soon as the priests had placed it there and withdrawn, a cloud signifying God's presence filled the temple so thickly that the priests couldn't even work. And after the dedication of the temple, God again appeared to Solomon—renewing His promise to bless him, and reminding him of the importance of spiritual integrity and obedience (1 Kings 9:1–9).

Solomon also built a grand palace for himself and became widely known for his sayings, songs, and splendor. People came from all over the world to see and hear him. One special visitor was the queen of Sheba, who traveled from a distant location—perhaps on the Arabian peninsula near modern-day Yemen. Solomon answered all her hard questions, they exchanged gifts, and she returned home, much impressed with the king's wisdom (1 Kings 10:1–13, especially verses 6–9).

Solomon apparently had a way with women. He accumulated 700 "wives of royal birth" and 300 additional concubines. Many were no doubt marriages to seal deals with other countries for trade, commerce, and expansion. In many cases, the brides came from nations that God had forbidden the Israelites to intermarry with. And we are told, "As Solomon grew old, his wives turned his heart after other gods" (1 Kings 11:3–4).

Solomon was the exception to our assumptions that wisdom comes with age. He had the benefit of a

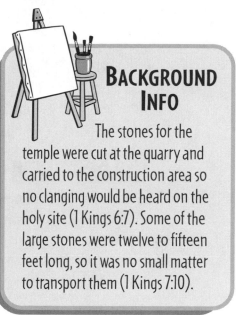

BACKGROUND INFO

The stones for the temple were cut at the quarry and carried to the construction area so no clanging would be heard on the holy site (1 Kings 6:7). Some of the large stones were twelve to fifteen feet long, so it was no small matter to transport them (1 Kings 7:10).

BACKGROUND INFO

Some people suggest the queen of Sheba's visit was more than merely a pursuit of intellectual curiosity. One theory is that she wished to get pregnant by Solomon and bear a child who would benefit from his gene pool. Others hypothesize that her visit was primarily to establish a business/trade alliance.

lifetime of wisdom, yet spurned all the godly insight at his disposal and brought to a quick end the magnificent, glorious, united kingdom of Israel. Because of God's great respect for David, Solomon was allowed to "ride out" the rest of his life as king. But during that time, Israel's enemies again became serious threats. And as soon as Solomon's son assumed the throne, the nation started to splinter.

The Beginning of the End

Solomon's son, Rehoboam, succeeded his father, but he had competition from another up-and-coming leader named Jeroboam. God had already sent a prophet to Jeroboam, "a man of standing," and told him that he would be given ten of the tribes to rule over. David's dynasty would continue, but only in the smaller area of Judah (which included the original tribes of Judah and Simeon). When Solomon realized there was another contender for king, he tried to kill Jeroboam but failed.

Samuel had previously alerted the people to the disadvantages of having a king, and most of those warnings had come to pass under Solomon. The massive building and expansion projects had required money and laborers, and many of Solomon's subjects had been "conscripted" to help: 3,300 foremen and 30,000 Israelite workers, with another 80,000 stonecutters and 70,000 carriers drafted from non-Israelites (1 Kings 5:13–18).

SWORD DRILL

Jeroboam had the larger kingdom, but the temple was still in Rehoboam's domain of Jerusalem. What old icon did Jeroboam reestablish to prevent his people from returning to Jerusalem to worship? (See 1 Kings 12:26-30.)

When Rehoboam came to power, the people requested relief from the "heavy yoke" Solomon had imposed on them (1 Kings 12:3–4). Solomon's advisers said Rehoboam could endear himself to the people if he granted their request. But when Rehoboam asked his own peer group, they advised imposing even greater requirements from the people—just to prove who was now the boss.

Rehoboam went with the advice of his own age-group . . . and most of the people immediately rejected his leadership. When he sent a royal official to change their minds, they stoned the guy to death. So the kingdom was irrevocably split. Rehoboam retained authority over Judah, and Jeroboam became king over "Israel" (the ten northern tribes).

Jeroboam knew the temple in Jerusalem was a lure that would keep drawing people out of his territory to go worship. So he immediately set up shrines throughout the northern kingdom and designated priests so that the people's desire to worship would be easily accommodated. Before long, the people were worshiping, but they had forsaken their true God.

The same apostasy was taking place in Judah. Although the temple was there, they set up additional shrines and began to worship other gods, even incorporating male shrine prostitutes (1 Kings 14:22–24).

A Long, Hard Reign Is Going to Fall

After such an inauspicious beginning, it's no surprise that few of the following kings were any better at leading the people. The rulers of Israel and Judah are listed throughout the books of Kings and Chronicles, but few are truly memorable. Except for a brief period of spiritual revival here and there, the entire span of the kings after Solomon was little better than the period of judges had been. The people were spiritually active, but active in idolatrous religions. They continued to ignore the God who had given them so much.

The chart on the next page lists the kings of Israel (the northern kingdom) and Judah (the southern kingdom). Don't feel badly if you don't recognize a lot of the names.

Several of these kings "earned" their thrones by assassinating their predecessors. Some faced strong opposition from invading enemies, resulting not only in warfare, but also terrible famine. The lone female ruler, Athaliah, was no better than the rotten men who preceded her. And while a few kings had moderate military success, most remain on record as men who "did evil in the eyes of the LORD."

Kings of Israel	Kings of Judah
Jeroboam I	Rehoboam
Nadab	Abijah
Baasha	Asa
Elah	Jehoshaphat
Zimri	Jehoram
Tibni	Ahaziah
Omri	Athaliah *(A queen rather than a king)*
Ahab	Joash
Ahaziah	Amaziah
Joram	Azariah
Jehu	Jotham
Jehoahaz	Ahaz
Jehoash	Hezekiah
Jeroboam II	Manasseh
Zechariah	Amon
Shallum	Josiah
Menahem	Jehoahaz
Pekahiah	Jehoiakim
Pekah	Jehoiachin
Hoshea	Zedekiah

The few exceptions who had varying degrees of spiritual integrity and success as kings were:

➤ Asa (1 Kings 15:9–24; 2 Chronicles 14–16)

➤ Jehoshaphat (1 Kings 22:41–50; 2 Chronicles 17–21:3)

➤ Jehu (2 Kings 9–10, the only good ruler of the northern kingdom)

➤ Joash (2 Kings 12; 2 Chronicles 24)

➤ Amaziah (2 Kings 14:1–22; 2 Chronicles 25)

➤ Azariah , a.k.a. Uzziah (2 Kings15:1–7; 2 Chronicles 26)

➤ Jotham (2 Kings 15:32–38; 2 Chronicles 27)

➤ Hezekiah (2 Kings 18–20; 2 Chronicles 29–32)

➤ Josiah (2 Kings 22:1–23:30; 2 Chronicles 34–35)

WHAT'S THE GOOD WORD?

"When one rules over men in righteousness, when he rules in the fear of God, he is like the light of morning at sunrise on a cloudless morning, like the brightness after rain that brings the grass from the earth.'… But evil men are all to be cast aside like thorns, which are not gathered with the hand."

– 2 SAMUEL 23:3-4, 6

When you read these stories, you'll see that even this approximately 20 percent of "good" kings tended to run hot and cold, in a spiritual sense. Few were stellar examples of leadership. After repeated warnings by God of what would happen if the people of Israel and Judah didn't return to Him, He allowed Israel to be defeated by the Assyrians in 722 B.C., followed by the conquest of Judah by Babylon in 605 B.C.

All that David had worked for and that Solomon had accumulated was stolen and carried off by peoples who couldn't care less about God. The temple, the royal palace, and all the important buildings were looted and burned. Most of the people who would be of value were marched off into captivity, with only a few of the poorest ones allowed to remain and tend to the crops (2 Kings 25:8–12).

WHAT'S THE GOOD WORD?

Unless the LORD builds the house, its builders labor in vain. Unless the LORD watches over the city, the watchmen stand guard in vain.

–PSALM 127:1

In Spite of Everything Wrong, A Strong Prophet Margin

Yet even in these bleak and seemingly hopeless times, a few of God's people stand out as glowing examples. If you're looking for a series of good stories that offer faith and optimism during this historic period, don't look at the kings. Look instead to the lives of God's prophets, Elijah and Elisha. God was speaking clearly through the prophets, whether or not the kings chose to heed what they had to say.

Elijah first shows up during the reign of one of the very worst kings—Ahab, who ruled with Queen Jezebel (who appears to have been even more wicked than the king). Elijah's first assignment was to tell Ahab that God would be withholding rain for three years.

Meanwhile, Elijah used the power of God to remind the common people that God was still attentive and compassionate. Elijah found a widow preparing a last meal for herself and her son, and miraculously provided food for them until after the drought (1 Kings 17:7–16). When her son became so sick he stopped breathing, Elijah brought him back to life. He did many other great things as well, but is probably best known for his impressive showdown against 850 idol-worshiping priests on top of Mount Carmel, when fire fell from heaven to verify the reality of Elijah's God and announce the return of rain to the land (1 Kings 18:19–46).

SWORD DRILL

How was a good prophet like Elijah supposed to find regular meals during a time when there was no rain on the land? (See 1 Kings 17:1–6.)

After Elijah rode a fiery chariot into heaven, his trainee, Elisha, had a ministry that was no less impressive. Essentially everything Elijah had done was repeated by Elisha, and more: miraculous supplies of food, resurrection of the dead, healings of leprosy and mass poisoning, making an ax head float, and even taking an entire army captive (2 Kings 2–8:6).

Elijah and Elisha were the two prophets who were singled out in this portion of the Bible, but there were others serving with them and after them. We'll take a look at several others in the next chapter.

BACKGROUND INFO

While Elijah and Elisha are generally the most recognized prophets during this string of wicked kings, they were by no means the only ones. In a rare moment when Elijah was feeling afraid, alone, and depressed, God assured the weary prophet that he was not a solo act. In fact, God knew of 7,000 other faithful followers (1 Kings 19:9-18).

Chapter Flashback

1. Saul should have *looked* like a good king because:
   a. He was already a head of state.
   b. His head was bigger than anyone else's.
   c. He was a head taller than anyone else.
   d. He was ahead of everyone else in most of the Kish triathlons.

2. David made a good king because:
   a. He followed another king who did a lousy job.
   b. He was a man after God's own heart.
   c. He was a man after Uriah's wife.
   d. He was a man without a country.

3. Solomon's primary achievements included:
   a. Building the temple and expanding the kingdom
   b. Visiting the queen of Sheba
   c. Winning many great battles
   d. Keeping all his wives and concubines happy

4. Israel and Judah each had a series of about how many kings?
   a. Ten
   b. Twenty
   c. Thirty
   d. Three wee kings

5. Two outstanding minority examples of faithfulness, power, and hope during the days of the divided kingdom were:

a. Jehoiakim and Jehoiachin

b. Pekah and Pekahiah

c. Delilah and Delovely

d. Elijah and Elisha

Answers: (1) c, (2) b, (3) a, (4) b, (5) d

FATHER
↓
SON

Faithful People in Awful Times

EZRA THROUGH ESTHER, AND ISAIAH THROUGH MALACHI

SNAPSHOT

"Michael! What are you doing with Dad's car keys? You know he said if he caught you going out without his permission again he would take away your driving privileges until you were on Medicare."

"Yeah, I know, Sis, but that's just it. Last time I disobeyed, all he did was give me a big huffy warning. I don't plan on getting caught, but if I do, all I have to do is sit through another barrage of threats. By the way, what are *you* doing?"

"I'm on hold on the Shopaholic Gotta-Have-It Retail line. They just advertised a combo set of diamond earrings with a large stuffed emperor penguin."

"A real penguin?"

"No, you goof. It's a plush toy. But the earrings are real diamonds."

SNEAK PREVIEW

1. God sent prophets both to warn people of coming calamity and to see them through those difficult times.

2. Prophets are found throughout the Bible, but the "writing prophets" are defined as those whose writings are included in the Old Testament.

3. Esther, Ezra, and Nehemiah weren't prophets, yet their stories demonstrate God's work among His people during their captivity and as they started rebuilding what they had lost.

"Where are you getting the money for real diamonds?"

"I'm, uh, using Mom's credit card," Sis said.

"I thought she locked it up after the last purchase you made. What was it . . . oh, yes . . . the Buffy the Vampire Slayer Home Extermination Kit. You charged $39.95 plus shipping and handling to get a plastic hammer and a stick."

"I don't need the actual card as long as I have the number committed to memory. Besides, I was just an immature kid when I did that."

"It was last Thursday!"

"I'm older and more mature now. That's why I need the earrings."

"Well, you'll probably be okay," Michael conceded. "Mom would never think to check her credit card receipts, just like Dad won't check the odometer . . . ."

"Oh, gotta go. They're taking me off hold. See ya later."

"Goodbye . . . and good luck."

* * * * * * * * * * * * * *

Most teenagers learn the hard way that it's not as easy as they think to pull one over on Mom and Dad. Still, there is something in human nature that makes us determined to learn the hard way. Even as adults, many people are unwilling to choose right over wrong until faced with imposed punishment. Sometimes such punishment is delayed for long periods, but it almost always catches up with us.

Don't Scoff at the Prophets

Throughout their history, God had informed His people of His plan to take them from slavery to freedom in a promised land, and how essential it would be for them to remain faithful to Him. He warned them of terrible things that would happen if they disobeyed. Yet over and over they spurned His warnings and acted in defiance of His clear instructions. After the era of judges and a long line of mostly evil kings, God's tolerance of His people's sins had come to an end.

In addition to giving the written law that recorded general rules to live by, God also sent a series of prophets—personal messengers who foretold future events, proclaimed His specific warnings, and reminded the people of His promises. Prophets were distinct from priests, though some men served both functions. And unlike the prophets and seers of ancient Greece and other nations, Hebrew prophets did more than simply interpret signs. Their messages originated from God. Sometimes the messages were critical of the prophet's own people, and the prophet found himself alone performing an unpopular task. But as a spokesperson for God, the prophet had little say-so in either his message or the people's response.

WHAT'S THE GOOD WORD?

"I am sending you to the Israelites, a rebellious nation that has rebelled against me; they and their fathers have been in revolt against me to this very day. The people to whom I am sending you are obstinate and stubborn. Say to them, 'This is what the Sovereign LORD says.' And whether they listen or fail to listen—for they are a rebellious house—they will know that a prophet has been among them."

–GOD TO EZEKIEL (EZEKIEL 2:3-5)

Early Prophets in the North

After the kingdom divided, prophets were sent both to Israel and Judah. We took a brief look at Elijah and Elisha at the end of the previous chapter. They are fairly well known, but other faithful prophets are found tucked away in short passages of Scripture, such as Nathan, who, during the united kingdom, set David straight after his sin with Bathsheba (2 Samuel 12) and a fellow named Ahijah, who took God's messages to Jeroboam (1 Kings 11:29–39; 14:1–20). Some "prophets" who pop up in Scripture are false prophets—men who made a name for themselves (and sometimes a pretty good living) by telling people what they wanted to hear even though they claimed to be speaking for God.

Other Prophets of the North

Perhaps some of the most memorable prophets are those known as "writing prophets" who have books of the Bible ascribed to them. Although these books are gathered together at the end of the Old Testament, and though all these prophets had similar jobs to take God's word to God's people, they came from

SWORD DRILL

How could people tell a prophet of God from a false prophet? And what penalties could be invoked if a prophecy turned out to be false? (See Deuteronomy 13:1–5; 18:18–22.)

WHAT'S THE GOOD WORD?

You lie on beds inlaid with ivory and lounge on your couches. You dine on choice lambs and fattened calves.... You drink wine by the bowlful and use the finest lotions, but you do not grieve over the ruin of Joseph. Therefore you will be among the first to go into exile; your feasting and lounging will end.

–AMOS 6:4, 6–7

a variety of backgrounds and were sent to various places.

Elijah and Elisha, for example, had served in the northern ten-tribe coalition of Israel. Following them came the prophets Amos and Hosea, who did their writing before Israel was defeated by Assyria.

Amos

Amos was a shepherd and fig grower from Tekoa, a city in Judah, and he was called to prophesy in Israel during a rare period of prosperity and confidence. But even though things were outwardly good, the inner spiritual condition of the people was rapidly deteriorating. They worshiped other gods and participated in rituals that included drunkenness, violence, and sensuality. In addition, social injustice was widespread, as rich people had their way at the expense of the poor. Amos warned them of captivity to come, and was so emphatic he received a personal rebuke from a high-ranking priest (Amos 7:10–17).

Hosea

Hosea had a long ministry but a turbulent personal life. His very marriage was an allegory that demonstrated the fickle lack of devotion Israel showed for God. At God's instruction, he married "an adulterous wife" named Gomer, who bore three children before leaving him to live with other men. God named Hosea's children for him—the Hebrew equivalent of "God scatters," "Not loved," and "Not my people" (Hosea 1:4–8). Whether these three were all Hosea's biological offspring is sometimes questioned.

But after leaving Hosea, Gomer apparently had to sell herself into slavery. God then instructed the prophet to redeem his wayward wife, not only buying back her freedom, but also expressing his love and forgiveness. The first three chapters of the Book of Hosea describe the prophet's personal struggles, and the remainder of the book shows how the relationship of the people toward God mirrored the struggling relationship between Gomer and Hosea. God's people were about to stray away from Him and would need to be forgiven and rescued when no longer able to fend for themselves.

Jonah/Nahum

While Amos and Hosea warned Israel of the threat of Assyria, Jonah was sent to Ninevah, the capital city of Assyria itself. If you think it seems difficult to confront your own people with their sins, imagine marching into enemy territory and telling a hostile and powerful nation to repent.

It's understandable when Jonah decided to try going the opposite direction, but he couldn't run away from God. The wayward prophet had his mind changed in no uncertain terms after being hurled over the side of a ship during a violent storm, swallowed by an enormous fish, and hurled up (in a different sense of the word) on shore three days later. But after he finally got around to delivering God's message to Assyria, the Ninevites amazingly responded and repented. Later, however, they reverted to their wicked ways, and the prophet Nahum was sent to alert them that their proud city would soon fall.

SWORD DRILL

Most people know how God used a fish to get Jonah going in the right direction. But later, in Ninevah, what other creature did God use to teach the prophet another lesson? (See Jonah 4:1–11.)

Obadiah

Similarly, the prophet Obadiah was sent to Edom, another enemy of Israel and Judah. As a rival nation, the Edomites took sadistic satisfaction as they witnessed the fall of Israel/Judah. Obadiah's message was that soon Edom would fall as well. And lest the Edomites think that event would even the score, God would soon enough deliver *His* people.

Prophets with Southern Accents

So Hosea and Amos prophesied to Israel, Jonah and Nahum to Assyria, and Obadiah to Edom. No less than six other writing prophets were sent to Judah, the southern kingdom, *before* the Babylonians came storming in. And although repeated attempts were made to persuade the people to change their ways, the residents of Judah were not so inclined.

Isaiah

While Amos and Hosea were operating in the northern area of Israel, Isaiah was active in the southern land of Judah. As the Assyrians were growing stronger as a threat to the north, Isaiah foretold that Judah's disregard for God would eventually result in their downfall at the hands of the Babylonians. And although these events wouldn't occur for another century and a half, he saw even beyond the eventual destruction of Jerusalem and predicted God's deliverance of His people from Babylon, comparing it to their previous release from Egypt.

Isaiah has been called the evangelist of the Old Testament because he not only dropped the bomb about terrible events to come, but also went to great lengths to offer consolation by describing God's redemption of His people—both short-term in their promised release from Babylon and long-range in the anticipation of a Messiah. Isaiah is quoted in the New Testament more than all the other writing prophets put together.

SWORD DRILL

At one point God sent Isaiah to King Hezekiah with the message that it was time for the king to die. What happened when the king asked for more time? (See Isaiah 38:1–8 and 2 Kings 20:1–11.)

Among other significant passages in his writing, he included a descriptive account of his call by God (chapter 6), a frequently quoted passage about the coming Messiah (9:2–7), a cryptic passage which many believe pertains to the fall of Satan from heaven (14:12–17), a favorite chapter of comfort (40), and a prediction of how the Messiah would suffer (53).

We know little about the personal life of Isaiah. Several references to his father, Amoz, suggest Isaiah may have come from a prominent family. We also know he was married and had a couple of children (Isaiah 7:3; 8:3). And according to one Jewish tradition, Isaiah went afoul of the authorities and died by being sawed in two (a mode of death mentioned in Hebrews 11:37).

BACKGROUND INFO

A **cistern** is a well-like reservoir for storing water. When dry, these reservoirs were sometimes used as makeshift prisons, as Joseph (Genesis 37:23-24) and Jeremiah (Jeremiah 38:6) could tell you.

Jeremiah

In contrast, Jeremiah tells us quite a bit about himself, and his was no enviable life. His ministry began during the rule of Josiah, the last decent king of Judah, who initiated something of a spiritual revival. But Jeremiah's message from God was that Judah's spiritual state would soon deteriorate once more and that the people would be overtaken by the Babylonians. Their captivity would last seventy years, after which God would surely deliver them. Still, this message made him quite an unpopular person, and the series of less-than-decent kings who succeeded Josiah gave Jeremiah varying degrees of hassle.

During his lifetime, Jeremiah was jailed frequently, once after being formally charged with treason. Friends rescued him from a plot to have him killed. His prophecies were read by a king who, not liking what he heard, sliced up the scroll bit by bit and tossed the pieces into a fire. Jeremiah was at one point tossed into a mucky cistern and left for dead until, again, someone rescued him. And he lived to see many of God's predictions come true as Babylon stormed into Judah and carried off many of its best people.

Ironically, the Babylonian leaders gave him more respect than most of the Hebrew kings had. Jeremiah is sometimes called "the weeping prophet," though he was steadfast and faithful throughout some terrible times. Nor is his writing entirely pessimistic. His book offers some wonderfully encouraging messages of hope amid the obstacles of his personal life and his prophetic announcements of coming defeat.

Joel

Joel doesn't provide a date or name a specific king by which to fix a definite time period for his book. Based on his references to what's going on, some people

believe he lived prior to the exile of Judah; others think his might be the last of the prophetic accounts from a chronological perspective. But Joel's message transcends the need to set a date.

He writes of a devastating locust plague: "What the locust swarm has left the great locusts have eaten; what the great locusts have left the young locusts have eaten; what the young locusts have left other locusts have eaten" (Joel 1:4). In other words, there's nothing left.

While some take an allegorical perspective and argue the locusts represent invading armies, most Bible scholars prefer a literal translation. After all, not even invading armies were as deadly as a locust plague to a culture purely dependent on agricultural life.

And since a locust plague was about as terrible as things could get, Joel compared the event to the coming "day of the LORD" (Joel 1:15) which would be "great and dreadful" (2:31). He called for repentance from the people. God would certainly take pity on them, but only after they experienced a horrendous level of destruction.

Joel's prophecy of God's Spirit being poured out on His people was recalled by Peter on the Day of Pentecost (Acts 2:16–21). This event will be further examined in chapter 12.

Micah

Micah is another prophet we know little about. Like other prophets, he spoke God's message of impending destruction—in this case, for Samaria and Jerusalem (the capital cities of Israel and Judah). And like others, he offered assurances that, in the long run, God would prove Himself faithful to His people and see them through all their trials.

One of the distinctives in the writing of Micah is his identification of Bethlehem as the city from which the coming "ruler over Israel" will come (Micah 5:2–4).

Habakkuk

Another prophet of whom little is known is Habakkuk. Yet his writing is unique in that he and God appear to have a conversation. The prophet asks questions, and God answers.

Habakkuk first wanted to know why sin could become so prevalent throughout Judah without God doing anything about it (Habakkuk 1:2–4). God's response was surprising: He was going to bring judgment on His sinful people by using the "ruthless and impetuous" Babylonians (1:5–11).

God's answer raised Habakkuk's next question: Why would God use a nation even worse than the people of Judah as His emissaries (1:12–2:1)? God assured His prophet that the Babylonians would have their own turn at experiencing "woe" (2:2–20). While people may tend to satisfy themselves with the lesser of two evils, evil is always evil to God. Both His people who drifted away from Him—and those who never acknowledged Him in the first place—would discover that He was always in control. And as a result of his dialogue with God, Habakkuk ended his writing with a type of song/psalm (Habakkuk 3).

WHAT'S THE GOOD WORD?

Though the fig tree does not bud and there are no grapes on the vines, though the olive crop fails and the fields produce no food, though there are no sheep in the pen and no cattle in the stalls, yet I will rejoice in the LORD, I will be joyful in God my Savior.

–HABAKKUK 3:17–18

Zephaniah

At about the same time Habakkuk and Nahum were speaking out for God, so was Zephaniah—the last of the minor prophets before the seventy-year captivity of Judah. And like other prophets, Zephaniah was looking ahead to a dreadful "day of the LORD" in which the nations would face God-sent tribulation. Judah would not escape this judgment but would indeed be restored, thanks to the ultimate mercy of God.

Prophets During the Exile

All the writing prophets described so far in this chapter had publicly warned God's people of coming tragedy. But self-concern was the rule of the land, and rampant idolatry continued. Even after Israel fell to the Assyrians and the people of Judah could see that God meant what He had been telling His prophets, they still didn't change. So Babylon led a siege on Jerusalem.

When the Babylonians finally broke through the walls, it wasn't a pretty sight. The Book of Lamentations, traditionally ascribed to Jeremiah, describes mothers cooking their own children to eat (4:10), women being ravished and princes hung up by their hands (5:11–12), and other disturbing images summed up with the statement, "Joy is gone from our hearts; our dancing has turned to mourning" (5:15). This state of mourning would continue for seventy years, as the people waited for God's divine timing when they would be released and return to their land. But even after returning, life would never be the same for them.

Still, even while the people were in captivity, God designated prophets who kept them informed of His plans. And now that the worst had happened and the people were again ready to turn to God for help, much of the news from the prophets was hopeful and encouraging.

All things considered, life could have been much worse for the people of God in Babylon. They were driven away from their homeland, yes, but once in Babylon, they were allowed to resettle and live pretty much as they pleased. In fact, even when freed seventy years later, many of the people chose to remain right where they were.

Ezekiel

While Jeremiah had been allowed to stay in Judah when the Babylonians whisked away many others, Ezekiel was among those who went to Babylon. In fact, it was in Babylon where God called him to be a prophet (Ezekiel 1:1–3).

These were trying times, because many people were deported prior to the fall of Jerusalem. The exiles would receive news from home from time to time—little of it good. Ezekiel had been in Babylon about ten years before the city of Jerusalem actually fell.

Ezekiel stands out from some of the other prophets in his methods of communicating God's message to the people. It was Ezekiel's assignment, while in Babylon, to use a number of object lessons to demonstrate God's judgment to the people. For example, God told him to build a model of Jerusalem complete with battering rams and siege ramps surrounding it, and to place an iron pan between himself and the model city—probably to symbolize the barrier between God's people and Himself. In addition, Ezekiel was to lie on his left side for 390 days to "bear the sin of the house of Israel" and another forty days on his right side to symbolize the sins of Judah (Ezekiel 4:1–8).

In connection with this assignment, the prophet was told to cook his food using human excrement for fuel, but he negotiated with God for permission to use animal manure instead (4:9–15). He was told to shave his head and burn a third of his hair, strike a third with a sword, and scatter the rest to the wind (5:1–2).

BACKGROUND INFO

The last holdouts in Jerusalem were being forced to eat food that was, according to their law, "unclean." Using human excrement for fuel would have defiled Ezekiel's food as well, which was God's intention. Yet Ezekiel came from a priestly family and was eager to maintain all the laws regarding cleanliness. Therefore, God granted his request to use a less offensive source of fuel.

Just as the siege on Jerusalem was coming to a close, God told Ezekiel his wife would die suddenly, after which the prophet was not to mourn her death (Ezekiel 24:15–27). The mourning process would normally initiate aid and comfort from other members of the community. But as Jerusalem fell, the entire nation was affected, and in their wide-scale despair they had no comfort to offer one another. Again, Ezekiel's personal life symbolized the events of the nation as a whole.

And there are many more such instances recorded in the Book of Ezekiel. Throughout it all, Ezekiel remained faithful. He is credited by some as being instrumental in turning the people permanently from their previous obsession with pursuing other gods. It seems that while in exile their widespread idolatrous ways at long last came to an end.

Daniel

Another of the brightest and best of the Hebrew youngsters carted off to Babylon was Daniel. Upon arrival, he was drafted into a Babylonian recruitment program to be immersed into the new culture. But Daniel refused to "defile" himself with

SWORD DRILL

The writing on the wall read: MENE, MENE, TEKEL, PARSIN. What was the meaning of this cryptic message? (See Daniel 5:26–28.)

foods and practices he considered inappropriate. He and his friends negotiated for a vegetable diet and were soon the standouts in their crowd of exceptional achievers.

God was with Daniel, and he made a name for himself with a long series of powerful kings. He interpreted Nebuchadnezzar's dream without even being told what it was (Daniel 2). It was Nebuchadnezzar who built a ninety-feet-tall statue of himself before which Daniel's friends—Shadrach, Meshach, and Abednego—refused to bow. As a result, they were tossed into a fiery furnace, and walked around amid the flames with no harm done (Daniel 3). The next king, Belshazzar, saw a bodiless hand write on the wall, and Daniel interpreted the message (Daniel 5).

As the Medes and Persians rolled in and conquered Babylon, Daniel remained an authority figure and simply continued his services for a new boss—King Darius. It was Darius who reluctantly tossed Daniel into the lions' den, where God kept His prophet safe (Daniel 6).

The last half of the Book of Daniel details his own visions of the future. Many interpreters feel that much of what Daniel saw is still in *our* future, and this book is invaluable in making sense out of certain portions of the Book of Revelation.

The Right Woman, the Right Place, the Right Time

You'll find no mention of any prophets in the Book of Esther. As a matter of fact, you won't even find a mention of God. Yet Esther's story stands as one of the most fascinating and faith-inspiring in all of Scripture.

Esther was among the Jews who had been relocated to the Persian city of Susa. She was most likely born in captivity because she lived during the reign of Xerxes, a successor of his father Darius. When Xerxes became displeased with his current wife, Vashti, he initiated a national search for "beautiful young virgins" to audition to be his new queen (Esther 2:2–4). Esther's cousin, a man named Mordecai, convinced her to participate.

Esther was chosen over all the other contestants, and then things really began to get interesting. An exalted noble named Haman had a hatred of all Jews, and Mordecai in particular. In a bizarre string of "coincidences" that surely had to have been divinely planned, Mordecai discovered a plot that saved the king's life, but was not rewarded. Meanwhile, Haman was plotting to destroy all the Jews and even had a gallows built on his land on which he planned to execute Mordecai. It just so happened, however, that one night the king couldn't sleep, decided to catch up on his reading, and discovered Mordecai's heroic deed.

The next day Haman met with Xerxes, and the king asked what he would do to reward a specially favored person. Thinking the king was talking about him, Haman spouted off a long list of public honors, after which the king told Haman to go do all those things for Mordecai. He complied, but he also set up a meeting with the king to get permission to eliminate all Jews once and for all.

Mordecai encouraged Esther to intercede with the king. She initiated a meeting with Xerxes, though it could have cost her life, and requested permission to host a dinner for Haman, the king, and herself. Haman, of course, was flattered. (Neither he nor the king had a clue that Esther was Jewish.) During the dinner, Xerxes offered to grant Esther any favor. She asked only for her life, because "I and my people have been sold for destruction and slaughter and annihilation" (Esther 7:4). When Xerxes demanded to know who was responsible for such a horrendous threat, she pointed across the table to Haman.

The king was irate and left the room to compose himself. Haman threw himself at Esther's feet to beg for his life just as Xerxes returned and assumed he was attempting to molest the queen. At that point, one of the king's servants piped up and said something to the effect of, "You know what? Haman has a great big gallows in his backyard." (See 7:9.) Xerxes immediately ordered Haman put to death on it.

The Jewish feast of Purim was instituted to commemorate this act of heroism on Esther's part. Between Daniel and Esther, some of the Bible's most thrilling and intriguing stories take place while God's people were supposedly helpless and in exile.

Back Home to Ground Zero

After seventy years in exile, the people were allowed to return to their homeland. They didn't go back in *en masse,* but in several caravans. And when they got there, they faced a depressing mess. The temple was in ruins, the protective walls were now piles of rubble, and many of the people who had remained had intermarried with the local non-Hebrew peoples.

Ezra, one of the priests, was among the leaders of an early-returning group, receiving both permission and supplies from King Cyrus. He set about rebuilding the temple and even returned a number of the original gold and silver artifacts that had been donated by the Persian king.

Ezra also responded to complaints that even the priests had intermarried with women from heathen tribes and were committing "detestable practices" (Ezra 9:1). In a zero-tolerance decision, all the foreign wives and their children were sent away in an attempt to purge the threat of further idolatry from the newly resettled people of God (10:10–17).

A while later Nehemiah returned with a group released by Artaxerxes. His goal was to rebuild the walls around Jerusalem. In spite of much verbal abuse and even death threats by their enemies, Nehemiah's group courageously continued working and accomplished their task in fifty-two days (Nehemiah 6:15).

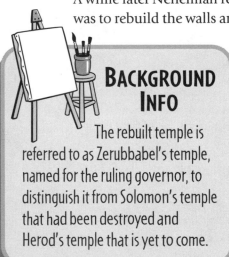

BACKGROUND INFO

The rebuilt temple is referred to as Zerubbabel's temple, named for the ruling governor, to distinguish it from Solomon's temple that had been destroyed and Herod's temple that is yet to come.

Three More Prophets: Last but Not Least

As the people came out of captivity and settled once again in the area of Judah, God continued to send prophets to guide them. He provided clear direction before the Exile (which was largely ignored), during the Exile, and, as we are about to see, afterward.

Haggai

As the people sifted through the ruins of their former civilization and began to rebuild, the scene was somewhat depressing. Neither the rebuilt temple nor the walls were as glorious and expansive as they once had been. The people quickly became unmotivated and turned their attention to their own homes. Not surprisingly, their personal habitats turned out quite nicely. Haggai's message from God was to the point: "Is it a time for you yourselves to be living in your paneled houses, while [the temple] remains a ruin?" (Haggai 1:4).

Haggai was not only a prophet but a motivational speaker as well. His promise was that once the people got their priorities in order, they would see God do great things among them again. God assured them that, "The glory of this present [temple] will be greater than the glory of the former house" (2:9).

Zechariah

Zechariah was younger than Haggai, and his ministry picked up right where Haggai's left off. Both priest and prophet, as Ezekiel and Jeremiah had been, Zechariah was doubly concerned with the spiritual status of the returning exiles. But in addition to the immediate needs of the people to get to work on restoring the temple and strengthening their commitment to God, Zechariah had a series of visions and had much to say concerning the coming Messiah. Among other things, he foretold this Messiah riding into Jerusalem on a donkey (Zechariah 9:9), being sold out for thirty pieces of silver (11:13), and His return to the Mount of Olives—the very place from which Jesus would one day ascend into heaven (14:4–9; Acts 1:9–12).

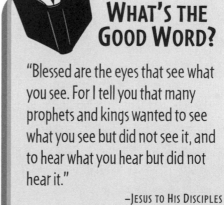

WHAT'S THE GOOD WORD?

"Blessed are the eyes that see what you see. For I tell you that many prophets and kings wanted to see what you see but did not see it, and to hear what you hear but did not hear it."

–JESUS TO HIS DISCIPLES
(LUKE 10:23–24)

Malachi

It had been a struggle for the people of Judah. They faced great trials, went into captivity, but eventually made it back home where they rebuilt their temple and put their walls back up. Still, they comprised

BACKGROUND INFO

Malachi was a Hebrew word meaning "my messenger." Therefore, some people speculate the author was some unknown prophet using the pen name of Malachi, and that no person by that name actually existed. No proof exists to confirm this speculation, however.

only a small cluster on the extensive map that marked the Persian Empire. The prophets had made sweeping predictions about great things to come, but the promised Deliverer of the nation had not yet arrived. There was little to get excited about, and Malachi wrote to address this mentality.

He addressed a number of spiritual concerns. The people were again intermarrying with idolatrous nations (Malachi 2:11). They offered God not their best animals, but those that were blind, crippled, and diseased (1:7–8). They refused to tithe (3:8–12). They complained and spoke against God (3:13–15).

Malachi, like all the prophets before him, attempted to turn the people's vision to the future where they could expect both a better time, and beyond that to a "great and dreadful day of the LORD." Specifically, Malachi told the people to watch for the coming of Elijah (Malachi 4:5–6). Jesus would later identify this "Elijah" as John the Baptist (Matthew 11:11–14).

SWORD DRILL

From which of the prophetic books did Jesus read in the synagogue after which He proclaimed, "Today this scripture is fulfilled in your hearing"? And what happened after He claimed to be the person the passage referred to? (See Luke 4:16–30.)

Most of us don't know nearly as much about the prophets as we should. You probably don't know much more about them now than you did at the beginning of this chapter. But as you have opportunities to go back and devote time to these men as individuals and to what they wrote, perhaps their words will make more sense to you. The prophets, along with Esther, Ezra, and Nehemiah, were God's men (and women) who faithfully represented Him during some of the darkest years of Old Testament history. And as you pay attention to what they have to say, you'll quickly discover that their writings are not merely for the benefit of Israel and Judah. You'll find an abundance of promises and encouragements for yourself as well.

Chapter Flashback

1. Which of the following lists contains names of the Old Testament writing prophets?
   a. Nathanael, Bartholomew, Thaddeus, and Alphaeus
   b. Josiah, Hezekiah, Hoshea, and Ahaz
   c. Jonah, Habakkuk, Hosea, and Amos
   d. Mariah, Aaliyah, Alicia, and Erykah

2. When confronted by prophets of God, the people usually:
   a. Did exactly as they said
   b. Studied the Scriptures to make sense of what they said
   c. Engaged them in intelligent and reasoned debate
   d. Just ignored them, but occasionally threw them in cisterns, tossed them overboard where they were swallowed by big fish, placed them in lions' dens, and hassled them in many other ways

3. Which of the following was *not* an area where prophets were sent?
   a. Babylon
   b. Abyssinia
   c. Judah
   d. Israel

4. Esther was:
   a. A good Jewish girl who became a Persian queen
   b. An anesthetic used by Israelite surgeons
   c. An embarrassing nickname for the prophet Jeremiah
   d. Babylonian goddess of the kumquat harvest

5. Ezra and Nehemiah are most remembered for:
   a. Their bold escapes from Babylonian captivity
   b. Their prophecies about Jesus
   c. Writing books of the Bible hardly anyone ever reads
   d. Rebuilding the temple and walls of Jerusalem after the captivity

Answers: (1) c, (2) d, (3) b, (4) a, (5) d (and shame on you if you chose c)

Rich Man, Poem Man

JOB THROUGH SONG OF SONGS

SNAPSHOT

"Jeff? What's with the outfit?" Michelle asked.

"What outfit?"

"Black jeans. Black turtleneck. Black jacket. Black sneakers. Let me guess. You're planning on supplementing our income by becoming a cat burglar."

"These are just clothes, dear. I never make a big deal about what *you're* wearing."

Michelle sighed. "Don't I know it! But . . . wait a minute. Are you growing a goatee?"

"If you really must know, I'm working on some poetry," Jeff explained. "It's something I've always wanted to do, and I don't appreciate being made fun of. I'm attempting to cast off the normal trappings of our society and look inside myself. I want to express my feelings in a deep and meaningful way."

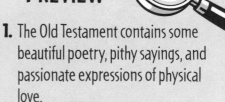

SNEAK PREVIEW

1. The Old Testament contains some beautiful poetry, pithy sayings, and passionate expressions of physical love.
2. Much of the writing in this portion of Scripture expresses surprisingly honest feelings.
3. The authors of these deeply emotional writings included men who were otherwise mighty warriors and highly logical thinkers.

"Let's see what you've written," Michelle replied.

"I, uh, haven't actually written anything yet. I'm searching for a deep and meaningful way to say that my boss is a mean, sadistic, money-grubbing, self-centered, incompetent oaf. But I can't find a good word that rhymes with *oaf*."

"Well, you just keep at it, dear, if it makes you happy. After disappearing for half a century, the hipster beatnik look might come back any day now."

"You really think that could happen?"

"Maybe so, Daddy-o."

* * * * * * * * * * * * * * *

You don't find a lot of full-time poets these days. The sensitivity and feelings required to translate one's innermost feelings into words on a page may be a full-time job, but few poets are able to pay the bills without taking on another "career" to support their artistic endeavors. The poet may also be a waiter, banker, nurse, construction worker, or member of any other profession, but only as a means to a living. If given the opportunity and funding, most poet/waiters and poet/bankers would gladly become simply poets.

SWORD DRILL

The Bible contains a number of Solomon's proverbs and other writings, but exactly how many songs and proverbs was he credited with writing in all? (See 1 Kings 4:29–34.)

So far in this guide, we have maintained essentially a chronological start-to-finish look at the major events of the Old Testament. In doing so, however, we skipped five books that contain some beautiful poetry and various other styles of creative expression. Yet the authors were not exclusively, or even primarily, writers. David might be out tending sheep, defeating giants, or ruling a kingdom on any given day, and then go home that night to pour out his aches and triumphs to God in a heart-on-his-sleeve psalm. Solomon was building empires and settling disputes, but he managed to make plenty of time for his writing pursuits. Not only did he knock off quite a few songs and proverbs, he is also credited with some of the Bible's most sexually explicit literature. But before we get to David and Solomon, let's take a look at someone remembered for his riches-to-rags story.

Job: The Right Man for the Job

The Book of Job is frequently grouped with Psalms, Proverbs, Ecclesiastes, and Song of Songs under the umbrella category of "Wisdom Literature." It appears to be an account of a man who lived very early in history, but recorded by someone who lived considerably later. Perhaps this was a story handed down orally for generations until someone finally put it down on parchment. Or maybe God simply inspired someone to record this story for posterity. If taken literally, the opening of the Book of Job must certainly be divinely inspired because it contains things no human could otherwise be aware of. And that being the case, it would be no difficult matter for God to relate the entire story (rather than simply the opening chapters) to someone.

The date of Job's life can be fixed to some extent based on the culture in which he lived and certain other references. The basic fact that his financial bottom line is not expressed in gold and silver but in livestock would establish a setting prior to David and maybe even before Abraham (1000 to 2000 years B.C.).

God's MVP (Most Valued Person)

Job is described as "blameless and upright; he feared God and shunned evil" (Job 1:1). He had a wife, ten children, and ample flocks and herds. In addition to maintaining his own proper spiritual condition, each day he made an offering for each of his children just in case one of them had slipped during the day (1:5).

Job stood out from the average human being, so much so that God targeted him for special recognition. God and Satan were having a conversation at the time, and Satan immediately looked to find bad where God saw good. Satan's argument was something along the lines of: "Well, who wouldn't be a good little camper after accumulating so many riches, a loving family, great health, and everything else he wanted?"

Satan's MVP (Most Vulnerable Person)

In response, God allowed Satan to strike everything Job had; He only restricted Satan from taking Job's life. So in a day's time, Job lost all his oxen, donkeys,

BACKGROUND INFO

Job is the original source of one of our quirky sayings: "I am nothing but skin and bones; I have escaped with only **the skin of my teeth**" (Job 19:20, emphasis added).

sheep, camels, and children. And the only servants he had left were the ones who came running back to tell him the horrible news about everything that had gone wrong.

Satan proved to be wrong about Job. In the midst of such overwhelming calamity, Job still "did not sin by charging God with wrongdoing" (Job 1:22). But Satan wasn't finished. He next solicited permission from God to afflict Job's health. Again, God allowed Satan to wreak havoc in Job's life.

Overnight, Job was plunged into a state of constant pain. Various symptoms of his disease are mentioned throughout the Book of Job, including weight loss, bad breath, nightmares, and fever. But worst of all, perhaps, were "painful sores from the soles of his feet to the top of his head." All he could do to medicate himself was sit in the ashes amid a pile of broken pottery and scrape his lesions (2:7–8).

At least Job's wife had been spared. Maybe she would be a great comfort to him in this terrible time of need. Then again, maybe not. Her advice to Job is not exactly what he needed to hear: "Are you still holding on to your integrity? Curse God and die!" (2:9).

Job was perplexed as to why all these terrible things were happening to him. Most of the rest of the Book of Job contains a dialogue among Job and four friends (three at first, and later a fourth shows up) exploring the possible reasons for Job's great dilemma. But, to be honest, his friends were most valuable during the first week they arrived because they didn't say a word (2:11–13). After that, they kept giving Job the third degree, trying to get him to confess to sins he hadn't committed (as if he didn't have enough problems already).

Throughout this account, Job asks hard questions. If he were going to be unable to experience peace and comfort again, why had he even been born in the first place (3:11–19)? Did he have any basis to maintain hope and patience (6:11)? Why do wicked people prosper while people like me suffer (21:7–15)? And perhaps the biggest question of all: Why do my misguided friends keep accusing me of stuff that isn't true? After a lengthy dialog, Job finally stops talking, but that doesn't stop one of his friends from rambling on for a long time (31:40–37:24).

In a Quest for Answers, More Questions!

After Job finally gives up his arguments and his windbag friends begin to wind down, suddenly we are told, "Then the LORD answered Job out of the storm" (38:1). But rather than go point by point through each of the issues that had been raised by Job and his friends, God simply asks a long series of questions of His own. Job 38–41 is primarily a barrage of question after question, none of which Job has any clue how to answer.

WHAT'S THE GOOD WORD?

"But I desire to speak to the Almighty and to argue my case with God. You, however, smear me with lies; you are worthless physicians, all of you! If only you would be altogether silent! For you, that would be wisdom"

–JOB TO HIS FRIENDS (JOB 13:3–5)

God wasn't angry with Job, but He was making a point. Job (and the rest of us) can see only the smallest percentage of what's going on in the universe. God oversees the whole thing the whole time. Yet people have the audacity to question His authority and want to determine for themselves what is fair and proper. Did Job (or do we) really think God doesn't notice when righteous people suffer—or do we dare doubt that He will ultimately do something about it?

Job was no longer looking for answers. After God appeared to him, he said simply, "My ears had heard of you but now my eyes have seen you. Therefore I despise myself and repent in dust and ashes" (42:5–6).

WHAT'S THE GOOD WORD?

"I know that my Redeemer lives, and that in the end he will stand upon the earth. And after my skin has been destroyed, yet in my flesh I will see God."

–JOB 19:25–26

As far as we know, Job never discovered why he was being tested—or that it was Satan, not God, who had initiated all his suffering—yet he passed the test with flying colors. In addition, Job was told to intercede and make offerings for his friends because their accusations had been way off base. And God gave Job more children and blessed the latter portion of his life even more than the former. After this extraordinary experience, Job enjoyed four generations of offspring and died "old and full of years" (Job 42:17).

Psalms: 150 of Israel's Greatest Hits in One Collection

Job must have felt like singing. Too bad the psalms weren't yet around for him to use. But by the time of the Exile, the people were using a number of "hymnbooks" with some of their favorite compositions. The Book of Psalms is a gathering of five previous collections:

> Book I: Psalms 1 to 41
>
> Book II: Psalms 42 to 72
>
> Book III: Psalms 73 to 89
>
> Book IV: Psalms 90 to 106
>
> Book V: Psalms 107 to 150

You'll find that the last psalm in each of these five "books" tends to wrap up its section. Many Bibles include notations indicating the breaks between these books within the Book of Psalms, as well as mentioning the authors where available. (Some authors remain unknown.) David is credited with almost half of the 150 psalms in this collection, with other psalms attributed to Asaph and Korah (musicians), Solomon, Moses, and a few others.

The Hebrew title for the Book of Psalms is translated "praises," but due to the numerous authors and various circumstances that inspired them, the psalms offer great diversity. While the underlying goal of the psalms was to offer praise to God, they served numerous other purposes as well: lamenting, reviewing Israel's history, confessing sins, emphasizing the importance of wisdom, and more.

Praise and Passion

Probably the most familiar of the psalms is Psalm 23. It is David's expression of utmost confidence and faith in God to protect him "even though I walk through the valley of the shadow of death." His enemies are within view, yet David remains fearless as he is aware of God's presence. And the psalm closes with warm and fuzzy thoughts of goodness, love, and dwelling in the house of the Lord forever. Not surprisingly, many church congregations like to recite this psalm together, and many Christians commit it to memory.

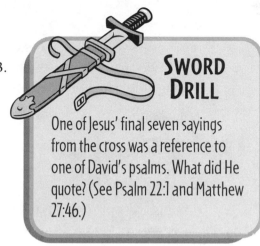

SWORD DRILL

One of Jesus' final seven sayings from the cross was a reference to one of David's psalms. What did He quote? (See Psalm 22:1 and Matthew 27:46.)

But if you read through some other of David's writings, you might be surprised at how anti-fuzzy his comments can be. Here are some:

> Strike all my enemies on the jaw; break the teeth of the wicked. (Psalm 3:7)

> I am worn out from groaning; all night long I flood my bed with weeping. (Psalm 6:6)

> My guilt has overwhelmed me like a burden too heavy to bear. My wounds fester and are loathsome because of my sinful folly. I am bowed down and brought very low; all day long I go about mourning. (Psalm 38:4–6)

> You have rejected us, O God, and burst forth upon us; you have been angry— now restore us! You have shaken the land and torn it open; mend its fractures, for it is quaking. You have shown your people desperate times; you have given us wine that makes us stagger. (Psalm 60:1–3)

The Book of Psalms is filled with additional similar examples. David's "praise" to God didn't entail ignoring or downplaying the unpleasant emotions he was feeling. He was passionate about glorifying God at times, yet he was equally passionate in his confession, his desire for vengeance, and his heartfelt expressions of pain and despair.

By reviewing the life of David as we read his psalms, we can gain additional insight. We see a number of places where David asks God to remedy a problem with David's enemies. But we can also recall that when given opportunities to personally do away with one of his biggest enemies—King Saul—David refused to do so. He left that decision in God's hands.

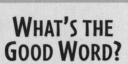

WHAT'S THE GOOD WORD?

May the words of my mouth and the meditation of my heart be pleasing in your sight, O LORD, my Rock and my Redeemer.

–PSALM 19:14

When David saw Bathsheba taking a bath, his lustful passions led to adultery and murder. But in Psalm 51 we see that his confession and plea to God are just as passionate as his sin had been. The brutally honest expressions of David's feelings are tempered by his willingness to submit to God's will for his life. Similarly, we shouldn't fear expressing our genuine emotions to God, even if those emotions are unpleasant and perhaps even embarrassing or awkward to admit.

Just as you might look through a modern hymnal and find a section of songs around a Christmas theme, so you might also find similar grouped themes within the Book of Psalms. One of the best examples is the grouping known as "Songs of Ascents" (Psalms 120–134), which pilgrims traditionally sang as they rode "up" to Jerusalem for special holidays and events.

A Book of Promise

Many people cite the Book of Psalms as their favorite biblical book, and it is quoted from more frequently in the New Testament than any other. For people just beginning to explore the Bible for themselves, Psalms is a book filled with promise. As the writers were seeking to connect with God at deeper spiritual levels, so will the readers. In addition to Psalm 23, many other of the psalms have widespread appeal:

> ➤ Psalm 1: the blessings of righteousness versus the fate of wicked people

> ➤ Psalm 8: good to read at night beside a telescope

> ➤ Psalm 22: assurance for those being oppressed

> ➤ Psalm 24: putting everything in perspective

➤ Psalm 63: from David in the desert, for your own "dry spells"

➤ Psalm 100: for Thanksgiving and other celebratory times

➤ Psalm 119: a Hebrew acrostic, where each "stanza" begins with the next successive letter of the alphabet, all focused on the importance of God's Word

➤ Psalm 139: the intimacy of God in the life of an individual

Proverbs: A Few Words of Advice

Just as the Book of Psalms is a collection of songs by various authors, the Book of Proverbs is a collection of wise sayings. Solomon usually gets credit for most of them, but there are other contributors who aren't well-known (unless you know something about Agur or Lemuel that other Bible scholars don't).

BACKGROUND INFO

Reading through the Book of Psalms, you'll probably see the word Selah quite frequently. No one has figured out exactly what this word means, though it is frequently thought to be some sort of musical instruction.

The biblical collection of proverbs, while maintaining a theme of wisdom, is not there merely to make us more intelligent. Rather, the "wisdom" it promotes is spiritual and is based on the knowledge of God. If we consult one of the psalms we so quickly skipped over, we will discover: "The fear of the LORD is the beginning of wisdom; all who follow his precepts have good understanding" (Psalm 111:10). And Solomon agrees: "The fear of the LORD is the beginning of knowledge, but fools despise wisdom and discipline" (Proverbs 1:7).

Some people tend to approach Proverbs as they might a horoscope, fortune cookie, or Magic 8-Ball. But true wisdom—based on a proper respect for God—is too rare and valuable to be taken so lightly. The writers of Proverbs come right out and say so in places.

Wisdom will save you from the ways of wicked men. (2:12)

Do not be wise in your own eyes; fear the LORD and shun evil. (3:7)

Wisdom is supreme; therefore get wisdom. Though it cost all you have, get understanding. (4:7)

Wisdom is more precious than rubies, and nothing you desire can compare with her. (8:11)

Wise men store up knowledge, but the mouth of a fool invites ruin. (10:14)

In addition to these clear teachings, the same point is made using allegorical images. In Hebrew, the word for *wisdom* is a feminine noun, so it's not much of a stretch for the writers to personify wisdom as a woman:

Wisdom calls aloud in the street, she raises her voice in the public squares; at the head of the noisy streets she cries out, in the gateways of the city she makes her speech. (Proverbs 1:20–21)

Do not forsake wisdom, and she will protect you; love her, and she will watch over you. (4:6)

"Let all who are simple come in here!" she [wisdom] says to those who lack judgment. "Come, eat my food and drink the wine I have mixed. Leave your simple ways and you will live; walk in the way of understanding." (9:4–6)

And just as certain sections of Proverbs personify "wisdom" as a woman, others do the same for "folly." One of the most foolish things to get involved in, according to Solomon's advice to his readers/listeners, is adultery. Proverbs 7 contains a vivid portrayal of a young man being seduced by an adulteress. As he listens to her and finally gives in to her smooth talk, the description isn't pretty: "All at once he followed her like an ox going to the slaughter, like a deer stepping into a noose till an arrow pierces his liver, like a bird darting into a snare, little knowing it will cost him his life" (verses 22–23).

WHAT'S THE GOOD WORD?

The way of a fool seems right to him, but a wise man listens to advice.

—Proverbs 12:15

Uncommon Sense

As you read through Proverbs, you'll probably recognize some of them as common sayings, perhaps not even knowing they came from the Bible. Here are just a few to get you started:

Trust in the LORD with all your heart and lean not on your own understanding; in all your ways acknowledge him, and he will make your paths straight. (3:5–6)

Above all else, guard your heart, for it is the wellspring of life. (4:23)

He who spares the rod hates his son, but he who loves him is careful to discipline him. (13:24)

A gentle answer turns away wrath, but a harsh word stirs up anger. (15:1)

Pride goes before destruction, a haughty spirit before a fall. (16:18)

A friend loves at all times. (17:17)

A cheerful heart is good medicine. (17:22)

Train a child in the way he should go, and when he is old he will not turn from it. (22:6)

An honest answer is like a kiss on the lips. (24:26)

A word aptly spoken is like apples of gold in settings of silver. (25:11)

As iron sharpens iron, so one man sharpens another. (27:17)

> **BACKGROUND INFO**
>
> One more proverb, just for fun: "Better to live on a corner of the roof than share a house with a quarrelsome wife" (21:9). In light of the fact that Solomon had 700 wives and 300 concubines, maybe he was writing from experience.

Many of these statements may just sound like common sense. But when you see how few people actually try to apply them personally, they may more accurately be termed "uncommon sense." And perhaps some of the wise lessons were learned the hard way. For example, we are first told, "Eat honey, my son, for it is good; honey from the comb is sweet to your taste" (Proverbs 24:13). Okay, so we're supposed to enjoy the simple pleasures of life. But read a few more pages and you'll find: "If you find honey, eat just enough—too much of it, and you will vomit" (25:16). In this and other cases, if we can learn to heed the advice of Scripture, perhaps we will practice moderation and not have to learn the same lessons the hard way.

Ecclesiastes: Been There, Done That, Still Bored

Speaking of learning certain lessons the hard way, we come to the Book of Ecclesiastes. Again, credit is usually given to Solomon as the author, and if so, it becomes a potent message indeed. Imagine the richest and wisest person who ever lived setting off on the same mission most of us have pursued at one point or another—to identify the meaning of life.

Ecclesiastes, perhaps more than Psalms, seems to inspire and reflect the psyche of many musicians. It's where we find the inspiration for "Turn! Turn! Turn!" ("To Everything There Is a Season"), made popular by the musical group The Byrds (3:1–8). The repeated complaint of the writer is that he can't get no satisfaction (pardon the rock 'n' roll grammar). And Ecclesiastes would be a greatly depressing book if the author didn't eventually come to the same conclusion as yet another Rolling Stones song: You can't always get what you want. But if you try sometimes, you just might find you get what you need.

Working from a personal opinion that "everything is meaningless" and "there is nothing new under the sun" (Ecclesiastes 1:2, 9), the author used his vast knowledge and resources to attempt to make sense of his life. He accumulated unparalleled knowledge (1:12–18). That didn't do it. Maybe outlandish pleasures would do the trick, so "I denied myself nothing my eyes desired; I refused my heart no pleasure" (2:10). Still no satisfaction. Maybe the secret was hard work; so the writer threw himself into "toilsome labor" (2:20). Nope, that wasn't it, either.

WHAT'S THE GOOD WORD?

Remember your Creator in the days of your youth, before the days of trouble come and the years approach when you will say, "I find no pleasure in them."

–ECCLESIASTES 12:1

Here was a person who had riches, intelligence, position, relationships, and everything else most of us spend our whole lives attempting to accumulate. Yet after all Solomon's (or maybe someone else's) effort and searching, he made quite a simple discovery: "Nothing is better for a man under the sun than to eat and drink and be glad. Then joy will accompany him in his work all the days of the life God has given him under the sun" (Ecclesiastes 8:15). And the concluding lesson is: "However many years a man may live, let him enjoy them all. But let him remember the days of darkness, for they will be many" (11:8).

If we leave God out of the equation, no amount of substitutes will bring fulfillment in life. With God, however, every simple blessing yields great joy and contentment.

Even the best of us occasionally feel that life is meaningless. But maybe we're just looking so hard to uncover deep mysteries that we miss the simple, satisfying events of life. And if we try sometime, we just might find that with God's presence, that's all that we need.

Song of Songs: Something Worth Singing About!

Of course, sometimes the right human relationship can make a big difference in the level of satisfaction with one's life. Ask anyone in a bad marriage how much influence one person can have, and then ask someone who has been happily married for decades. We should choose wisely to whom we commit ourselves.

Solomon is traditionally accepted as the author of Song of Songs, to add to Ecclesiastes and the bulk of Proverbs on his résumé. The title given to this work, however, suggests that of the 1,005 songs written by Solomon (1 Kings 4:32), this one is his best. This particular book seems almost out of place tucked between the Wisdom Literature that precedes it and the long list of prophetic books that follow. In fact, much debate has taken place over exactly how to view and interpret the Song of Songs.

Is it an allegory about the relationship between God and His Old Testament people of Israel? Is it a prophetic look into the future to describe how God will relate with His people, the church? Is it simply what it appears to be: a bold and sensuous love story between a man and a woman as they approach their wedding day? Or, like numerous other passages in the Old Testament, is it both a historically accurate account that also has a spiritual significance?

Any way we want to interpret it, we have to read the Song of Songs as we would a play. Look for the different roles as you read:

➤ The "Beloved" (a young bride)

➤ The "Lover" (the prospective groom, probably Solomon)

➤ "Friends" who observe and comment on the love between the two

Even though interpreters and translators have "cleaned up" the explicit language a bit for the general Bible-reading public, the Song of Songs is still quite blunt in its description of each person's physical attributes through the eyes of the other. It includes detailed descriptions of eyes, hair, lips, necks, breasts, legs, strength, and more. The passion of togetherness and ache of separation are described as well.

But the physical detail leads to the underlying significance of the glory of love itself. While we tend to speak so much of "Christian love" that we can do so dispassionately, the Beloved and her Lover demonstrate what kind of emotions should be evoked when love is genuine. In the concluding chapter of the book we read: "Place me like a seal over your heart, like a seal on your arm; for love is as strong as death, its jealousy unyielding as the grave. It burns like blazing fire, like a mighty flame. Many waters cannot quench love; rivers cannot wash it away. If one were to give all the wealth of his house for love, it would be utterly scorned" (Song of Songs 8:6–7).

If this is the lesson we bring away from the Song of Songs, it is indeed well positioned among the other Wisdom Literature. Wisdom without love is just a bunch of facts. Love without wisdom risks becoming folly and sexual deviance, and can lead to a world of hurt. But when love combines with wisdom, marvelous and joyous things happen. In the next chapter, we will see what happened when an all-wise God so loved the world. It's such a big deal that it will require a whole New Testament.

Chapter Flashback

You know the drill by now. Match the appropriate book of the Bible with the descriptions that follow.

(1) The hymnal of the Old Testament

A. Job

(2) A collection of pithy writings about wisdom

B. Psalms

(3) A book about two people who start off separate, make some bold and explicit expressions of love, and end up anticipating a wonderful life together

C. Proverbs

(4) A book about a guy who started off good, had some horrible experiences with pain and isolation, and ended up okay again

D. Ecclesiastes

(5) A book by a guy who started off good, had some trouble finding the meaning of life, and ended up (reasonably) okay again

E. Song of Songs

Answers: (1) B, (2) C, (3) E, (4) A, (5) D

The Fulcrum of History

Matthew, Mark, Luke, John

SNAPSHOT

"Joseph?"

"Yes, Mary? I thought you were asleep."

"No, I've been lying here pondering."

"Pondering? You've just had a baby after a long journey to an unfamiliar city. You're sleeping with donkeys and sheep, for goodness sake. And after all that, you're *pondering?*"

"Actually, I was wondering how the world will celebrate the birth of our son—well, my son—I mean, God's Son. Oh, you know what I mean."

""Relax. I know whose Son you mean, but I don't know what you mean by the world celebrating His birth."

"Well, the angel told me my, uh, God's Son will be given the throne of His father David and will reign

SNEAK PREVIEW

1. The life, death, and resurrection of Jesus Christ form the pivot point of human history.

2. While upholding every part of the Old Testament law and fulfilling the prophecies of the promised Messiah, Jesus also made clear God's emphases on forgiveness, mercy, grace, and salvation (among other things).

3. As much as we are told about Jesus in the Gospels, we still know relatively little about His approximately thirty-three years spent on earth.

forever. And you were told that He would save His people from their sins."

"So what does that have to do with celebrations?" Joseph asked.

"I was just thinking of some of those parties given in honor of the birth of Caesar Augustus that we read about in the *Nazareth Enquirer*. And I was pondering how people might celebrate the birth of Jesus in the future."

"I suppose everyone will spend the day at the temple worshiping God."

"Do you really think so? Of course, now that the moneylenders and animal salesmen spend so much time there, more people seem willing to go to the temple once in a while. But I wouldn't want to see the celebration of Jesus' birth become commercialized."

"Commercialized? In what ways? Like songs and feasts?"

"I suppose songs would be okay, as long as they honored God. Lyrics about shepherds watching their flocks by night and angels being heard on high would be suitable."

"Well, Mary, I don't know what else you would expect people to sing about."

"Joseph, this is the first century we're living in. People do strange things. I wouldn't be surprised to hear songs along the lines of 'No Place Like Rome for the Holidays,' or 'Grandma Got Run Over by a Musk Ox.'"

"Mary! You're just being ridiculous now. Go to sleep before you suggest that people will start cutting down trees, decorating them with gaudy ornaments, and spend the day watching games down at the arena."

"Don't be silly, Joseph. No one would ever think of going that far. . . . But now that you mention it, maybe I'll ponder on that just a bit longer."

* * * * * * * * * * * * * *

Our goal in this chapter will be to ponder (however briefly) the significance of the birth, life, death, and resurrection of Jesus. We are told that shortly after the visit by the shepherds and their account of angels spanning the nighttime skies, "Mary treasured up all these things and pondered them in her heart" (Luke 2:19).

Most of us don't do nearly enough pondering about spiritual things. Even at Christmas, our specially designated time to commemorate the birth of Jesus, the usual flurry of shopping, traveling, cooking, and other commitments make it difficult to do any significant pondering. Yet sometimes during the year, at regular intervals, it is quite beneficial to set aside time simply to find a quiet place and think about how much God has provided that we should treasure.

Jesus Shows Up in the Strangest Places

Foremost on our lists of why to be thankful should be the fact that Jesus took human form, stepped out of the heavenly realms for a short time, and humbled Himself by becoming human. Our minds are incapable of imagining what it would be like to be supreme, eternal, omnipotent, and perfect in every way, only to be thrust into the body of an infant and then experience humanity with all its sin, pain, death, and separation from God.

We're relatively familiar with the biblical Christmas story, from annual Charlie Brown specials if not from Scripture. In fact, we may think we know more than we actually do. For example, the Bible says nothing about an innkeeper or a stable where Jesus was born. We infer both because Jesus was placed in a manger when there was no room in the inn, but the dwelling was just as likely a cave. We sing of three kings visiting Him, but nowhere are they called kings (translations lean toward "magi," "wise men," or "band of scholars"), nor do we learn their number. Christmas plays traditionally portray three because three gifts are mentioned. And our Christmas plays are probably in error when they show the wise men around the manger. By the time the travelers got to Bethlehem, Jesus may have been almost two years old (because in Herod's mania to get rid of potential rivals, he had all boys under two killed). Whatever Jesus' age, by the time the wise men saw Him, He was in a "house" (Matthew 2:1–12).

WHAT'S THE GOOD WORD?

The Word became flesh and made his dwelling among us. We have seen his glory, the glory of the One and Only, who came from the Father, full of grace and truth.

–JOHN 1:14

After both the wise men and Jesus escape from King Herod, the next we hear of Jesus is when He is twelve. After a family trip from Nazareth to Jerusalem to celebrate Passover, Jesus turned up missing during the return trip. His parents U-turned back to Jerusalem and finally found their adolescent boy in the temple, asking questions and holding His own with the religious teachers. Of course He got a scolding, and in His defense said only: "Why were you searching for me? Didn't you know I had to be in my Father's house?" (Luke 2:49).

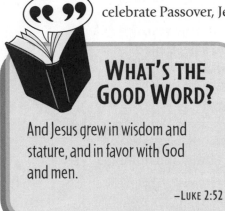

WHAT'S THE GOOD WORD?

And Jesus grew in wisdom and stature, and in favor with God and men.

−Luke 2:52

While Matthew's and Luke's stories of a young Jesus provide us with a good human perspective of what was going on (and Mark skips His childhood altogether to dive right into Jesus' adult ministry), John's gospel gives us God's perspective. Jesus' birth was no less than God's "Word" becoming flesh and taking up residence among human beings (John 1:1–18). But all the stories agree on one critical point: Jesus would be unlike any other person who ever lived. You don't find most babies in feed troughs. You don't find most teenagers reluctant to leave church. And you don't find gods of other religions willing (or able) to take on human form in order to sacrifice themselves for humanity. Later we will see why this distinction is so very essential.

Between Testaments: Revolting Developments

The last we heard of the chronological flow of biblical history in the Old Testament, God's people were just coming out of their period of captivity and beginning to rebuild in their homelands. Persia was the ruling empire at that time.

Between the Old Testament and New Testament, however, four centuries passed while Greece defeated Persia, taking control of Palestine in 332 B.C. During this time, a ruthless leader named Antiochus IV Epiphanes came to power. His method of imposing Greek rule was to destroy everything Jewish, emphasizing his mandates by erecting a statue of Zeus in the temple itself, and then slaughtering a pig on the altar as a sacrifice. Eventually the Hebrew people grew so incensed that they took up arms in resistance.

A Jewish man named Mattathias Maccabeus rose up in revolt, spurring his five sons and others to fight back. Twenty-four years later, Judah was free again. But less than a century went by before the Romans rolled into the area and imposed *their* rule. They took Jerusalem by force, slaughtered priests, and defiled the Most Holy Place of the temple.

So as the New Testament begins, you will see clues of a seething hatred of the Romans as the Jews are forced to yield to yet another bigger and bossier nation. Still, they have a certain degree of freedom to worship as they please since Rome has installed local "governors" over the people. A series of rather nasty Herods had been placed over Judea beginning with Herod the Great (37–4 B.C.), the one who had attempted to have the baby Jesus put to death.

Sects and the City of Jerusalem

Also during the past several centuries, a number of religious groups had been gaining followers, all within the confines of Judaism. Among them were:

➤ *Pharisees.* Primarily merchants descended from some of the heroes who fought against Antiochus IV Epiphanes, this group of about 6,000 promoted strict (frequently legalistic) adherence to oral and written Jewish law. They endured the Roman presence as long as the Romans didn't impede the Jews' ability to worship as they wished.

➤ *Sadducees.* Descendants of Solomon's high priest, this aristocratic group maintained a priestly role in their culture. However, their religious commitment was only to the Torah—the first five books of Hebrew Scripture. They rejected the oral traditions and were at odds with the Pharisees on a number of matters, especially concerning the resurrection of the dead, which the Sadducees didn't believe in.

BACKGROUND INFO

Alexander the Great and his successors desired to "Hellenize" the world by imposing a standard of Greek language and culture. Those who attempted to enforce this change could be quite emphatic, but so could some of those who resisted it.

➤ **Essenes.** Perhaps disgruntled members from both the Pharisees and Sadducees, the Essenes became a separatist group that withdrew to the wilderness where they shared meals and possessions. Feeling that much of the worship in Jerusalem had become corrupted, they had their own rituals as they studied and copied the Torah.

➤ **Zealots.** Rather than withdrawing from things they didn't like, the Zealots were an activist group that fought back. Theologically, they were most like the Pharisees, yet they wanted nothing to do with the Romans. Not only did they refuse to pay taxes to Rome, they weren't above committing terrorist acts when the opportunities arose.

It was in this diverse and delicate mix of cultures and beliefs that the thirty-year-old Jesus began His public ministry.

Out of Nazareth, into the World

One day Jesus showed up at the Jordan River to be baptized by His relative, John the Baptist. John's sermons in the wilderness had promoted repentance, and his listeners had wondered if indeed *he* might be the Messiah they had been told to expect. But John made it clear that he was only preparing the way for someone else who would follow him (John 1:19–28).

BACKGROUND INFO

The primary religious council of the time was known as the Sanhedrin–sort of a religious Supreme Court. The majority membership on this council belonged to the Sadducees.

Not long after Jesus' baptism, He was led by the Spirit into the wilderness where He was tempted by Satan (Matthew 4:1–11). After Jesus had fasted for forty days, the devil appeared and made three very attractive offers, each with a catch that would have goaded Jesus into doing something inappropriate. Jesus simply chose an appropriate Scripture from the Old Testament to refute and decline each of the devil's temptations in turn.

Jesus began teaching and healing the sick, and quickly gathered a following. Many disciples were interested in working with Him, but after spending a night praying, He chose twelve who would become His apostles—those who would be especially close to Him (Luke 6:12–16). His "Top Twelve" list included:

(1) Simon (or Peter)

(2) Andrew (Simon's brother)

(3) James (son of Zebedee)

(4) John (another son of Zebedee)

(5) Philip

(6) Bartholomew (or Nathanael)

(7) Matthew (or Levi)

(8) Thomas

(9) James (son of Alphaeus)

(10) Simon the Zealot

(11) Judas the Younger (or Thaddaeus)

(12) Judas Iscariot

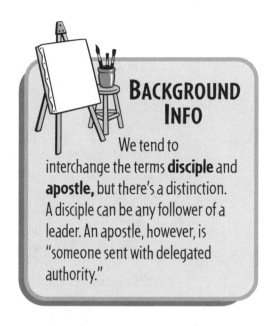

BACKGROUND INFO

We tend to interchange the terms **disciple** and **apostle,** but there's a distinction. A disciple can be any follower of a leader. An apostle, however, is "someone sent with delegated authority."

Jesus chose these men not only to help in His demanding ministry, but also to carry on after the time came for Him to leave them. They would listen to His teachings just as would the other crowds of people. But the apostles had the advantage of asking follow-up questions after the crowds had gone home. Several times in the Gospels we are told that they asked Jesus what in the world He had meant by a certain parable or difficult teaching. We get a few behind-the-scenes discussions and learn, as they did, more precisely how to interpret certain teachings.

And beyond a doubt, Jesus placed a new spin on the messages they had been hearing from other religious teachers. One of the first examples we see of His teaching is the Sermon on the Mount (Matthew 5–7). He started out by telling everyone how "blessed" they were if they happened to be poor in spirit, mourning, thirsting for righteousness, and otherwise in positions without power. He detailed a completely unheard-of system of priorities and rewards based on God's standards. Even today, the teachings in the Sermon on the Mount seem naïve and illogical at first. But as Jesus continued to teach, He further explained His perspective.

In many cases, we've been taught to be aggressive, to get ahead in this competitive world of ours, to seize the day, and to do whatever it takes to ensure our own place and position. As we're told in one popular bumper sticker, He [or she] who dies with the most toys wins.

But from Jesus' perspective, dying doesn't end anything. Physical death is simply another step toward spiritual eternity—as is each day of physical life. Therefore, our physical lives should reflect our spiritual commitments. We should care more about treasures in heaven than bank accounts on earth. And we should make decisions with the knowledge that Jesus has promised, "Many who are first will be last, and many who are last will be first" (Matthew 19:30).

If our lives are only lived "for show" to impress others, we already have our rewards. It's the things we do in secret—the fasting, giving, prayers, and such— that God sees and rewards. God hears our putdowns of others and equates it with murder. He knows of our lust and deems it little different than literal adultery. He grieves at the callous ways we get divorced, "swear to God" and make other oaths, and set out to take revenge on our enemies. (See Matthew 5:21–22, 27–37.)

It's not just outer behavior for which we will receive a heavenly performance review; it's our inner thoughts and intentions as well. The process of spiritual maturity is lifelong, a journey that no one gets exactly right. The ongoing goal is to "Be perfect, therefore, as your heavenly Father is perfect" (Matthew 5:48). This involves turning the other cheek when struck, volunteering additional help for someone who has already demanded our service, and even loving our enemies. It's not enough to be nice to people who are nice to us first. Followers of Jesus are expected to set new standards in showing love to those who don't seem to deserve it (see Matthew 5:38–48).

You Can't Convince All the People All the Time

The hard teachings of Jesus lost Him a big group of followers. (They still do.) Even though Jesus was performing great miracles like healing all kinds of physical maladies and sicknesses, and casting out evil spirits, not everyone was willing to become a believer in Him.

In one account, He had just fed 5,000 people using only a kid's sack lunch—five small barley loaves and two small fish (John 6:1–15). The people were so amazed they wanted to make Jesus their king on the spot. But when they followed Him to see what He would do next, they were disappointed when He decided to teach rather than feed them again. He wanted them to see that He was more than a meal ticket and was the very "bread of life" itself (John 6:35). After making the comment that eternal life would come to "whoever eats my flesh and drinks my blood," a large group of His followers were turned off. Rather than thinking about or asking what He meant, they simply stopped following Him (see John 6:54–63, 66).

WHAT'S THE GOOD WORD?

"Do not store up for yourselves treasures on earth, where moth and rust destroy, and where thieves break in and steal. But store up for yourselves treasures in heaven, where moth and rust do not destroy, and where thieves do not break in and steal. For where your treasure is, there your heart will be also."

—MATTHEW 6:19–21

In another account, a wealthy young man approached Jesus and inquired about eternal life. The man showed great respect for Jesus, and Jesus felt love for this seeker. But Jesus also saw into the heart of the man, and forced a decision out of him. Jesus told him all he had to do to join the ranks of the disciples was first sell all he had and give it to the poor. But the young man just couldn't do it. He was quite wealthy and was unwilling to make that particular sacrifice (Mark 10:17–22).

Even Jesus' top twelve disciples were perplexed that some kind of arrangement hadn't been worked out for this guy. But Jesus made clear two things to them: (1) Certain sacrifices would be expected from those who wanted to be His followers;

and (2) God would more than compensate for any sacrifices based on commitment to Jesus (Mark 10:23–31).

Jesus' teachings and practices also got Him into a lot of trouble with the religious leaders who were suspicious of Him from the beginning. It wasn't long before they were doing all sorts of things to try to trick Him into doing or saying things that they could prosecute Him for. They challenged Him about paying taxes to Caesar (Matthew 22:15–22). They dragged a woman out of bed and paraded her in front of Him to see if He would enforce the death penalty for adultery (John 8:1–11). They derided Him for spending so much time with "sinners" (Matthew 9:11). But Jesus had no trouble evading each of their traps, and He even promoted mercy and compassion as He did.

BACKGROUND INFO

Jesus used a lot of parables in His teaching because only people who were spiritually attuned would understand the message. Many of His thickheaded opponents could see what He was doing and hear what He was teaching but wouldn't "get it" and therefore couldn't accuse Him. (See Matthew 13:10-17.)

The Pharisees complained when Jesus and His disciples picked and ate a small amount of grain on the Sabbath, because harvesting wheat was forbidden (Matthew 12:1–2). They got perturbed every time Jesus healed someone on the Sabbath because they considered it "work." Yet Jesus pointed out that none of them would have any qualms about rescuing a sheep that had stumbled into a pit on the Sabbath—so what exactly was the "sin" in helping human beings in similar dire circumstances (Matthew 12:9–14)?

As conflict between Jesus and the religious leaders escalated during His three-year ministry, groups of Pharisees were eventually plotting to have Him killed (Matthew 12:14). Yet Jesus continued to call them on their hypocritical practices—making a pretense of outward prayer, tithing, formal worship, and ritual—all the while being misguided, self-centered, and full of hypocrisy and wickedness. Jesus didn't mince words with these so-called leaders who were misrepresenting the God of grace and mercy to the people who needed Him.

No Mere Miracles

Jesus' teachings might have been rejected by certain people, yet He continued to attract followers because His words were backed up with power that could only have come from God. He touched lepers, which should have been a big no-no. But instead of His becoming "unclean" due to the forbidden contact, the lepers were healed instead! No disease or affliction appeared to be too difficult for Him to cure. Blind people regained sight. Deafness yielded to hearing. People with paralysis and withered limbs became able to leap and use their hands again. Internal bleeding and other mysterious, lingering diseases were instantly cured at a word or touch of Jesus.

Not even death was an obstacle big enough to hamper Jesus' healing powers. His raising of Lazarus after his friend had been dead four days gets the most attention (John 11:1–44). But Jesus also raised a widow's son and a couple's daughter from the dead as well (Luke 7:11–17; 8:41–42, 49–56).

In one case, Jesus merely gave a command and someone a long distance away was cured (Luke 7:1–10). In another, a woman in a crowd displayed immense faith and touched Jesus, expecting to be healed and embarrassed to discover that He had even noticed (Luke 8:43–48). Jesus used a variety of methods to heal others: speaking, touching, spitting on the ground and applying the mud as a poultice, and so forth.

WHAT'S THE GOOD WORD?

"It is not the healthy who need a doctor, but the sick. But go and learn what this means: 'I desire mercy, not sacrifice.' For I have not come to call the righteous, but sinners."

–MATTHEW 9:12–13

If He had wanted, Jesus could have made quite a spectacle with His miracles, but these great healings always seemed to be somewhat understated. Early in His ministry, He begged people not to tell others what He had done for them, but they couldn't help it. His miracles seem to be inspired by the faith of those seeking help, and they were conducted due to the compassion He felt for people who were hurting. He refused Satan's temptation to use God's power to turn stones to bread for His own benefit, but twice

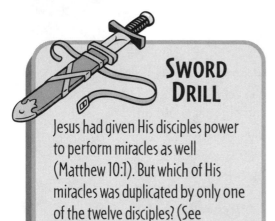

SWORD DRILL

Jesus had given His disciples power to perform miracles as well (Matthew 10:1). But which of His miracles was duplicated by only one of the twelve disciples? (See Matthew 14:22–33.)

He fed crowds of hungry listeners using miraculous means.

It's hard to imagine anyone else with such great power at his or her disposal being so low key in the use of it. If hurting people came to Jesus for help, He was readily available to them. But when people came along and just wanted Him to do something cool on cue, He not only refused, but became angry at such a lack of respect for God's power (Matthew 12:38–42; Luke 23:8–12).

In addition to His healing miracles and resurrections, Jesus demonstrated a surprising amount of control over "laws" of nature. His first miracle was turning water into excellent wine. He twice got the apostles' attention by bestowing on them a miraculously enormous catch of fish. He walked on water. He calmed violent storms with a spoken command. But even though the apostles were privy to many of the miracles that no one else saw, even they were slow to comprehend who Jesus was and what He was doing.

What a Friend They Had in Jesus

Both Jesus' teachings and His miracles were more significant than we usually realize. Yet some of the most outstanding accounts in the Gospels are those that describe Jesus' interpersonal relationships. We see Him patiently training disciples and showing compassion for those flocking to Him for healing. But that's just a start.

While we've seen intense animosity of the Pharisees as a group toward Jesus, we also see that Jesus made time to meet with and answer questions by curious individuals among them. During one private session, a Pharisee named Nicodemus was a bit slow in understanding everything Jesus was trying to tell him, but eventually he became a believer. It was Nicodemus who first heard the words so frequently quoted from Scripture: "For God so loved the world that he gave his one and only Son, that whoever believes in him shall not perish but have eternal life" (John 3:16). And, it was Nicodemus, along with another Pharisee named Joseph, who went to Pilate after Jesus' death and got permission to tend to the body (John 19:38–42).

Tax collectors were among the most despised people during Jesus' time—and for good reason. To begin with, they acted as agents of Rome, collecting money as tribute to keep the oppressive foreign power going strong. And in addition, they generally made a good living by overcharging people and keeping the difference. But when the tax collector Zacchaeus went out of his way to see Jesus (by climbing a tree, no less), Jesus invited Himself to Zach's home (Luke 19:1–10). Physically, Zacchaeus was height impaired. But after his meeting with Jesus, he stood tall as a child of God, ready to make amends to everyone he had cheated.

Perhaps even more hated than tax collectors were the Samaritans. It is believed that when many of the Israelites were carried into captivity, the poorer ones left behind had intermarried with other nations, eventually becoming the Samaritans. Over the centuries, the tensions between the Jews and Samaritans had evolved into political, religious, and even racial divisions. Yet Jesus sometimes chose to travel through Samaria, and on one trip He conducted an extended conversation with a lone woman at a well. Before long, she had brought others to hear Him, and many of the Samaritans placed their faith in Him (John 4:1–42).

SWORD DRILL

Which of Jesus' apostles had been a tax collector? (See Matthew 9:9-13.)

Women as a gender didn't generally receive a lot of respect from their male-oriented society, yet Jesus showed no discrimination. He rescued the woman caught in adultery from a mob eager to stone her (John 8:1–11). At a party, He allowed a prostitute to wet His feet with her tears, dry them with her hair, and anoint them with perfume as others watched in embarrassment and scorn (Luke 7:36–50). He offered spiritual salvation to women and men equally, and outside Judea first presented His identity as Messiah to a woman (John 4:4–42, especially verses 25–26). A group of women followed Him in His ministry, and it was the women who attempted to care for His body after His crucifixion.

Jesus even treated women as equals in terms of logic and debate. A non-Hebrew woman came to Him seeking help for her demon-possessed daughter. Jesus first refused to help, explaining that He had come to "the lost sheep of Israel" and that it was not right to "take the children's bread and toss it to their dogs." But nonplussed, the woman replied, "Yes, Lord, but even the dogs eat the crumbs that fall from their masters' table." Amazed at this woman's great faith, Jesus granted her request (Matthew 15:21–28).

Countdown to Agony

Jesus' three-year ministry of teaching and healing might have changed the world in itself, but His main purpose in coming to earth was to die as a sacrifice for the sins of the world. This had been the plan set in place from the moment of Adam's and Eve's original sin, and numerous Old Testament prophecies and symbols had reinforced this expectation (Genesis 3:15; Numbers 21:4–9; etc.).

Just because Jesus was God in the flesh didn't make this task any easier. He was sent to relate to us "in every way" and to be "tempted in every way, just as we are" (Hebrews 2:17; 4:15). Jesus felt great frustration with the incompetence and hypocrisy of the religious leaders of His time, as we would. He felt the same sorrow any of us would feel as He was betrayed by one of His closest friends, denied by others, and deserted by all. And surely His feelings of injustice were stronger than anything we're capable of feeling, because throughout His rigged trials and darkest moments, He could have put a stop to it. He had the power to escape His utter humiliation and painful anguish at any moment, yet He endured it all on our behalf.

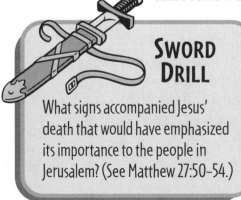

One Sunday He rides into Jerusalem to the cheers and acclaim of great crowds, yet by week's end He is totally alone. His best friends of the past three years have all fled to distance themselves from Him. His all-night prayers to somehow avoid this excruciating experience have gone unanswered as He realizes this is exactly why He has come (see Mark 14:41–42). So He goes through a series of humiliating trials where He is beaten, mocked, insulted, spat on, and forced to wear a regal robe along with a crown of thorns. He doesn't even have the strength to carry His cross to the execution site—and that's *before* He is nailed to that cross and lifted to become an object of scorn for those in attendance.

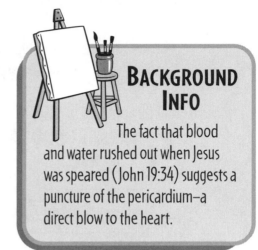

BACKGROUND INFO

The fact that blood and water rushed out when Jesus was speared (John 19:34) suggests a puncture of the pericardium–a direct blow to the heart.

Because He is bearing the sin of humankind, even His usual connection with God the Father has been severed and He feels, in His own words, "forsaken" (Matthew 27:46). His other proclamations from the cross emphasize His human limitations as well. He is thirsty, concerned for the care of His mother after He is gone, and able to find companionship only in one of the criminals with whom He has been sentenced to death.

His death comes sooner than expected. So rather than breaking His legs to hasten the process, a soldier spears Jesus to ensure He is indeed dead.

Undaunted: Dead or Alive

Jesus' body was placed in a borrowed tomb. The religious leaders knew He had said He would rise again, and they feared someone would tamper with the grave. To prevent any such foul play, they made sure the tomb was guarded—not by inexperienced volunteers but trained Roman soldiers posted to watch the officially sealed stone. But not even the Roman Empire was a match for a God-sent earthquake and the angel of the Lord who rolled the stone from the entrance (Matthew 28:2–15).

The guards, after failing to secure the tomb as they had been instructed to do, received a bribe from the religious leaders to spread the story that the disciples sneaked past them and stole the body (Matthew 28:2–4, 11–15). Of all the alternative attempts to "explain away" the resurrection of Jesus, this is one of the most ludicrous. The disciples were in such a state that Peter (their fearless leader) wouldn't even admit his association with Jesus to a servant girl (Matthew 26:69–75)—much less lead a commando raid against trained soldiers. And if either the Romans or Jesus' Jewish opponents had His body, surely they would have produced it rather than let the story spread that He had indeed risen from the dead.

BACKGROUND INFO

Some think the Roman guards deserted their post, allowing the disciples easy access to the tomb. But deserting one's post could easily have resulted in the death penalty for Roman soldiers. They were trained to complete their mission or die trying, even though in this case they "shook and became like dead men" (Matthew 28:4).

But Jesus' resurrection was much more than a story. There were no less than ten eyewitness accounts of His appearances after the crucifixion—several times to those who knew Him best (for example, John 20:26–29) and one time to a group of more than 500 people at once (1 Corinthians 15:6). One group even saw Him ascend into heaven after telling them to wait in Jerusalem for another big event God would provide (Acts 1:9–11).

Even though Jesus was back in heaven with God, He would remain active in world events. As we will see in the next chapter, He made a special appearance to the apostle Paul, and millions of people will attest today that He has been just as active in their own lives.

A Sense of Balance

Hundreds of prophecies and dozens of symbols in the Old Testament pointed forward to Jesus. Every doctrine of Christianity points back to His life, death, and resurrection. Jesus Christ is the fulcrum of history. He connects Old Testament law with New Testament grace and mercy. The very way humankind marks time is based on what occurred before Him and what happened after He arrived.

And, as we will see in future chapters, Jesus Christ is also the foundation and cornerstone of every believer's life. He is the One who makes possible abundant life, joy, peace, and other priceless qualities during times when no other source can. The gospels of Matthew, Mark, Luke, and John provide additional details in the life of Jesus. The books that follow build on those events and formulate doctrines based on them. Open your Bible to any of these books and soak in all you can. You'll find more than enough to keep you pondering for a long, long time.

Chapter Flashback

1. Jesus' twelve disciples included representatives from all but which of the following groups?
   a. Zealots
   b. Tax collectors
   c. Fishermen
   d. Pharisees

2. Jesus taught that the last would be:
   a. Hungry
   b. Least
   c. First
   d. Out of luck

3. Who did Jesus raise from the dead (that we know of)?
   a. Only one person (Lazarus)
   b. Three people
   c. A group of 500 people at once
   d. Moses and Elijah

4. The group of people who most opposed the ministry of Jesus were:
   a. The Greeks
   b. The Romans
   c. The Pharisees
   d. The disciples

5. The best explanation for Jesus' resurrection is:
   a. It really happened because the resurrected Jesus was seen by a great number of people.

b. The disciples suddenly became courageous and stole Jesus' body out of a sealed tomb guarded by trained Roman soldiers.

c. The Jewish opponents of Jesus conspired with the Romans to hide the body.

d. The Roman soldiers had run out to get some breakfast.

Answers: (1) d, (2) c, (3) b, (4) c, (5) a

CHAPTER 12

The Church Goes International

ACTS

SNAPSHOT

[Phone rings] "Hello?"

"Hey, Zach. It's me, Jonathan."

"Hey, man, where were you today?"

"I had a cold, so my mom made me stay home. Did we have any homework?"

"We're just supposed to keep reading and working on our book reports. And, oh yeah, we're supposed to start planning a history project."

"Rats! I hate history."

"Yeah, me too. So what did you do to pass the time at home today?"

"I watched my DVDs of *Pearl Harbor* and *Saving Private Ryan*."

"Oh, man. I haven't watched those in so long!

SNEAK PREVIEW

1. Shortly after Jesus ascended back into heaven, God sent "another Counselor": the Holy Spirit to indwell believers with power.
2. As persecution drove believers out of Jerusalem, they formed churches in various locations.
3. As the number of believers continued to grow, so did the need to establish more order and structure.

Saving Private Ryan was my favorite movie for a long time. Now it's anything I can find about the Old West. So what else did you do?"

"I played my new *Time Machine* video game. It's so totally cool. I went back to the Mesozoic Era, ancient Rome, Valley Forge, the moon landing, and the Battle at Little Big Horn."

"Are you going to be well enough by Wednesday to go the museum exhibit?"

"Are you kidding? No cold is going to stop me from seeing the stuff they found in that newly discovered Pharaoh's tomb! You can count on me. Besides, it gets us out of that crummy history class!"

"All right! See you then."

＊ ＊ ＊ ＊ ＊ ＊ ＊ ＊ ＊ ＊ ＊ ＊ ＊ ＊ ＊

Sometimes we just *think* we don't like something. Perhaps an inept teacher or one bad experience puts us off on a certain subject, but years later we find it's actually far more intriguing than we ever suspected. Maybe you'll find this to be true about church history.

The book of Acts is the sole history book of the New Testament. While it is far less intimidating than the five long books that introduce the Old Testament, some people still snarl up their noses at "history." But if we make an effort to actually enjoy the book of Acts, we'll discover this history lesson involves magicians, miracles, close calls, shipwrecks, murder plots, and much, much more.

Gone but Not Forgotten

The book of Acts picks up right where the Gospels left off. Jesus had risen from the dead and had made a number of appearances over a period of forty days, confirming many of the things He had already tried to prepare His disciples to expect. Matthew records His instructions in what has come to be known as the Great Commission. (See 28:18–20.)

And if you read straight through the gospel of Luke and then skip to Acts, you get the same author following the same story for the benefit of the same person, an influential (probably Roman) man named Theophilus (Luke 1:3; Acts 1:1). It is believed Luke was a doctor (see Colossians 4:14), and his writings are filled with detail. In addition, if you read the book of Acts closely, you'll notice a couple of pronoun shifts as Luke's third-person account suddenly becomes first person at points, suggesting that he became personally involved in portions of this history and didn't just report what other people told him.

As Acts begins, it helps to put oneself in the place of Jesus' disciples. Jesus had come and gone, and they found themselves standing around on top of a mountain. Now what? Two angels assured them that one day Jesus would return to earth in the same way He had left, but what should they do in the meantime?

Some of them were convinced that something truly incredible had taken place, so maybe they needed to let other people know the significance of what had happened. However, some of Jesus' closest dozen followers doubted what they had seen—even when the resurrected Jesus had been in full view (Matthew 28:16–17).

WHAT'S THE GOOD WORD?

Then Jesus came to [the eleven disciples] and said, "All authority in heaven and on earth has been given to me. Therefore go and make disciples of all nations, baptizing them in the name of the Father and of the Son and of the Holy Spirit, and teaching them to obey everything I have commanded you. And surely I am with you always, to the very end of the age."

—MATTHEW 28:18–20

They had always been "the Twelve," but Judas' betrayal of Jesus and subsequent suicide had reduced them to eleven. So they nominated a couple of replacements and cast lots to see which of the two God would select. The winner was a man named Matthias, but we never hear anything about him after this appointment (Acts 1:12–26).

The process of casting lots is mentioned several times in the Bible but never explained. It probably involved tossing stones to see how they landed, not unlike the way we might roll dice (Proverbs 16:33). For the Roman soldiers who cast lots to see who got Jesus' clothes, it was just a method of gambling (Matthew 27:35). But for devout followers of God, it was a solemn method of letting God determine crucial decisions. The clothing of the high priest contained two stones called the Urim and Thummim, thought to be used for this very purpose.

SWORD DRILL

What were some of the crucial decisions made as a result of casting lots throughout the Old Testament? (See Leviticus 16:6–10; Joshua 18:8–10; 1 Samuel 10:20–22; and Jonah 1:4–7. You may also come up with others.)

However, the selection of Matthias is the last mention of casting lots in the Bible. God was about to provide a better way of letting people know what He wanted.

Rebirth, Wind, and Fire

After three years of teaching, performing miracles, and all the other marvelous things Jesus did, His following of "believers" still numbered a paltry 120 (Acts 1:15). We might expect this number to be considerably larger, but perhaps it reflects the oppression the people felt from the Romans, the opposition Jesus had received from the Jewish religious leaders, and other factors that would have diminished enthusiasm for any rabbi claiming to be the Messiah and promoting such drastic new teachings.

But it was about to be confirmed that Jesus had not been just any rabbi. He had promised His disciples that although He would have to leave them, He would not leave them alone in a hostile world. He had promised to send a "Counselor" in His place—God's Holy Spirit (John 14:26; 16:7, 13–16). And He had even kept appearing to them over a period of forty days after His resurrection (Acts 1:3). But after His ascension into heaven, for about a week and a half the disciples had no direction. Jesus had told them to wait in Jerusalem, which is what they were doing.

Of course, Jesus had said a lot of things that seemed to have been forgotten by the disciples in the wake of His death, resurrection, and ascension. But their memory was certainly jogged on the Day of Pentecost, a Jewish festival held fifty days after Passover. While gathered together, a violent wind from heaven blew down on them. Immediately following came "what seemed to be tongues of fire that separated and came to rest on each of them" (Acts 2:1–3).

The effect of this mysterious phenomenon was that the Holy Spirit enabled the disciples to speak in various languages. Apparently, they were gathered in or near the temple, and people visiting from around the world for Pentecost were able to hear of the wonders of God in their native languages.

If something like this were to happen today, we could certainly expect scoffers, and it was no different for the first-century believers. Some of the onlookers were making fun of the multilingual disciples and accused them of being drunk.

At this point, Peter stepped into the sandals of leadership. He didn't cower as he had previously done when quizzed about his relationship with Jesus. This time he stood boldly and addressed the entire crowd, assuring them that his peers were certainly not drunk at 9 A.M.! What was actually happening, he realized, was a direct fulfillment of an Old Testament prophecy that one day God would pour out His Spirit on men and women. Then he gave a short sermon that established the connection between the life of Jesus and the coming of the Holy Spirit. As he concluded with an opportunity for his listeners to repent and be baptized, another 3,000 people became believers (see Acts 2:14–41).

And what a group this was! They met together every day in the temple courts, sharing meals and possessions with one another. The same Spirit that bound them together also enabled the apostles to perform "many wonders and miraculous signs" (Acts 2:43; see also 2:42, 44–47; 4:32–37). Consequently, their numbers increased day by day.

> ## WHAT'S THE GOOD WORD?
>
> "And afterward, I will pour my Spirit on all people. Your sons and daughters will prophesy, your old men will dream dreams, your young men will see visions. Even on my servants, both men and women, I will pour out my Spirit in those days."
>
> –JOEL 2:28–29; SEE ALSO ACTS 2:17–18

Growing Pains

But as you might expect, with this rapid growth also came the first occasions of things not going quite as they should. One couple sold some land and claimed they had donated the proceeds to the apostles, when really they had held back some of it for themselves. Keeping what was theirs would have been perfectly okay, but lying about it while trying to look good to others turned out worse than they could ever have expected. Their action was considered "lying to the Holy Spirit," and both guilty parties died as a result (Acts 5:1–11).

SWORD DRILL

Why would hurting people hang around hoping to see Peter, especially on sunny days? (See Acts 5:12–16.)

In another instance, a magician offered to pay the apostles if they would "sell" him the Holy Spirit. He was strongly chastised and begged them to intercede for him before something drastic happened to him as well (Acts 8:9–24).

Just as Jesus had become a target of criticism by the religious leaders when His miracles began to draw crowds, so now did the other apostles. After Peter and John healed a crippled beggar and began teaching the crowd that had gathered, they soon found themselves arrested and imprisoned. They were released the next day, but the conflict between the new followers of Jesus and the religious "establishment" would continue and intensify as the apostles kept performing miracles and the traditional leaders took offense. However, before long we hear that even "a large number of priests became obedient to the faith" as well (Acts 6:7).

And as the group of believers grew, so did the need for leadership. In addition to the burgeoning numbers of believers, their sharing of food and such was attracting widows and others in need. The apostles couldn't take care of all the physical needs and still attend to the preaching and healing they had been doing, so they appointed seven other men who are frequently referred to as deacons. They too were "full of the Spirit and wisdom," and they were capable of doing "great wonders and miraculous signs" (Acts 6:3, 8). Their primary responsibility, however, was to oversee the food distribution and other logistical needs of the new church.

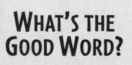

WHAT'S THE GOOD WORD?

"Silver or gold I do not have, but what I have I give you. In the name of Jesus Christ of Nazareth, walk."

—PETER, TO THE CRIPPLED BEGGAR (ACTS 3:6)

One of these men, Philip, is credited with an assist in a key conversion of someone who may have first carried the gospel to Africa (Acts 8:26–40). Another deacon named Stephen was soon singled out as a target by certain synagogue members. They falsely accused him of heresy, after which he eloquently defended himself. When he accused them of being "stiff-necked" and refusing to listen to Jesus, they became irate. And when he added, "Look, I see heaven open and the Son of Man standing at the right hand of God," they began to stone him. On his knees as the stones were pelting him, his last words were a prayer: "Lord, do not hold this sin against them" (Acts 7:54–60).

The Rise and Fall of Saul (or Paul)

In attendance at the stoning of Stephen was a young man named Saul. All we know about him at first is that the people stoning Stephen "laid their clothes at the feet of [this] young man" (Acts 7:58) and that Saul was cheering on Stephen's death (8:1). Some people suggest that Saul may have been the person in charge of the stoning.

When next we hear of Saul, he "was still breathing out murderous threats against the Lord's disciples" (Acts 9:1). He had secured permission to go to Damascus to roust any followers of Jesus he might find in the synagogues there—whether men or women. Any such people would be arrested and returned to Jerusalem. But before he made it to Damascus, he had an unexpected change of plans.

A light from heaven surrounded him and a voice addressed him. The men with Saul heard a noise but couldn't detect the words that Saul heard: "Saul, Saul, why do you persecute me?" (9:4). The voice then identified Himself as Jesus, who told him to continue into Damascus and wait for further instructions. As Saul got up, he discovered he was blind.

Meanwhile, Jesus spoke to a believer named Ananias in Damascus and told him to prepare to meet Saul. It must have been a daunting task to voluntarily approach the "murderous" individual who had come looking to arrest believers, but Ananias did as

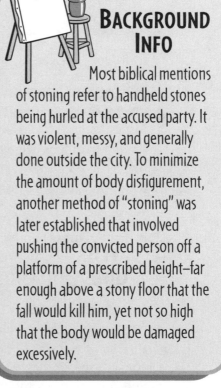

BACKGROUND INFO

Most biblical mentions of stoning refer to handheld stones being hurled at the accused party. It was violent, messy, and generally done outside the city. To minimize the amount of body disfigurement, another method of "stoning" was later established that involved pushing the convicted person off a platform of a prescribed height–far enough above a stony floor that the fall would kill him, yet not so high that the body would be damaged excessively.

BACKGROUND INFO

Saul's name change is not really explained in Scripture, though it was not unusual for people to adopt a name different than the one given them at birth. A common suggestion is that since Saul's ministry would take him to many Gentile groups, he went with a more Greek-sounding name.

he was instructed. After meeting with Saul, "something like scales" fell from Saul's eyes (9:18).

Not only had his physical sight been restored, but Saul was seeing things differently from a spiritual perspective as well. After spending several days with the Damascus disciples, he began to get up in the synagogues and preach that Jesus is the Son of God. And with his prior religious training, he was quite convincing.

Now, instead of Saul doing the arresting and interrogation, the Jewish leaders started looking for opportunities to have *him* killed, and even posted guards at the city gates to make sure he didn't get away. However, the disciples whom Saul had gone to arrest ended up covering for him by helping him escape in a basket lowered through an opening in the city wall.

Things were still confusing when Saul got back to Jerusalem. Who would really believe that Saul, of all people, had joined the ranks of the followers of Jesus? But just as Ananias had risked helping Saul in Damascus, another faithful disciple named Barnabas helped him meet and settle into that group of Jerusalem believers. When another group of Jews planned to kill Saul, the believers sent him to stay in Tarsus, his hometown, for a while.

This isn't the last we'll hear about him. This Saul will enter full-time ministry and be known more familiarly as Paul.

Ladies and Gentile-men, a New Gospel!

Meanwhile, Peter and most of the other apostles were going strong, even though persecution against them was intensifying. In addition to the external pressure they felt, the Jewish-based believers were seeing that the Holy Spirit was converting Gentiles to belief in Jesus as well. This was no small concern. All the Old Testament prohibitions against intermingling with "heathen" cultures had been emphasized for centuries. But God made it quite clear to Peter that His forgiveness and salvation would now extend to non-Jewish peoples as well. Three times in a vision, Peter was commanded to partake from an all-you-can-eat buffet that included formerly prohibited foods (Acts 10–11). As repulsed as Peter felt at this invitation, he came to see that it was a graphic representation of his need to welcome Gentile as well as Jewish believers into the newly forming church.

Christianity was spreading, not only to the Gentiles, but also to peoples in various portions of the world. Peter had been doing some traveling to areas around Jerusalem where, among other things, he healed a paralytic man and raised a woman from the dead (Acts 9:32–43). Not long afterward, at the prompting of the Holy Spirit, Saul and Barnabas were sent to places farther outside Jerusalem to proclaim the Word of God, attend to believers, and establish churches. Their first trip took them to Cyprus, Pisidian Antioch, Iconium, Lystra, and Derbe—a little venture west that involved both land and sea travel.

On this trip they temporarily blinded a pesky magician (Acts 13:6–12), did other miraculous signs and wonders (14:3), and at one point were even thought to be incarnations of the Greek gods Zeus and Hermes (14:11–12). They also incurred the wrath of the Jewish leaders most places they went. After a couple of near misses with local authorities, at one point Paul was stoned and left for dead but recovered after the angry crowd had dispersed (14:19–20).

Paul and Barnabas reported back to a council being held in Jerusalem. A major dispute had arisen about whether to acknowledge Gentile belief in Jesus without the Gentiles first conforming to Jewish traditions (especially circumcision). Some believers were also Pharisees, and it was very disconcerting to

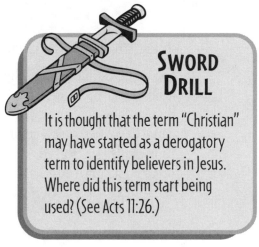

SWORD DRILL

It is thought that the term "Christian" may have started as a derogatory term to identify believers in Jesus. Where did this term start being used? (See Acts 11:26.)

BACKGROUND INFO

A few of the place names in Acts are still familiar to us (Rome, Cyprus, etc.). Others are no longer around or have had name changes. If you want to follow the geographic meanderings of Paul on his journeys, many Bibles contain a map with his separate routes marked out.

find themselves worshiping alongside people they considered "heathen."

However, both Peter and the Paul/Barnabas team had witnessed God's power among Gentiles—just the way they were. As a result, it was decided that Gentile believers need not be circumcised. However, they were challenged to adhere to certain practices to avoid unnecessary conflict with their Jewish peers. Sexual immorality was forbidden, of course, and they were also asked to avoid eating meat retaining the blood of the animals or that had been offered to idols (Acts 15:19-21, 28-29). There would continue to be certain tensions between Gentile and Jewish believers, but the fact that they worked out this problem with so little controversy was an admirable and significant accomplishment.

On the Road Again

After the council, Paul and Barnabas thought it would be fitting to make another lengthy journey to encourage the churches they had previously visited and maybe even branch out a little farther. But a disagreement arose that split them up. Barnabas teamed up with his young relative, John Mark (the source of the argument). Paul paired up with a man named Silas, and the two teams went their separate ways.

SWORD DRILL

What, exactly, caused the division between Paul and Barnabas? Who do you think was right, or did they both have a valid point? (See Acts 15:36-41.)

On Paul's second tour of the area, he fanned out to visit Philippi, Thessalonica, Berea, Athens, Corinth, Ephesus, Troas, and a few other places in Greece and Macedonia. So later, when Paul writes his letters to the Philippians, Thessalonians, Corinthians, Ephesians, and such, he is following up on this initial trip.

Paul tried to make the most of his time in each location. He would traditionally go to the synagogue, where visitors were usually invited to speak. He would tell the members about Jesus, after which some usually responded and others usually tried to run him out of town. Sometimes his stay would be just for a day or two, but other times he would get such a good response he would stay much longer—occasionally even a year or more (Acts 18:9–11; 20:31). In Athens he found a good opportunity to speak when he came upon an altar erected "To an unknown God" (Acts 17:22–23). He simply told the people there about the God he knew, whom they hadn't yet heard about.

In addition to teaching, Paul had been given power to do great things as well. In Ephesus, for example, people could take handkerchiefs or aprons touched by Paul to sick or possessed people and the people would be immediately cured (19:11–12). Paul was so convincing that large numbers of people were repenting of their sinful ways and believing in Jesus, and a great number of sorcerers even brought out their mystical scrolls and had a public bonfire. In response, a guild of local silversmiths (who made a good living selling images of the goddess Artemis outside the temple devoted to her) feared they would be driven out of business. They incited a citywide riot, but after a few hours the city clerk settled the matter without incident.

BACKGROUND INFO

The perspective of the book of Acts first shifts in chapter 16. The author begins by referring to Paul and his companions as "they." But after a stop in a place called Troas, the group suddenly becomes "we." It is generally assumed that Luke joined the group for a while at this point. Another member of the party is a young man named Timothy, to whom Paul writes two letters found in the New Testament (verses 1–3).

Paul was headed back to Jerusalem, so the next place he stopped he spoke for a long time. (Who knew if he would ever be back?) By midnight, a youngster named Eutychus just couldn't stay awake anymore. The trouble was, he was seated in a third-story window well, and when he fell asleep, he tumbled forward and onto the floor below, dead. Paul paused, placed his arms around the young man, and his life was restored. Everyone took a meal break, and then Paul kept talking until daybreak (20:7–12).

In addition to the major events taking place, Acts introduces us to a number of people—both good and bad. We've mentioned a number of Paul's

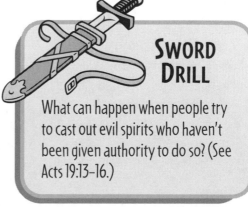

SWORD DRILL

What can happen when people try to cast out evil spirits who haven't been given authority to do so? (See Acts 19:13–16.)

SWORD DRILL

Sometimes God's people in similar dire circumstances can experience very different results. For example, Acts tells of several believers who were sent to prison. What was the outcome for James? (Acts 12:1-2). For Peter? (Acts 12:3-19). For Paul? (Acts 16:22-40).

companions—Barnabas, Silas, Luke, and Timothy. Others involved in his ministry were Lydia (16:13-15), a couple named Priscilla and Aquila (18:1-4), Apollos (18:24-28), and others. Meanwhile, the Herod who had killed James and tried to do the same to Peter died a most undignified death (12:18-23). Other Roman officials would soon make life more challenging for Paul.

Paul and Silas made their way back to Jerusalem to complete this second journey, even after a prophet of God warned that Paul would be taken prisoner there (21:10-14). But before his arrest, he shared with the local believers the great things God was doing in other parts of the world.

Arrest for the Weary

Sure enough, the prophecy came true and Paul was arrested soon after getting back to Jerusalem (21:27-36). But Paul's incarceration didn't change his lifestyle all that much. He was still able to tell crowds (along with top-level government officials) about Jesus. And he had hoped to get to Rome someday to spend time with the believers there (19:21). By appealing his arrest, he got a free trip (25:12). In addition, he was protected from a group of more than forty hostile enemies who had sworn not to eat or drink until Paul was dead (23:12-22). Twice during this period he was able to share his personal conversion experience (22:1-21; 26:9-18). Not many of the higher officials chose to respond, but at least they heard the truth.

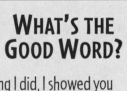

WHAT'S THE GOOD WORD?

"In everything I did, I showed you that by this kind of hard work we must help the weak, remembering the words the Lord Jesus himself said: 'It is more blessed to give than to receive.'"

—ACTS 20:35

Paul's trip to Rome was not without incident, however. A terrible storm hit and sank his ship. But the Roman officials eventually heeded Paul's instructions and everyone survived. In Malta, where everyone was washed up on the shore, Paul was able to speak and to heal many sick people (27:9–28:10). And when he finally made it to Rome and was under guard for two years, Paul lived in "his own rented house" where he was free to preach, write, and even receive visitors (28:17–31).

The book of Acts concludes without the happy ending we might desire, where Paul is released. But from all indications, that's exactly what happened at some point thereafter. Many think he even journeyed as far as Spain later in his life.

Paul would eventually die in prison, but not yet. First he would pen a number of letters that not only inspired the people and churches of his own time period, but continue to do so even today. We'll look at those letters in the next chapter.

Chapter Flashback

Match the people mentioned in the book of Acts with their descriptions. (Stephen and Barnabas are found in multiple pairings. The two listings for Ananias, however, refer to different men who happened to have the same name.)

(1) Ananias and Sapphira

(2) Aquila and Priscilla

(3) Barnabas and Ananias

(4) Barnabas and Silas

(5) Mark and Eutychus

(6) Stephen and James

(7) Stephen and Philip

A. Two of the seven first "deacons"

B. Paul's two primary traveling companions

C. Two young men who made mistakes but later recovered from them

D. Two people put to death for their beliefs

E. Two people put to death for lying to the Holy Spirit

F. A married couple who helped Paul in his ministry

G. Two believers who took a big risk in bringing Paul into the church

Answers: (1) E, (2) F, (3) G, (4) B, (5) C, (6) D, (7) A

Paul: A Man of Letters

ROMANS THROUGH PHILEMON

"See you later, Mom; I'm going to play some tennis."

"Wait just a minute, Jeremy. I said you couldn't do anything until you had finished every one of your thank-you notes for your graduation presents."

"They're done."

"How about putting your résumé together to mail out to prospective employers so you can get a part-time job when you get to college?"

"Done."

"The letter you've been promising to write Granddad?"

"Finished."

"And Aunt Selma?"

"Check!"

SNEAK PREVIEW

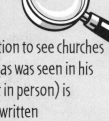

1. Paul's determination to see churches grow and thrive (as was seen in his eagerness to visit in person) is confirmed by his written correspondence that taught, motivated, and encouraged them.

2. Some of Paul's letters were for the benefit of churches as a whole; others were targeted more to individuals.

3. Though Paul's letters to churches and individuals began primarily as personal correspondence, they quickly were included in the canon of inspired Scripture.

"Jeremy, I'm really surprised at your initiative. That must have taken hours of work. I'm going to the post office later if you want me to mail everything out for you."

"No need. For the thank-you notes I pulled the E-mail addresses out of my master list, made a file, clicked 'Send,' and was done in five minutes. For Granddad and Aunt Selma, I did the same. Then I loaded the printer with résumé paper and it's printing right now—highest quality. Then I took a nap and now I'm ready to play tennis. Anything else?"

"A little personal thought and individual attention might be nice."

"Good grief, Mom. Come out of the Dark Ages. I gotta go. See you."

SWORD DRILL

Paul's letters are filled with encouragement and persuasive arguments to get the most out of life. But can you identify two Old Testament figures who wrote letters leading to death? One was usually a good king, but he once sent a letter with instructions to have a man killed—and sent it by the doomed man himself! Another letter was written by a wicked queen willing to have a man killed just to acquire a vineyard for her husband. (See 2 Samuel 11:14-15 and 1 Kings 21:7-10.)

* * * * * * * * * * * * * * *

So far in the New Testament, we've covered four gospels and a book of history. The next stretch includes a series of letters, traditionally called the Epistles. In fact, twenty-one of the twenty-seven New Testament books fit in this category, and at least thirteen of them were authored by Paul. (The author of the Letter to the Hebrews remains a mystery. It may have been written by Paul as well.) This chapter addresses Paul's epistles, not his E-pistles. They were done the old-fashioned way—handwritten and hand delivered (if not by Paul himself, by one of his representatives).

As you might expect if you sat down and wrote a letter to thirteen different friends, you might cover a lot of the same subjects in each letter. You'd let everyone know how you were doing, what had been going on in your life, and so forth. And then, more than likely, you would personalize each letter based on what was taking place in the other person's life, acknowledging what you knew had occurred. Some would reflect joy based on a recent marriage, new child, or other festive occasion. Some would express sorrow at a death or tragedy. Some might contain warnings and admonitions if you have information the recipient is unaware of.

Paul's letters aren't so different. If he were writing today, a click of the mouse would save Paul from having to pay a scribe or getting writing cramps. But it's refreshing to note the individual attention given to each of Paul's letters. As we will see, they express a wide range of emotions over situations he was unable to attend to personally. Some of his letters repeat what other letters had already said, which should be expected. Some were intended to be shared with an entire church; others were more private. Along with deep thoughts and explanations of biblical doctrine, we find personal greetings and comments. Yet these letters were almost instantly accepted as divinely inspired writings that belonged with the rest of the Holy Scriptures.

WHAT'S THE GOOD WORD?

Bear in mind that our Lord's patience means salvation, just as our dear brother Paul also wrote you with the wisdom that God gave him. He writes the same way in all his letters, speaking in them of these matters. His letters contain some things that are hard to understand, which ignorant and unstable people distort, as they do the other Scriptures, to their own destruction.

–2 PETER 3:15–16

When in Romans . . .

The book of Romans has been called the Constitution of the New Testament because it covers a wide range of foundational truths of the gospel of Jesus. It isn't thought to be the first epistle written chronologically, but it's a good beginning because it covers so many essential themes. Paul writes in anticipation of a personal visit to Rome (Romans 1:10–13; 15:23–29). He also seems to be aware of the tensions between the Jews and Gentiles, and explains how the righteousness of God is crucial to both groups (Romans 1:16–17).

It is in Romans where we learn that everyone has sinned and falls short of the glory of God (3:23) and that "the wages of sin is death" (6:23). No one is personally righteous enough to overcome the problem of sin and death. However, God freely makes available an otherwise unattainable status of righteousness to all who believe in Jesus, and that righteousness effects a transition from death to eternal life.

People will continue to struggle with sin and will feel overcome at times, but the Holy Spirit is active in our lives and keeps clear the connection between sinful humankind and a perfect, sinless God (8:5,15–17, 26–27). Consequently, believers can expect no condemnation from God (8:1), are more than conquerors in their struggles (8:37), and cannot possibly be cut off from the love of God that Jesus made possible (8:38–39). It is as if God has legally adopted those who place their faith in Him, and believers are actually coheirs with Jesus to receive everything God offers (8:17).

WHAT'S THE GOOD WORD?

For I am convinced that neither death nor life, neither angels nor demons, neither the present nor the future, nor any powers, neither height nor depth, nor anything else in all creation, will be able to separate us from the love of God that is in Christ Jesus our Lord.

–ROMANS 8:38–39

Our part, in return, is to behave appropriately, remembering whose family we now belong to. While no longer required to slaughter animals as sacrifices (because Jesus was the ultimate and final blood sacrifice), we are still to consider ourselves as "living sacrifices" to God (12:1). And since sacrifices weren't supposed to be blemished in any way, we need to work on being "transformed by the renewing of [our] minds" (12:2) to becoming the people God wants us to be—for our own good, not because He can possibly gain anything from it.

We are to practice love in real and relevant ways (12:9–21; 13:8–10). We should respect human authority, even when we don't agree with our leaders (13:1–4). And as we mature spiritually, we must take great care not to become proud or feel superior. We are to always be aware of those who may be weaker, and ensure that our own habits and freedoms don't interfere with anyone else's spiritual growth (14:1–15:7).

More to the Corinthians Than Fine Leather

Older readers may recall car ads on TV where Ricardo Montalban promoted "rich

Corinthian leather," and that may be all many of us know about Corinth. But in Paul's day, Corinth was a mighty commercial city in Greece. The members of the church there, however, were dividing into cliques (1 Corinthians 1:11–12). Much of Paul's writing addressed the need for unity within the church.

While Romans emphasized doctrine, the tone of Corinthians is more personal. We know that some earlier correspondence had taken place between Paul and this church (1 Corinthians 5:9–11; 7:1), though it has never been discovered. That being the case, it makes sense that what we know as 1 Corinthians would naturally be less formal and more intimate. And a few years later, when Paul got around to writing what we know as 2 Corinthians, he shared some very revealing details about his own life.

Come Together—Right Now!

But he begins with the most urgent matter, calling on the church members to use their God-given wisdom and heal the divisions that had been occurring (1 Corinthians 1:1–4:20). And then he confronts a specific incident he has been told about. One of the members was attending on a regular basis after marrying "his father's wife"—an offense that "does not occur even among pagans" (5:1). Paul's advice was to expel this man from the church, temporarily at least, so that after being "handed over to Satan" (out in the world) he would repent and return to church fellowship.

Other potentially divisive issues among the believers were lawsuits (6:1–11), sexual impropriety (6:12–20), divorce and marriage problems (7:1–40), whether or not it was okay to eat food bought in the marketplace that had been sacrificed to idols (8:1–13), lack of respect during church worship (11:2–16), and inappropriate behavior during the Lord's Supper (11:17–34). Paul provided clear guidelines for each of these matters. A rule of thumb was that even things that some people felt free to do should probably be avoided (in public, at least) to prevent anyone from "stumbling" in his or her walk with God (10:13–33).

BACKGROUND INFO

The offensive member of the Corinthian church had probably married his stepmother, not his biological mother. Still, it was a direct violation of the law (Deuteronomy 22:30).

All this leads up to Paul's explanation of the diversity of spiritual gifts, and the importance of each person doing his or her part and allowing others to do so as well (12; 14). It is in this context that he writes the "Love Chapter" of the Bible, 1 Corinthians 13. All or portions of this chapter are read at many weddings, though many people have no idea it pertains directly to our attitudes in using spiritual gifts.

Finally, just prior to his closing personal greetings (1 Corinthians 16), Paul addresses the issue of resurrection. The good news is that when believers are resurrected, their sinful, degrading, human bodies are replaced with eternal, perfect ones. The bad news is that we have to die before we get to be resurrected. Yet Paul's reminder is that for believers, death has no lasting "sting" (1 Corinthians 15:12–58).

Mr. Big Shot: Who Do You Think You Are?
The book of 2 Corinthians was written primarily as a response to a bunch of false teachers who had no respect for Paul and who were attempting to turn the church against him. In reply to their accusations, Paul wrote his most personal and self-revealing letter. He referred to the infiltrators somewhat sarcastically in places. Various translations refer to them as "super-apostles" or "big-shot apostles" (2 Corinthians 11:5), and Paul compared them to Satan, who "masquerades as an angel of light" (11:14).

Paul didn't hesitate to go head-on with his opponents. He briefly summarizes the credentials of his own harsh life in a short paragraph in 2 Corinthians 11:22–29— and his résumé includes beatings, stoning, whippings, shipwrecks, and more. He was somewhat embarrassed to have to spell everything out, but these events were the best possible proof that he was a genuine apostle who served Jesus tirelessly.

He also wrote of God's ongoing grace in dealing with a physical "thorn" that caused him chronic suffering, and of a mysterious vision he had waited fourteen years to mention (12:1–10). None of the phonies who opposed Paul could even approach his accomplishments, and the people in the Corinthian church quickly vindicated Paul's reputation.

The Galatian Situation

While Romans has been called the Constitution of the Bible, Galatians has been compared to the Magna Carta. With the significant body of Old Testament law to contend with, some of the religious teachers of the time had created quite a legalistic system. "Do this. Don't do that . . . or that . . . or that." Most of Jesus' disagreements with the Pharisees had arisen out of their nitpicky adherence to their own interpretation of what the law meant—which was faulty to begin with. And as the church grew out of Judaism, many people remained firm about continuing a strict legalistic system of worship. Galatians is an emancipation proclamation for Christians who might feel their faith is little more than a heavy yoke.

Ill Legalism

Galatia was a territory in Asia Minor between the Black Sea and Mediterranean Sea. The letter to the Galatians is addressed to the *churches* there (Galatians 1:2) and is the only epistle so addressed to more than one specific location. In this letter, Paul again is forced to defend himself from accusations—this time by legalistic teachers.

BACKGROUND INFO

The Pharisees had gone through the entire Old Testament law and had written out a list of 248 "to do" commandments and 365 "don't you dare" prohibitions. In doing so, they had imposed unyielding interpretations that weren't necessarily accurate.

The legalism issue had penetrated into even the inner circle of Christian leadership. Peter had at one time felt the freedom to eat with Gentile believers and treat them as equals. But in time even he and Barnabas—two forerunners in the acceptance of "outsiders"—had been pulled back into "the circumcision group" of legalistic Jewish believers (Galatians 2:11–21). Paul had confronted Peter to his face and had set him straight.

Paul accused the Galatians of "foolishness" (3:1–5). He referred them to Abraham, a figure they highly respected, and reminded them that he had been declared righteous by God simply because of his faith. The law hadn't even been written yet! Is it so surprising, then, that God still responds to the simple faith of people rather than mere adherence to a long list of laws? The law can never justify and save anyone; but faith in God can.

Freedom: The Real Thing

And since God declares us righteous, we are freed from the requirements other people attempt to impose—circumcision being at the top of the list for those in the Galatian churches. Paul was fed up with teachers who insisted that being circumcised was key to being accepted by God—so fed up, in fact, that he wrote: "As for those agitators, I wish they would go the whole way and emasculate themselves" (5:12). Ouch!

WHAT'S THE GOOD WORD?

But the fruit of the Spirit is love, joy, peace, patience, kindness, goodness, faithfulness, gentleness and self-control. Against such things there is no law. . . . Since we live by the Spirit, let us keep in step with the Spirit.

—GALATIANS 5:22–23, 25

To their credit, some of the legalistic leaders feared that, as had occurred so many times in the past, granting people any degree of religious freedom would very likely send them down a slippery slope into immorality. But Paul explained that true freedom comes from responding to the Holy Spirit in our lives, and the results of doing so are only positive. We continue to struggle with the strong desires of our natural, sinful natures, and if we give in to them, we can indeed misuse and/or lose our God-given freedoms. But if we keep in step with the Holy Spirit, we discover great freedom within a lifetime of service and satisfaction.

Breezin' Through Ephesians

On his travels, Paul had parked himself in Ephesus longer than anywhere else—for three years, as a matter of fact (Acts 20:31). Yet the letter to the Ephesian church is not nearly as personal as some of Paul's other messages. This leads some people to suspect Paul didn't really write it, but it is just as likely that the message may have been meant for a number of churches in the area, with Ephesus being the primary recipient.

The content is certainly relevant for any church in any age. While 1 Corinthians dealt with a lot of people problems (marriage, lawsuits, food, and other everyday stuff), Ephesians begins with a reference to God's blessings (1:3), and most of what follows keeps the focus on God. Though God has always been, and will continue to be, a mystery to us, much of the mystery has been explained in the coming of Jesus to earth. Thanks to the human life of Jesus, we have a much better understanding of what God is really like (1:9–10; 3:2–6).

It is Jesus who infuses life into our otherwise dreary worlds, guarantees eternal life afterward, and is the common bond of all believers whether Jew or Gentile (2:1–22). Paul considered himself "the prisoner of Christ Jesus" (3:1; 4:1) and planned his life and ministry accordingly. He also challenged his readers to attempt to "grasp how wide and long and high and deep is the love of Christ, and to know this love that surpasses knowledge" (3:18–19). Such knowledge results in unity, an enlightened life rather than living in darkness, and strengthened relationships.

WHAT'S THE GOOD WORD?

For it is by grace you have been saved, through faith–and this not from yourselves, it is the gift of God–not by works, so that no one can boast. For we are God's workmanship, created in Christ Jesus to do good works, which God prepared in advance for us to do.

—EPHESIANS 2:8–10

Christians are called to "submit to one another out of reverence for Christ" (5:21). Basic guidelines are provided for husbands and wives, children and parents, and masters and slaves. But such guidelines prove unnecessary if we can learn one basic lesson: "Be imitators of God . . . and live a life of love, just as Christ loved us and gave himself up for us as a fragrant offering and sacrifice to God" (5:1–2). To help us in this endeavor, God provides us with full spiritual armor: the belt of truth, breastplate of righteousness, feet guarded with the readiness that comes from the gospel of peace, shield of faith, helmet of salvation, and the sword of the Spirit, which is the word of God (6:10–18). Because Jesus died for us, we are called to live for God.

Philippians: Fillin' Up on Joy

Imagine yourself in a prison cell, held for a crime you had not committed and having done no wrong to anyone. How would you feel? What would you do?

Perhaps, like Paul, you would shoot off a few letters. You might write to acquire good lawyers, appeal to the governor, threaten lawsuits, seek comfort from loved ones, and gripe about the injustices of the penal system. Paul, however, wrote his epistle to the Philippians to remind them how much they all had to rejoice over. Although it's clear he is incarcerated (Philippians 1:12–14), this letter is one of the most upbeat portions of Scripture.

Even the reports of others who "preach Christ out of envy and rivalry" (1:15) couldn't stifle the joy Paul felt as he contemplated his relationship with Jesus and his human friendships. Jesus was the joy of his life, and death would only take him closer to his Savior (1:20–26).

Joy, however, must begin with humility (2:1–11). As we yield ourselves to God, He lifts us higher than we could ever lift ourselves. Paul knew the emptiness of a legalistic lifestyle, for he had been "a Hebrew of Hebrews" and a zealous devotee of the law (3:2–6). In light of his knowledge of Jesus, however, he considered everything else a loss—a pile of rubbish (3:7–11).

BACKGROUND INFO

Gnosticism was a philosophy that completely separated the material world (which was perceived as all bad) from the spiritual (all good). So taken to extremes, it didn't much matter what sins your material body was committing as long as you considered your spiritual self to be strong. This philosophy also placed much value on "secret knowledge" that was attainable by only a small minority of insightful people.

Paul wanted his joy to be contagious, so he pleaded for his readers to "press on" toward the goal of eternal life with Jesus. A couple of women were having a spat that affected the church, so he called them by name and asked them to patch things up. By replacing worry with joy and keeping our minds on excellent and praiseworthy things, he wrote, we can experience a peace of God that defies explanation (4:2–9). And that's something to rejoice about!

Colossians: For Better or Worship

Colossians is another letter Paul penned from the pen. He addressed a false doctrine he had heard was being promoted, but he never stated exactly what it was. Some think it might have been an early form of

Gnosticism, which developed soon thereafter. Others suggest some people might have been promoting the worship of angels (Colossians 2:18)—another religious movement of the time that lasted several centuries.

Paul cut to the core of whatever this false teaching happened to be by establishing Jesus Christ—the material human Being interwoven with the perfect spiritual eternal Being—as preeminent in all of creation. The humanity of Jesus was by no means a limitation of who He was, but rather the best possible representation of the invisible God (1:15). No one could see God and live (Exodus 33:20), but by observing Jesus we could comprehend to a much greater degree "all the fullness" of God (Colossians 1:19–20).

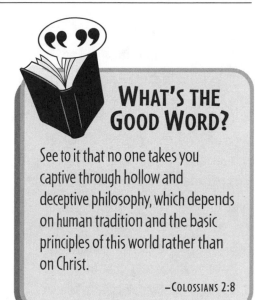

WHAT'S THE GOOD WORD?

See to it that no one takes you captive through hollow and deceptive philosophy, which depends on human tradition and the basic principles of this world rather than on Christ.

—COLOSSIANS 2:8

Other portions of the letter to the Colossians are similar to portions of Ephesians, which suggests that Paul may have written them at about the same time.

Bless Those Thessalonians

Chronologically, Paul's two letters to the Thessalonians may have been the first of all his writings that have been preserved. (Perhaps Galatians was written earlier.) Like other of his letters, some of the content is Paul's response to hearing that other leaders have questioned his authority. He was forced to defend himself again (1 Thessalonians 2:1–16). But he moved quickly into topics more beneficial to the church.

1 Thessalonians: Going but Not Forgotten
One of the specific issues at the Thessalonian church was concern that people were dying before the anticipated return of Jesus. Would that disqualify them from anything promised to believers? Had they missed the boat?

Paul assured them of the reality of resurrection and that, in fact, the "dead in Christ" would precede the living whenever Jesus returned and gathered His

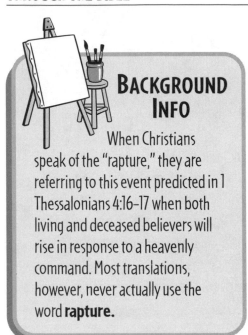

BACKGROUND INFO

When Christians speak of the "rapture," they are referring to this event predicted in 1 Thessalonians 4:16-17 when both living and deceased believers will rise in response to a heavenly command. Most translations, however, never actually use the word **rapture.**

people into heaven (4:13–18). Expectation of resurrection was to be an encouragement, not a dreadful or worrisome concept (4:18; 5:11).

2 Thessalonians: Working While You Wait

The second letter to the Thessalonians continued this train of thought. The church was facing some persecution, and someone had sent them a letter purportedly from Paul saying that Jesus had already returned and they had missed it (2 Thessalonians 2:1–2). Paul explained that trials would become status quo for the church. In fact, believers could expect even worse times and the eventual coming of a "man of lawlessness" (2:3–12)—frequently thought to be the same antichrist John would describe later in the book of Revelation.

It is also suggested that after hearing about the promised return of Jesus, some of the church members were sitting around twiddling their thumbs and waiting for the big party. Paul, therefore, warned them to "stand firm and hold to the teachings we passed on to you" (2:15) and encouraged them to remain faithful and busy (3:6–15). They had no way of knowing exactly how long the wait might be.

Some of Paul's Epistles Were Put out to Pastors

The letters of Paul we've covered so far were intended for entire churches or even groups of churches. But in addition to writing to whole congregations, Paul also acted as mentor for some of the younger men being called into leadership over the churches. So his "Pastoral Epistles" are comprised of two letters to Timothy and one to Titus—all relatively short.

Another distinction of these epistles is that they were written considerably later in Paul's life. As he saw what appeared to be his imminent death, portions of these letters are quite personal.

1 and 2 Timothy

Timothy would seem a good choice to lead the church because his mother and grandmother were Jewish believers and his father was a Gentile (probably a nonbeliever, based on Acts 16:1). Consequently, Timothy could relate to both segments of the church. Paul commended Timothy's faith but prodded him to be a bit bolder in his approach (2 Timothy 1:3–10).

The bad times the believers were currently facing would only get worse, so Paul urged Timothy to cling to the truth of Scripture and remain faithful. In spite of Paul's sense of his impending death, he could see beyond to his reward: "For I am already being poured out like a drink offering, and the time has come for my departure. I have fought the good fight, I have finished the race, I have kept the faith. Now there is in store for me the crown of righteousness, which the Lord, the righteous Judge, will award to me on that day—and not only to me, but also to all who have longed for his appearing" (2 Timothy 4:6–8).

> ## BACKGROUND INFO
>
> Timothy had traveled with Paul before, and had been placed over the church in Ephesus as Paul continued his journeys. So Paul's letters to Timothy contain advice relevant to most pastors— public worship expectations, how to choose good leaders, seeing through false teachings, and dealing with specific groups within the church (widows, older and younger groups, slaves, etc.).

How many of us will be able to say the same when our time comes?

Titus

Titus had also traveled with Paul for a while before being placed over a church. He was a child of Gentile parents who placed his faith in Jesus after hearing Paul's teaching. Titus's church was in Crete, a Mediterranean island known primarily for the dishonesty, greed, immorality, and general nastiness of its inhabitants. But the believers there were making a difference, and Titus held his own as a positive model amid this culture. Later he had an equally challenging assignment in Dalmatia (which became Albania/Yugoslavia), where the people tended to be belligerent and combative.

The content of Paul's letter, not surprisingly, is similar to what he wrote to Timothy. It is the challenge and encouragement of an older, experienced pastor/evangelist to a younger peer in a difficult but rewarding job.

SWORD DRILL

Timothy and Titus had certain similarities, yet one key difference made Titus stand out as an example for all Gentiles. What was that crucial distinction, and why was it so significant? (See Acts 16:1–3 and Galatians 2:3–5.)

Philemon: Short Book, Big Favor

Though not categorized as a pastoral letter, the epistle to Philemon is also addressed to an individual, though added to the salutation is the intention that it also be read by the church that met at Philemon's house (v. 2). The essence of this short letter is Paul's request that Philemon, a wealthy man, forgive and reinstate a slave named Onesimus, who had stolen from him and then had run away. Paul had met the runaway slave during his travels, and Onesimus had become a believer. Paul was interceding on the slave's behalf for mercy and the right to return and serve once again.

On a broader scale, the story of Onesimus is something of an object lesson for all of us. The name "Onesimus" meant "useful." So someone who should have been useful proved to be useless until an encounter with God and a change of heart. Similarly, we can be Christians in name only and be in great need of a genuine divine encounter before we are truly useful for the kingdom of God.

The Law of the Letter

So there we have a short summary of thirteen letters penned by the apostle Paul. A careful reading of this section of Scripture will show that he covered a great many important topics and provided thorough explanations of exactly why faith in Jesus is so essential for a Christian's spiritual development.

But Paul wasn't the only letter writer in Scripture. The next chapter will move on to some other important authors, and we'll see what they have to say. As a matter of fact, we should get the rest of the way through the Bible. Stay awake. We're approaching the end—and what an end it is!

Chapter Flashback

1. Which group of people did *not* receive a letter from Paul?
   a. The Galatians
   b. The Ephesians
   c. The Filipinos
   d. The Colossians

2. In more than one of his letters, Paul had to:
   a. Remind people who he was
   b. Defend himself against accusations of false teachers
   c. Solicit funds for the continuation of his ministry
   d. Ask the recipient to send a drachma to the top name on the list

3. The joy-filled letter to the Philippians, as well as other letters, were written while Paul was:
   a. In prison
   b. At Club Med
   c. On the road
   d. In Corinth

4. Paul's letters to Timothy and Titus are called:
   a. Rural Epistles
   b. Casual Epistles
   c. Castor Oil Epistles
   d. Pastoral Epistles

5. Paul's short letter to Philemon was primarily in regard to a runaway:
   a. Best-seller
   b. Chariot
   c. Child
   d. Slave

Answers: (1) c, (2) b, (3) a, (4) d, (5) d

CHAPTER 14

More Epistles to Pique Your Interest ...(And a Peek into the Future)

HEBREWS THROUGH REVELATION

SNAPSHOT

"Wanda, what are you doing?"

"I'll be with you in a second, dear. I'm just trying to read these tea leaves."

"Say what?"

"It's a way of telling the future, Steve. I'm supposed to take my nurse's exam tomorrow, and I need to know how I'm going to do. So if you can't say anything helpful, don't say anything at all."

"I do have one suggestion you may find useful: I don't think most people who read tea leaves use *tea bags.*"

"I wondered why this wasn't working. My horoscope wasn't much better."

"Your horoscope?"

"Today's reading for Libra: 'Unanticipated surprise

SNEAK PREVIEW

1. In addition to Paul's letters, the Bible includes correspondence from James, Peter, John, Jude, and the author of Hebrews.

2. Revelation was John's record of his God-given insight into the present state of a number of churches as well as future events.

3. Whether we're reading gospels, history, epistles, or even the apocalyptic book of Revelation, the New Testament books all offer encouragement to believers.

in store for you.' I don't know if that means I'll be surprised at how well I will do . . . or surprised at how badly I'll bomb."

"I have a Magic 8-Ball, if you think that will help," Steve said, thinking she was joking.

"I already tried. 'Reply hazy. Try again later.' And my fortune cookie was equally vague: 'She with wrinkled clothes rides dragon in great pain.' Do you suppose that means I should at least *look* good when I take the test? It makes you wonder, doesn't it?"

"All I wonder is why you don't use the time and effort you're putting into fortune-telling and apply it to studying instead. If you are well prepared, can't you predict how you'll do on the big test?"

"Steve, if you're not going to be serious I can't waste my time talking to you. By the way, have you seen our copy of the *Total Nitwit's Guide to Palmistry?*"

* * * * * * * * * * * * * * *

WHAT'S THE GOOD WORD?

Let no one be found among you who sacrifices his son or daughter in the fire, who practices divination or sorcery, interprets omens, engages in witchcraft, or casts spells, or who is a medium or spiritist or who consults the dead. Anyone who does these things is detestable to the LORD.

—DEUTERONOMY 18:10–12

Some people will do almost anything (and spend almost any amount) to get the slightest hint at just what might happen to them at some undetermined moment in the future. Eager (or perhaps desperate) people consult Tarot card readers, mediums, self-titled experts at "crossing over," Ouija boards, and any number of other sources to attempt to know the future.

Many of these same people scoff at what the Bible has to say about the future, yet it is more specific than most of their other sources. In addition, the Bible has proved that it can be trusted. We've already looked at a number of Old Testament prophets who looked into the future and saw a coming Savior who would be both Messiah and Redeemer. Jesus fulfilled hundreds of their prophecies with His life, death, and resurrection.

Jesus also spoke authoritatively about things still to come. The apostle Paul wrote of the resurrection of believers, the Rapture, and other future events. And in this chapter we will see still other writers who foretell both great and dreadful things—including John's grand vision in the book of Revelation. But before we look to the future, first we're going to spend some time looking backward.

Hebrews: More Than Nostalgia

Who wrote the book of Hebrews? Who, exactly, was the intended audience? Bible scholars can't say for sure. While the content certainly doesn't conflict with anything Paul wrote, the writing style doesn't appear to be his. (For one thing, he almost always identified himself at the beginning of each letter, and Hebrews just dives right into a deep theological discussion.)

Out of the Shadow, Thanks to the Son

However, we need not know the author or intended location because Hebrews is a classic work and a credit to whoever wrote it. We know the church at the time was continually being tugged back toward the older, traditional ways of Judaism. Some people were intentionally trying to impose strict legalistic standards; others were simply sliding back to familiar habits.

SWORD DRILL

Which biblical character consulted a medium (or **witch,** in some translations) seeking insight into his future . . . and how did that little escapade turn out? (See 1 Samuel 28:4–20.)

The Letter to the Hebrews helps the reader make the connection between those old ways and the new freedoms made possible through Jesus. The opening sentences contrast "in the past" with "in these last days," and the author continues this back-and-forth consideration throughout the book. One by one, he (or maybe even she) brings up revered people and symbols: angels, Moses, priests, animal sacrifices at the temple, and so forth. And in each case, a convincing argument is made to explain how Jesus is superior.

But far from disparaging the significance of Old Testament worship, the writer of Hebrews shows how it was specially designed as a precursor of more intimate worship yet to come. The Old Testament law was intended as only a "shadow"

of the New Testament gospel of grace (Hebrews 10:1). As the temple signified God's mysterious presence, Jesus demonstrated God's very real presence among us. As the bloodshed of sacrificial animals was an annual installment against sin, Jesus' sacrifice was "once for all" (10:10).

Eyes Forward!

Hebrews gives us a classic definition of faith (11:1) and continues with ways that faith was demonstrated by a long list of great Old Testament figures that includes Abel, Noah, Abraham, Moses, and many others. Special credit is given to these men and women of the Old Testament because their faith was based on God's *promise* of a future deliverer, not the actual fulfillment of that promise. As the author says: "These were all commended for their faith, yet none of them received what had been promised. God had planned something better for us so that only together with us would they be made perfect" (11:39–40).

The New Testament church has it much easier because members can look

backward at what God has already accomplished. They can experience His Holy Spirit in their lives in a way unknown to most Old Testament saints. Yet the crucial factor remains the same: faith.

BACKGROUND INFO

The seven letters found between Hebrews and Revelation (James, 1 Peter, 2 Peter, 1 John, 2 John, 3 John, and Jude) are called the General Letters because they weren't addressed to specific people or locations as Paul's letters were.

Therefore, we should be highly motivated to "throw off everything that hinders and the sin that so easily entangles, and . . . run with perseverance the race marked out for us" (12:1). With faith, we even come to see our hardships as a form of spiritual discipline that toughens us up like nothing else can. And we learn that when the discipline comes from God it is because He loves us. Even though our trials might be unpleasant and even painful, they can produce "a harvest of righteousness and peace" (verse 11).

You don't have to read the entire Old Testament to get to the heart of Hebrews, but it helps. And just as Hebrews looks back to so many significant traditions, it teaches us to look forward as we "fix our eyes on Jesus, the author and perfecter of our faith" (12:2). After all, Jesus is "the same yesterday and today and forever" (13:8).

James: Just Do It!

The New Testament mentions four men named James. The apostle of Jesus by that name was the first of the eleven (after Judas took his own life) put to death by the ruling powers and didn't get to have a writing career. Two others weren't in high positions in the church. So by process of elimination, the author of the New Testament letter almost has to be James, the half brother of Jesus. While Jesus' brothers didn't at first believe what He was telling them about Himself (John 7:5), James later became a believer and a prominent church leader (Galatians 1:19; 2:9).

Working Your Faith

The letter of James is one of the most practical and easy to understand portions of the Bible. James echoes some of the themes of Hebrews about the necessity of enduring suffering. (Most of the Christians were being persecuted during this time, so many of the writers address the issue.) But James doesn't want Christians to make things worse for each other by showing favoritism to rich people while putting down poor people who show up at church (James 2:1–10).

Paul's letters emphasize the clear truth that all anyone needs in order to come to God is simple faith. God's forgiveness and mercy take care of the rest, and no amount of human striving can ever accomplish what God freely bestows on repentant people. But James adds the observation that faith should result in some obvious changes in a person's life. He asks, "What good is it, my brothers, if a man

WHAT'S THE GOOD WORD?

When tempted, no one should say, "God is tempting me." For God cannot be tempted by evil, nor does he tempt anyone; but each one is tempted when, by his own evil desire, he is dragged away and enticed. Then, after desire has conceived, it gives birth to sin; and sin, when it is full-grown, gives birth to death.

–JAMES 1:13–15

claims to have faith but has no deeds? Can such faith save him?" (2:14).

James isn't elevating our own actions above God's saving faith, but he is challenging us to consider that if we have had a *genuine* experience with God's saving faith our actions should certainly take a turn for the better. This observation emphasizes his previous instruction: "Do not merely listen to the word, and so deceive yourselves. Do what it says" (1:22). Salvation doesn't come in merely *hearing* God's Word but in responding to it.

Barring Verbal Barrages

And one of the hardest changes we'll face, says James, is controlling our words. Your tongue, he says, is like a rudder of a ship, a spark that starts a raging fire, a deadly poison, and more (3:1–12). We tend to consider verbal sins minor in comparison to more physical ones. But both James and Jesus (Matthew 5:21–26) beg to differ.

James continues to write of practical displays of faith—submitting oneself to God in order to prevent a lot of problems: senseless arguments (James 4:1–12), incorrect assumptions about the future (4:13–15), dependence on wealth instead of God (5:1–6), and swearing unnecessary oaths (5:12). Rather than these old, natural ways of handling stressful situations, he emphasizes the importance of patience and prayer (5:7–18). Genuine faith results in not only actions that benefit others, he says, but also a strong trust in God that gets the believer through the toughest challenges of life.

Peter: Remember Him?

When we were going through the book of Acts, it was Peter who stood up on the Day of Pentecost to address the crowd. It was Peter who was active in the formation of the early church. It was Peter who had the vision to include Gentiles in the newly forming congregations, and who had a miraculous release from prison. But almost as soon as we read of Paul's dramatic conversion experience, Peter fades from sight. Now we look at his two New Testament letters, and they can seem short and perhaps insignificant compared to Paul's string of writings. Yet Peter provides insight on Christian living and Christian doctrine we get nowhere else.

Peter's writings reflect his biography, to some extent. He had started as a simple fisherman, but Jesus had called him to be a "fisher of men" instead. And even though he made a lot of mistakes along the way, including three flagrant denials of Jesus when his Lord most needed support, Jesus had forgiven him and had done great things through him.

SWORD DRILL

One time Peter caught a single fish that supplied enough money for two people's taxes. How did that happen? (See Matthew 17:24–27.)

1 Peter

Early in Peter's first letter, he wrote, "Praise be to the God and Father of our Lord Jesus Christ! In his great mercy he has given us new birth into a living hope through the resurrection of Jesus Christ from the dead, and into an inheritance that can never perish, spoil or fade—kept in heaven for you" (1 Peter 1:3–4). Peter urged his readers to keep this promise of new birth and inheritance in mind as they suffered through "all kinds of trials" (1:6).

He explained that Christians aren't supposed to fit in among the ever-present sinfulness of humankind. They are "strangers here" (1:17), a "spiritual house," a "holy priesthood," (2:5), and, above all, "a people belonging to God" (2:9). Christians will suffer, yes, but so will people who do evil. So, logically, he concludes, "It is better, if it is God's will, to suffer for doing good than for doing evil" (3:17).

Peter pointed to the nearness of "the end of all things" (4:7). Rather than fret about present sufferings or future fears, it is far better to simply live a decent life, he noted. People are looking at us to see how we behave, so therefore we should "Live such good lives among the pagans that, though they accuse you of doing wrong, they may see your good deeds and glorify God on the day he visits us" (2:12).

Submission to authority is crucial. We are to "show proper respect to everyone" (2:17)—including government officials, marriage partners, and our elders. Not only are other people watching us; so is Satan (5:8). Only humility and obedience to God will get us through all the obstacles we face.

2 Peter

Peter's second letter turns from the sources of suffering outside the church to some of the threats within. Just as Paul had been forced to deal with teachers who corrupted truth, so too was Peter, who strongly rebuked false teachers and boldly defended God's true prophets (2 Peter 1:12–2:22).

Again, Peter urged his readers to look to the future when "the day of the Lord will come like a thief" (3:10). But rather than merely portraying Jesus' eventual coming as a spiritual sword of Damocles hanging over the heads of every hopeless nonbeliever, Peter explained that God hasn't given up on *anyone* yet. That's exactly why Jesus hadn't yet made a hasty return: "The Lord is not slow in keeping his promise, as some understand slowness. He is patient with you, not wanting anyone to perish, but everyone to come to repentance" (3:9).

When Jesus returns, it will be all over for those who have rejected Him. Until then, however, time remains for people to discover the truth and act on it. And perhaps it will be the "holy and godly lives" of believers (3:11) that make a difference for many such people.

John, John, John

John, the apostle of Jesus, wrote five New Testament books. One was his gospel account of Jesus; the others are four of the final five books of the Bible. We'll look at his three epistles here and just a bit later at Revelation.

Unlike most other letter writers, John never identified himself. This is not unusual, however, for in his gospel he always referred to himself simply as, "the disciple whom Jesus loved."

1 John

The First Letter of John starts at "the beginning" (1:1), just as the gospel of John does. And like his gospel that called Jesus "the Word," this letter describes God in bold, broad terms. God is "light" (1 John 1:5). He is "truth" (2:20–23). He is "love" (4:16). And as "children of God" we should reflect those same traits in our own lives (3:1–3). It's a simple teaching to understand, but considerably harder to enforce on a daily basis in real life. Loving others sounds warm and fuzzy . . . until those others don't love us in return, or until they do things that appear to be unlovable.

But John doesn't let us off easy. Loving others, when it doesn't come naturally, must become a spiritual discipline. The bottom line is this: "If anyone says, 'I love God,' yet hates his brother, he is a liar. For anyone who does not love his brother, whom he has seen, cannot love God, whom he has not seen" (4:20).

Like several of the letters we've already examined, the First Letter of John warned of the encroachment of false teachers, using the term "antichrists" to describe them (2:18–29). John also warned readers that they (and we) will face other obstacles while attempting to live a Christian life; yet none of those obstacles is insurmountable. With God's help, we can overcome each one and continue to grow and mature.

2 John and 3 John

John's second and third letters were almost short enough to have been written on Post-It Notes, had they been available during the first century. Both were encouraging reminders to remain faithful in light of obstacles such as unnamed deceivers (2 John 7) and specific people who were making life harder than it ought to be (3 John 9–10).

SWORD DRILL

Jesus gave John and his brother James a nickname: Boanerges. What did it mean? (See Mark 3:17.)

WHAT'S THE GOOD WORD?

Who is it that overcomes the world? Only he who believes that Jesus is the Son of God.

–1 John 5:5

Hey, Jude, Don't Make It So Obscure

The Jude who wrote the next to last book of the Bible is most likely the brother of the author of James—another half brother of Jesus. Although his letter is among the shortest in the New Testament, it is one of the more challenging ones to understand. In his mere twenty-five verses, he drops in Old Testament references to the Exodus, Sodom and Gomorrah, Moses, Cain, Balaam, Korah, and Enoch. And in a very cryptic note, he mentions in passing a dispute between the archangel Michael and the devil concerning the body of Moses (Jude 9). This reference is to an apocryphal work called "The Assumption of Moses." A few verses later he alludes to a book of Enoch (Jude 14), an apocryphal book not found in Scripture. Obviously, his readers were more up-to-date on such writings than most people today.

BACKGROUND INFO

Just because Jude (and other) writers of Scripture used source material that isn't in our "official" Bible should not be too disturbing. Just as we might quote Shakespeare or Andy Warhol without necessarily endorsing everything about their works or their lifestyles, biblical authors could reference other writings without meaning to suggest they were on par with God's Word.

Still, Jude's message comes through. He had intended to speak of salvation and positive things, yet once again false teachers necessitated a warning letter (which is why so many of his Old Testament references recalled unpleasant stories). He spent his short epistle focused on what such heretical teachers could expect, and closed with a challenge for his readers to "keep yourselves in God's love as you wait for the mercy of our Lord Jesus Christ to bring you to eternal life" (Jude 21).

Revelation: Talk About a Big Finish!

With the long string of letters behind us, we now turn our attention to the final book of the Bible. Just as the Old Testament finished with books of prophecy, the New Testament concludes with a final, prophetic look at the end times. And even though the Old Testament contains seventeen books in this category and the New

Testament but one, the book of Revelation has plenty to keep prophecy lovers busy for decades.

John's Revelation stands out for other reasons as well. It is the only biblical book written primarily in the apocalyptic style. This unusual technique involved the use of much symbolism, supposed access to previously unknown mysteries of God, predictions of the end of the world, and in most cases, pen names by the authors (because much apocalyptic material was clearly not inspired by God). Many such books were little more than fictional flights of fancy written anonymously.

Revelation is definitely written in this style, but is a singular exception to most apocalyptic literature. John not only identifies himself as the author but also provides enough details about his life and settings to verify what he is saying. (It isn't nearly so easy to do "fact checking" on other apocalyptic writers.) John is also helpful by providing interpretations for many (but not nearly all) of the symbols he uses.

BACKGROUND INFO

Many apocalyptic books originated after the years of Israel's captivity. The land was ruled by a series of mean and powerful nations. And although the people still had the promises of their former prophets, there were no new prophets being sent by God. Much apocalyptic literature was an attempt to keep everyone looking ahead and remaining somewhat optimistic.

For those who are somewhat new to reading the Bible, Revelation contains what they may find to be both the most fascinating and the most frustrating passages they will come across. It clearly contains a message of great importance, yet all the symbols allow for a wide variety of interpretations. People aren't likely to ever agree on exactly what it all means.

We will spend just a few pages describing what is contained in the book of Revelation, but when you get ready to read through it on your own, you may not want to stray too far from a good commentary or two.

Busted Flat on Patmos

The conditions that led to the writing of Revelation were unique as well. While most of Jesus' apostles were eventually martyred when they wouldn't quit talking about Him, John had avoided the swords and crosses that others had faced. However, his fervor for Jesus had landed him in exile on the Aegean island of Patmos. It was there that Jesus appeared to him in a marvelous vision (Revelation 1:9–20).

The Not-So-Magnificent Seven

The first item of business was to record Jesus' message to seven churches in the area: Ephesus, Smyrna, Pergamum, Thyatira, Sardis, Philadelphia, and Laodicea. These weren't necessarily the biggest or best or worst churches, but they were the ones designated by Jesus Himself.

BACKGROUND INFO

Some people believe the sequence of the seven specific churches in Revelation symbolizes "the church" throughout history, beginning with much persecution and ending with apathy, with a few bright spots along the way.

In the address to each church, Jesus began with a reference to Himself, followed by an acknowledgment of the things the church was doing well, followed by any problem areas within the church, followed by a promise of what could happen if only the church would persevere and "overcome" its problems. A couple of the churches were doing quite well; others had significant shortcomings that needed to be addressed.

Not surprisingly, many of the problems already mentioned by Paul and other New Testament writers show up in these churches—infiltration by false teachers, intense persecution, pride, favoritism, and so forth.

In this case, one of the worst was saved for last. The church at Laodicea was proud, spiritually lukewarm, and had lost the sensitivity to care. Jesus presents an image where He is standing and knocking on the door but receiving no response from the callous church members. Some people suggest that is a picture of the church today.

A Strange Place to Visit, but I Would Die to Live Here

But John's attention was suddenly diverted to another, more accessible door, even though this one was in heaven. He received an invitation to "Come up here"

(4:1), and his writing shifts abruptly from the faults of the earthly church to the glories of the heavenly realms. The rest of his writing is from a divine perspective, complete with angels, resurrected saints, God, Jesus, the Holy Spirit, and more.

He sees a scroll that no one is worthy to open except "the Lamb who was slain" (5:1–7, 11), an obvious reference to Jesus. The scroll was protected by seven seals, and as the Lamb began to remove the seals, earthly events went from bad to worse. The first four seals triggered the onslaught of horsemen bringing war, famine, conquest, and death (6:1–8).

BACKGROUND INFO

The breaking of each of the first four seals of this heavenly scroll releases a rider, each on a horse of a different color. Collectively, these four riders have come to be known as the four horsemen of the Apocalypse.

Next was revealed the martyrdom of many of God's people. Next came a massive earthquake. The seventh seal initiated a whole new series of judgments, each beginning with the sounding of an angelic trumpet. And the seventh trumpet judgment initiated a series of seven "bowl judgments" as John witnessed angels "pour out the seven bowls of God's wrath on the earth" (16:1).

Included in these judgments are demons from the Abyss (9:1–11), the rise of the Antichrist with the mysterious number 666 (13:1–18), a horribly bloody battle at Armageddon (16:16; 19:17–21), the great prostitute connected with Babylon (17:1–6), a fiery lake of burning sulfur (19:20; 20:10), great numbers of bad people killed and God's people martyred, numerous earthquakes and other (super)natural disasters, and at last the return of Jesus (19:11–16).

SWORD DRILL

When reading and studying the book of Revelation, it is possible to do two things that prompt a most severe response from God. What two things should we avoid at all costs? (See Revelation 22:18–19.)

The descriptions of this terrible time are graphic and specific. Spiritual lukewarmness is no longer an option. People are either with God, or they oppose Him. And to stand for God during this time very frequently leads to death.

Yet the Revelation of John never for a moment suggests that God isn't in control. He is allowing certain things to happen because He is about to restore a perfect relationship between Himself and His people. But in order to do so, those who don't want to be His people will be judged and separated from those who do.

Home Improvement

Satan and all evil will be destroyed at this time, paving the way for God to establish a new paradise for His people—the New Jerusalem (21:1–2). The final two chapters of the Bible are devoted to describing what believers can ultimately expect: streets of gold, pearly gates, no more tears, no more night, and direct access to their loving heavenly Father. All who read Revelation are invited to "come" and be involved in this eternal wonderland.

If we keep in mind that Revelation was addressed to the church, we should see it as a highly motivational message. Some people like to relegate things such as heaven and eternal life to the realm of fairy tales. But throughout the Bible we are assured of the absolute reality of everything God has promised.

It is Revelation that puts everything into context. In light of the misery so many of God's people will have to face before time as we know it winds to an end, the certainty of heaven and eternity with God is indeed a big finish for the world's greatest Book!

Chapter Flashback

1. The two half brothers of Jesus who (according to most people) wrote books of the New Testament were:
   a. Peter and Paul
   b. James and Jude
   c. Paul and John
   d. George and Ringo

2. The best reliable source for information about the future is:
   a. The first on-line Web site you happen to find
   b. Mr. Theo, telephone psychic
   c. Nostradamus
   d. The Bible

3. The book of Hebrews takes on deeper meaning if you happen to have a good working knowledge of:
   a. *The Old Man and the Sea*
   b. *The Old Curiosity Shop*
   c. The Old Testament
   d. This Old House

4. The book of Revelation is written in a peculiar writing style known as:
   a. Apocalyptic
   b. Apologetic
   c. Apoplectic
   d. Apodictic

5. The book of Revelation, with all its scary passages and perplexing symbols, was written primarily to:
   a. Scare unbelievers
   b. Annoy skeptics
   c. Encourage churches
   d. Inspire Stephen King

Answers: (1) b, (2) d, (3) c, (4) a, (5) c

PART THREE

Into the Bible

Now that you've seen why the Bible is so important and have been through its entire contents, you know it all by now. Right?

Hopefully not. The more we learn about the Bible, the more we realize we don't really know. The more our curiosity is piqued. The more we want to get a better grasp on the things we now *think* we know.

The goal of this section is to help you dig deeper into the Bible on your own. You'll learn what tools can help and how to use them. You'll discover the value of not only reading what's on the pages, but also becoming a conscientious observer of what a passage is saying. And more than that, you'll be challenged to then properly interpret the text and apply it to your own life in helpful and relevant ways.

Don't give up yet. This is where understanding the Bible gets really beneficial . . . and fun.

CHAPTER 15

The Next Step

FROM READING . . . TO STUDYING . . . TO ENJOYING THE BIBLE

SNAPSHOT

"Thanks for bringing over this Tupperware, Bernice. It's just what I need for our church potluck tomorrow."

"Anytime, Shannon. But I was wondering if, while I'm here, you could recommend a good book. I know you read something like a book a week."

"Closer to two or three a week. Come on in. I've got a couple of bookshelves full, and you can take what you want."

"You're not kidding! You've read all these?"

"Yep. As you can see, they're mostly fiction."

"That's great. What can you tell me about this one called *Some of All Fears*?"

"Let's see. I think that one is about a serial killer who . . . No, that was *Fear Comes to Some*. Maybe it's the one where the detective turns out to be . . .

SNEAK PREVIEW

1. Casual Bible reading is of some benefit, but intentional and regular Bible study is much more relevant and productive.
2. Jesus Himself helped us prioritize the teachings of Scripture.
3. If Bible knowledge isn't helping us strengthen our relationships, we're probably not paying enough attention to what the Bible really says.

or perhaps the one where the mystery writer solves crimes . . . or was that *Some Come to Call?*"

"The cover says it's a romance."

"Then I'm probably wrong on all counts. You know, I go through those books so quickly, to tell you the truth I can't really recall much about them after a while. They're so real as I read them, but when the next one comes along, the plots of previous ones just seem to evaporate."

"I know what you mean. I'm the same way with movies. I usually know which ones I've seen, but I don't always remember the storylines or even the main actors."

"Oh, well, what does it matter? Go ahead and take *Some of All Fears,* and after you read it you can remind me what it's about."

"Thanks. See you in Sunday school tomorrow?"

"I'll be there. We're supposed to discuss the fourth chapter of Galatians, aren't we?"

"Really? I thought it was Ephesians."

"Oh, well, what does it matter? I guess we'll find out when we get there."

"See you then. And thanks for the . . . uh . . . what did I come for?"

"Tupperware?"

"Yeah. Thanks!"

* * * * * * * * * * * * * * * *

If you've read the previous ten chapters of this *World's Easiest Guide,* you've propelled yourself all the way through the major action of the Bible. You've covered a lot of time, territory, and information. But is it now just a matter of days until you move on to something else and forget most of it?

What we've covered has been extremely condensed so we could move through it quickly. The trade-off is that we haven't covered anything in much detail, so it might not stick with you very long unless you go back and review what you've been learning. But if you go back and decide to read every word, from Genesis to Revelation, the Bible is such a comprehensive and thick Book that by the time you get to Revelation you're going to have forgotten many of the earlier people and events. Oh, well . . . does it really matter?

All You Need Is Love?

If the arguments of the opening chapters of this guide were at all persuasive, and if you're convinced that the Bible is the inspired Word of God and a unique Book, then it does indeed matter whether you retain what you read. It does matter whether or not you can differentiate biblical mandates from legalistic traditions and twisted, heretical teachings. Just because you've gone through the Bible doesn't mean you're through with the Bible.

But how are you supposed to absorb so *much* information? Where do you start? Now that you've skimmed through the hundreds (or perhaps thousands) of pages in your Bible, what now? If you want to go a bit deeper, what can you do? What, in fact, is most urgent for you to know?

Thankfully, we're not the first people to face this little dilemma. While Jesus was teaching one day, one of the other religious teachers interrupted him with a similar question: "Of all the commandments, which is the most important?" (Mark 12:28).

> ## WHAT'S THE GOOD WORD?
>
> Give me understanding, and I will keep your law and obey it with all my heart. Direct me in the path of your commands, for in Thee I find delight.
>
> —PSALM 119:34–35

Jesus didn't hesitate. He answered: "The most important one . . . is this: 'Hear, O Israel, the Lord our God, the Lord is one. Love the Lord your God with all your heart and with all your soul and with all your mind and with all your strength.' The second is this: 'Love your neighbor as yourself.' There is no commandment greater than these" (Mark 12:29–31).

How many of us, if asked the same question, could go straight to Deuteronomy 6:4–5 and Leviticus 19:18 to come up with the correct answer? We tend to dwell on familiar passages, such as the Ten Commandments. Yet while those big ten

BACKGROUND INFO

On another occasion, Jesus was asked to explain what, exactly, He meant by "neighbor." His definition turned out to include just about anybody who needs our compassion—whether friend or enemy. (See Luke 10:25-37.)

tend to dwell on what *not* to do, Jesus pinpoints two very clear and positive commands: (1) Love God as much as you can; and (2) Love others as much as you can.

These are two themes we see again and again in Jesus' teaching and ministry. He didn't just come from heaven to earth in order to deliver eloquent sermons. He was almost always surrounded by crowds that were attracted to Him because of His compassion for their suffering and the wonderful things He told them about God. God was no remote and indifferent figure. Rather, He was a loving Father, a great heavenly Friend, Someone who not only encouraged but also rewarded persistence in prayer. He was a God of great forgiveness and mercy.

And while many people were eager to capitalize on the close relationships with God that Jesus was describing, Jesus also made it clear that God expected the "trickle-down" theory to apply. Those who received God's wonderful mercy and other gifts and then refused to treat other people the way God had treated them, could not expect the gifts to keep coming. Instead, such selfish people were in danger of receiving God's justice—which always seems harsh in contrast to His grace and forgiveness (see, for example, the parable of the wicked servant in Matthew 18:23–35).

Why Bother?

Many things can motivate us to continue to pursue a deeper knowledge of Scripture—and some motivations are better than others. For some people, it's enough to keep finding more and more obscure characters and facts, adding to the mental trivia bank they are accumulating. Others sincerely seek to understand the entire Bible, from start to finish, and to be able to make good sense of it on a cognitive and logical level. Many others continue to read, not based so much on what they're getting out of it, but because of a persistent feeling of obligation. Bible study is on the "to do" list alongside "take out the garbage" or "scrub the toilet."

For the Love of God

It's amazing how much stamina and determination some people have in regard to Bible reading, yet many of them miss the point. Unless our interaction with Scripture is leading to a better interaction with God and with other people, it isn't actually doing us much good.

The best motivation for continuous, growing, deepening degrees of Bible study is better *relationships*. Foremost, of course, is one's relationship with God, and the Bible is the best way to get to know Him better. Have you ever spent an evening with close friends and wished it would just keep going on and on? If so, you know the power of intimate relationships. If we can foster similar feelings in response to spending time with God, then Bible study ceases to be a chore.

We never figure out everything about God, but Scripture provides us with a much broader and clearer picture of Him in contrast to the skewed perspectives of Him we might get from others. We are not only invited to see who God is but also to participate in His kingdom and discover His plan for us and for humanity. We are even promised gifts to use as we actively respond and get more involved.

To Boldly Love Where No One Has Loved Before

Then, as the relationship with God develops and strengthens, we face a much harder challenge: Go and show love to other people. God is perfect and has much to offer, so working on that relationship is usually a breeze. But when we try to develop the same love for others who bug us, slug us, or pull the rug from under us, we have a harder go of it. The Bible becomes very important as a guidebook of what is expected from us—as well as a reminder of what God will continue to do for us as we take on these more difficult challenges.

So understanding the Bible should help us understand God better and help us relate to other

WHAT'S THE GOOD WORD?

"Love your enemies and pray for those who persecute you, . . . If you love those who love you, what reward will you get? Are not even the tax collectors doing that? And if you greet only your brothers, what are you doing more than others? Do not even pagans do that?"

—MATTHEW 5:44, 46-47

people better (with time and practice). And if we look closely enough at Jesus' explanation of the greatest commandment, we notice He says that we should love our neighbors *as ourselves* (Mark 12:31). By extension, therefore, it is appropriate to have a proper degree of self-love and self-respect. Scripture also helps us in this regard by helping us differentiate between false pride and genuine, God-given gifts and talents. We come to see ourselves as truly unique and special because of who we are in relation to God, not due to anything we have accomplished on our own.

Love God. Love others. Love ourselves. What better reasons could we have to keep going back to the pages of the Bible and pondering its clear truths and deep mysteries?

"Study": Not a Bad Word

Yet when it comes to Bible study, some of us might have a problem due to bad associations with the word *study*. Many of us flash back to cramming for exams, doing without sleep, barely squeaking by with (or just missing) the grade we needed, boring or sadistic teachers, and other unpleasantries. After being forced to study trigonometry, European history, British poetry, or other things that interfere with our spring break plans, we may still foster a dislike for the very word *study* in any context.

Yet "study" need not carry such negative connotations. Recall, for instance, some of those times when you were more than willing to study the face of a new love or sleeping infant. When you're ready to invest your hard-earned money, you willingly study the market to see where it might make the most return. When you're out playing touch football in your neighborhood, you study the defense so your neighbor doesn't show you up too badly. Such opportunities to "study" are met with not only willingness, but also great eagerness. And that's the attitude we need as we approach Bible *study*.

The Attitude Preferred by One out of Ten Healed Lepers

Indeed, the proper attitude is essential if we want to take away everything possible from an encounter with Scripture. Perhaps you recall the story of the ten lepers who confronted Jesus on the roadside (Luke 17:11–19). They asked Him for healing, and He told them to go and show themselves to the priests. Their healing took place as they were on their way. One of the ten stopped, turned around, and went back to thank Jesus.

Have you ever wondered about Jesus' response? He asked, "Were not all ten cleansed? Where are the other nine?"

SWORD DRILL

Just after the captivity period, what leader "devoted himself to the study and observance of the Law of the LORD, and to teaching its decrees and laws in Israel"? (See Ezra 7:10.)

If you look at this story one way, the majority was doing *exactly* what Jesus told them to do. They had been given specific instructions, and lo and behold, they were obeying. Yet theirs is not the response Jesus praises. One single ex-leper stopped long enough to reconnect with Jesus, express heartfelt thanks, and then carry on with what he had been instructed to do—and he's the hero of the story.

Many of us approach Bible study with the attitude of the nine lepers. We're not resistant. We're eager to do what we've been told we should do because there's something in it for us. And maybe we even develop a degree of tunnel vision as we determine to read three chapters a day, get as far as we can in a half hour, or complete whatever we've committed to do. Yet too often sheer determination gradually replaces the joy and other positive responses that should come from spending time in God's Word.

Perhaps the boomeranging leper should teach us that we have a great deal of freedom on the road to obedience. We should never let adherence to a bunch of written words preclude a personal encounter with the living, eternal God. As long as those words are drawing us toward Him, we're doing fine. But if Bible study becomes nothing more than regular forced readings, it's time to pause long enough to find an attitude that will nudge us closer to our ultimate goal—a closer relationship with Jesus.

WHAT'S THE GOOD WORD?

Finally, brothers, whatever is true, whatever is noble, whatever is right, whatever is pure, whatever is lovely, whatever is admirable–if anything is excellent or praiseworthy–think about such things.

–PHILIPPIANS 4:8

God provides His Word, just as He provided the miraculous cleansing of leprosy. It's His free gift to people who seek His help. But as we clamor for more and more of what He has to offer, we are to supply the proper mind-set that keeps the focus on Him—not us.

Now that we've seen a few reasons *why* we are to go beyond casual Bible reading to more intentional Bible study, let's consider *how*.

Bible Study Breakdown

Some people tend to make *Bible reading* and *Bible study* interchangeable terms. Others may believe Bible study involves a group, whereas Bible reading is a solitary endeavor.

Neither of these perspectives is quite correct. Bible study involves more than simply Bible reading, and we can study the Bible as individuals, seeking to go deeper into its truths. Bible study may include consulting other resources to help us get more out of what we're reading (which is the topic of the next chapter). But before we get to that point, Bible study also includes some techniques that don't always apply when simply doing a little Bible reading. Let's break down Bible "study" into some distinctive elements.

Meditation

Meditation has become a suspicious concept for some people because it is so closely associated with Eastern religions where mantras are assigned and the practitioner repeats the same word or phrase over and over in an attempt to achieve some kind of spiritual high. But that's not the kind of meditation we're talking about here.

In regard to Bible reading, meditation essentially boils down to paying close attention. Effective meditation on Scripture requires ample time and alertness. All the other distractions clamoring for your mental attention must be tuned out for a period to allow you to concentrate *fully* on what God is saying in His Word. John Bunyan put it this way: "If we have not quiet in our minds, outward comfort will do no more for us than a golden slipper on a gouty foot."

Meditation involves absorbing the biblical content, reflecting on its significance in your own life, and personally applying those teachings. The Bible begins to make sense not only on a cognitive level, but a personal one as well. Through meditation, you uncover deeper meanings to passages, discover significant personal applications, and sense God's direction in your life in other ways.

Meditation is not a mysterious rite or a discipline achievable by only a chosen few. The Bible instructs us *all* to meditate on what it says. When the Israelites were making the crucial transition from their wilderness wanderings to taking possession of the Promised Land, God gave Joshua and the people specific instructions: "Do not let this Book of the Law depart from your mouth; meditate on it day and night, so that you may be careful to do everything written in it. Then you will be prosperous and successful" (Joshua 1:8). And in Psalm 119—a classic poetic treatise on the importance of God's Word—we find numerous references to meditating on Scripture (verses 15, 23, 27, 48, 78, 97, 99, and 148).

WHAT'S THE GOOD WORD?

Blessed is the man who does not walk in the counsel of the wicked or stand in the way of sinners or sit in the seat of mockers. But his delight is in the law of the LORD, and on his law he meditates day and night. He is like a tree planted by streams of water, which yields its fruit in season and whose leaf does not wither. Whatever he does prospers.

–PSALM 1:1-3

Meditation on God's Word provides wisdom that will never be discovered during a quick read through of the Bible. Just as a detailed study of a great painting yields a better appreciation for the artist, regular meditation on the Word of God reveals much about its heavenly Author. In time, your own personal meditation may even provide you with "more insight than all [your] teachers" (Psalm 119:99).

Illumination

Psalm 119 is also the source of the great reminder that, "Your word is a lamp to my feet and a light for my path" (v. 105). But exactly how brightly that light shines is more than a matter of personal Bible study or even devoted meditation. Illumination is another concept that, like meditation, has a different meaning in a Christian context. It is not to be confused with other religions that merely promote the pursuit of "enlightenment."

Illumination is a work of the Holy Spirit that enables believers to better understand the truths of Scripture. We can study Scripture by using all the resources at our disposal, and we can meditate on what it says until our gray matter hurts, but only God Himself in the form of the Holy Spirit can clarify certain passages so that they make sense to those who have placed faith in Him (1 Corinthians 2:14).

WHAT'S THE GOOD WORD?

However, as it is written: "No eye has seen, no ear has heard, no mind has conceived what God has prepared for those who love him"–but God has revealed it to us by his Spirit.

–1 CORINTHIANS 2:9–10

Much of the Old Testament was (intentionally) a mystery until Jesus appeared and revealed how He would make sense of it all. Similarly, other portions of Scripture remain vague and foggy until we connect with God through His Holy Spirit and are enabled to see more clearly what He is revealing to us (John 16:13–15).

If Christians seem like freaks to the rest of the world, it is largely because what we believe is perceived as "foolishness" by others (1 Corinthians 1:18–21). Jesus is seen as a misguided prophet, His death as a clumsy accident, His disciples as deceived zealots, and contemporary followers only naïve simpletons incapable of making their way through the big, mean world without some kind of fairy tale to believe in.

But for those with the willingness to reach out to God through faith in Jesus, the brilliant illumination of the Holy Spirit bores through the dark outlook of the rest of the world. Jesus is seen to be God in flesh and bone—the promised deliverer and the Savior of the world. His death was the "Paid in Full" stamp on the sin humankind had been struggling under for centuries. His resurrection was the reward that paved the way for all the rest of us who will follow Him into eternal life. And as His contemporary disciples, the least we can do is to put up with a little flak from our nonbelieving peers. After all, we have officially changed "citizenship status" and are no longer representing this world, but God's kingdom (Philippians 3:20–21).

And as our outlook toward God changes, so should our consideration of other people. While Christians are to be adamant opponents to the sin in the world, we are always to remember that other sinful people are still loved by God (and *should* be loved by us as well). Rather than secluding ourselves in Heavenly Home Estates, we are designated as "ambassadors" and instructed to be always ready and willing to help reconcile other people to God (2 Corinthians 5:16–21). The illumination of the Holy Spirit is so bright that after it opens Scripture to you like a floodlight, those around you may notice and want to know what's going on.

Bible study and meditation are steps we take to discover more about God and His mysterious truths; the illumination of the Holy Spirit is the reward believers get for their efforts, revealing much more than we would ever expect.

Memorization

People who work with numbers a lot are never far from some kind of calculator. Those who want to excel in music can't stray far from their chosen instrument. And as people get more serious about Bible study, many find it extremely helpful to not only keep Bibles nearby, but also to memorize favorite verses and passages for immediate recall.

SWORD DRILL

The apostle Paul could present the truths of the gospel as convincingly as anyone. Yet which resistant listener heard him speak and then accused him of being "out of your mind" and "insane"? (See Acts 26:19-32.)

If indeed the Word of God is to operate as "the sword of the Spirit" (Ephesians 6:17), we're unarmed without it. Bible memorization provides us with an arsenal from God's Word in the midst of stressful situations—not at some point afterward when it finally becomes convenient to find a Bible and look up helpful references.

It's in the midst of the argument when someone has called us terrible names that we need to be aware of our options, such as:

➤ a gentle answer to turn away wrath (Proverbs 15:1);

➤ a rebuttal of clear truth, yet spoken with love (Ephesians 4:15);

➤ turning the other cheek (Matthew 5:39); or

➤ any number of other appropriate biblical responses.

BACKGROUND INFO

At one time it was a common practice for male Jews to wear **phylacteries**–little boxes containing written-out Scriptures that were strapped to the left arm and forehead. That way the wearer would never be far from the Word of God. Some people see this literal act as symbolic of our need to "carry" God's Word in our memory. (See Deuteronomy 6:6-9; Matthew 23:5-7.)

We're not likely to call "time out" in the middle of a verbal confrontation to go consult the Bible. And if we wait until the argument is over, we very likely will have already done something that wasn't among the best of our options. Scripture memory provides "random access" to God's Word right when and where we need it.

Some people are far better at memorizing than others. And clearly it takes time to accumulate a good assortment of relevant memorized Scripture. But as your Bible study uncovers verses that speak clearly to you, and as the Spirit illuminates new and relevant truths, you can add to your ever-growing memory bank and have more and more of God's Word available in the time it takes a brain synapse to fire.

Application

Perhaps the biggest distinction between casual Bible reading and intentional Bible study is motivation. It's one thing to pick up the Bible, read a few pages, and think, *What a good story!* or *Isn't that nice?* But usually Bible study takes place with the desire to know, *What should I be learning from this?*

We're going to deal more with the importance of observation and application in chapter 17. But for now let's just say that the Bible is more than a record of what has been. As God's Word, it remains a constant standard for what should continue to be.

History passes and cultures come and go. The Bible covers many of those historic eras, now long gone. However, the importance of concepts such as love, compassion, mercy, grace, forgiveness, and such never diminishes. As the Bible deals with such truths, we see that they are still just as valid for us today as they were for Abraham, Moses, David, Peter, Paul, and all the rest of the biblical characters throughout history.

So What?

So while casual Bible reading can be helpful, it's no match for the potential benefits of genuine Bible *study*. That's our next step. We meditate until we find hidden treasures previously unseen. We let God's Spirit illuminate the text to reveal even more truths. We commit favorite portions to memory and use them during real-life situations. And we continually seek ways to personally apply the truths we uncover and make them relevant to our own lives. Bible study is never really complete until we put the *us* in studi*us*.

Maybe that's a lot to remember, so let's simplify it a bit. If you don't want to fool with steps and techniques, here are just two words to remember as you approach future Bible study: *So what?*

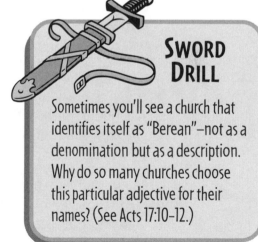

SWORD DRILL

Sometimes you'll see a church that identifies itself as "Berean"–not as a denomination but as a description. Why do so many churches choose this particular adjective for their names? (See Acts 17:10–12.)

If indeed *all* Scripture is God's Word—good for teaching, rebuking, correcting, and training in righteousness (as we have previously seen in 2 Timothy 3:16)—we ought not be able to skim through the Bible's pages very far before we find something that speaks directly to us. Whenever we read a story, a historical passage, a parable, a psalm, or any other section of Scripture, we need to ask ourselves: *So what? Why is that in the Bible? How does this part of God's Word apply to me?*

As we approach Bible study, we always need to remember that God gave us His Word for a reason. Some days it's easier than others to figure out how what we're reading applies to us, but with a little effort we can almost always come away with something that is personally relevant.

The chapters that follow will provide some helpful suggestions for gleaning more from each day's Bible study. Perhaps you're satisfied with a little occasional light Bible reading and don't care to go deeper. But if you have a desire to not only understand the Bible better but also to get closer to God, you'll discover Bible study isn't as difficult or complicated as you might think.

Chapter Flashback

1. The most important biblical commandments, according to Jesus, are:
   a. Don't steal, kill, or commit adultery.
   b. Love God and love others.
   c. Love God and love life.
   d. Eat, drink, and be merry.

2. Bible study should primarily be a(n):
   a. Chore
   b. Obligation
   c. Way to postpone homework or housework
   d. Way to strengthen one's relationship with God

3. What lesson about Bible study can we learn from the story of the ten lepers?
   a. Studying in a group of ten is better than individual study.
   b. We should seek help from priests.
   c. The right attitude makes a big difference.
   d. We should do exactly what Jesus says without thinking about it.

4. Bible study takes on new vitality as we attempt to integrate:
   a. Meditation, illumination, memorization, and application
   b. Mediation, illustration, visualization, and a vacation
   c. Hesitation, trepidation, reservation, and consternation
   d. Addition, subtraction, multiplication, and division

5. Two words to remind you to apply any passage of Scripture to your own life are:
   a. Who, me?
   b. Be prepared.

c. Tempus fugit.
d. So what?

Answers: (1) b, (2) d, (3) c, (4) a, (5) d

Tool Time

LEARNING TO USE COMMENTARIES, CONCORDANCES, AND OTHER STUDY HELPS

SNAPSHOT

"Dale, it looks like you're having some trouble with your snowblower. Can I help?"

"Thanks anyway, Hank, but I think I can get it."

"Are you sure?" Hank persisted. "It looks as if you're trying to remove a tight bolt by using a rubber band and a stick."

"Yeah, I'm trying my own method. I really don't like to use tools," Dale answered. "They just seem so unnatural. If I can't fix something myself, I don't feel worthwhile."

"Well, I've got a ratchet set that can have that thing off in seconds. Or I could bring my toolbox over and I'm sure we could get the whole snowblower fixed in no time. We're supposed to get between eight and twelve inches of snow tonight."

SNEAK PREVIEW

1. Bible study, like many other tasks, can go much smoother with the right "tools."
2. We all have a number of helpful, accessible, affordable Bible study aids at our disposal.
3. It requires very little effort to learn to use these study aids that can greatly enhance our understanding of the Bible.

"Oh, I don't plan to use it. I never have. It was a hand-me-down from my father-in-law after he got a new one. I'm just trying to get it fixed so I can pass it on to someone who wants it."

"Your driveway is huge! Don't tell me you still prefer the old-fashioned shoveling method to get rid of snow!"

"Oh, no. Shovels take all the challenge out of the job. I just strap on my boots and get out and tramp down all the snow by hand . . . or rather, by foot. Besides, the fire usually melts a lot of it."

"The fire?"

"Sure. How else do you think I'm going to cook my supper?"

* * * * * * * * * * * * * * *

A scene in the movie *Cast Away* shows the Tom Hanks character stranded and alone on a remote island. He finds coconuts to eat—or so he thinks. A long sequence of shots shows various ineffective methods he uses attempting to get through the thick husk to the actual coconut, and then trying to salvage the coconut milk without wasting the precious liquid. The movie portrayed, without words, the intense frustration he experienced as he was denied access to something he needed just because he had no basic tools to accomplish a simple task. (Sort of like cooking every meal over a campfire instead of using a stove.) Later, in contrast, he was shown using tools he had fashioned and getting the job done just fine.

In this chapter we want to look at a few simple tools that can help us get to "the meat" of the Bible. Rather than simply reading and reading and not ever getting beneath the surface, we want to discover ways to make Bible study not only a broad and rich experience, but also a deep and personally satisfying one.

Popular Subdivisions

Even without our realizing it, much has already taken place to help make Bible reading a more convenient experience. For one thing, the translating has already been done, so you don't have to learn Hebrew, Greek, and Aramaic before you can see what Scripture has to say.

For another, the text of each "book" of the Bible (whether narrative, letter, poetry, or whatever) has been divided into smaller units for easier reading and reference. In several cases, a block of text was first separated into more than one book. For example, we started with one book of Samuel, one book of Kings, one book of Chronicles, another single book that combined Ezra and Nehemiah, and some additional longer texts that have since been separated.

In addition, each of our "books" has now been further divided into chapters and verses. Those aren't in the original manuscripts, but we can certainly be glad they have been inserted. It's hard enough sometimes to follow a preacher when he says, "Turn in your Bibles to Jeremiah 33:3." Can you imagine the additional difficulty if he said, "Turn almost, but not quite, two-thirds of the way through Jeremiah and start looking for a verse about calling on God"? Even today, books like Jeremiah and Ezekiel are intimidating to lots of people. Without any kind of breaks, you have to wonder how many people would ever try to read these longer books.

Reading the Small Print

Footnotes are another rather obvious Bible study aid. Most Bibles contain footnotes that can enhance your understanding as you read through a passage.

Usually, the translators of any particular version will include notes of their own. For instance, you might be reading the *NIV Study Bible*, the *Serendipity Study Bible*, or the *Quest Study Bible*. Each has its own footnotes that provide additional information. But since these versions are all based on the *New International Version*, you can find additional

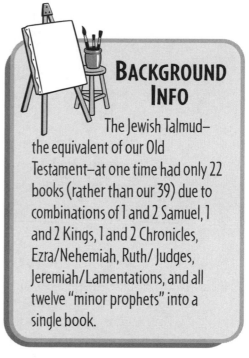

BACKGROUND INFO

The Jewish Talmud– the equivalent of our Old Testament–at one time had only 22 books (rather than our 39) due to combinations of 1 and 2 Samuel, 1 and 2 Kings, 1 and 2 Chronicles, Ezra/Nehemiah, Ruth/ Judges, Jeremiah/Lamentations, and all twelve "minor prophets" into a single book.

WHAT'S THE GOOD WORD?

"This is what the LORD says, he who made the earth, the LORD who formed it and established it–the LORD is his name: 'Call to me and I will answer you and tell you great and unsearchable things you do not know.'"

–JEREMIAH 33:2-3

footnotes common to all three versions. You may need to look closely to find them, but here are just a few examples among many:

➤ When you get to Matthew 18:24, you'll see that "ten thousand talents" (not exactly a current monetary standard) equates to "millions of dollars."

➤ In Mark 1:40, you learn through the footnote that the Greek word usually translated "leprosy" could actually represent a multitude of various skin diseases—not necessarily the single disease we know as leprosy.

➤ In John 3:3, you see that "born again" can also be interpreted as "born from above."

➤ In Acts 8:32–33, you discover that the passage being read by the man encountered by Philip is, in our Bibles, Isaiah 53:7–8. All the text tells you is that the man was reading "Isaiah the prophet" (Acts 8:30), but without the footnote you might have to read fifty-three chapters before you could connect the two passages.

When writing term papers in high school, we might come to despise the dreaded footnotes that are required. But when reading Scripture, footnotes are our friends. They save lots of time and provide much information we might otherwise miss. Through footnotes we are made privy to definitions, alternate ways the original languages might be translated, what other manuscripts (that aren't being used by the translators) might include or exclude, references to the original source of quoted material, geographic help (such as the location of Cush in Esther 1:1), and much more.

And these are just the footnotes that come with most translations. Even the most basic pew Bibles usually have a few such footnotes if we're looking for them. However, if you use a study Bible, you are likely to have a wealth of additional footnotes provided by the publishers of the Bible to add to those already available. Some Bibles add so much detail to explain the scriptural text that it's easy to get bogged down in the footnotes rather than paying attention to the Bible itself. We never want to let that happen, but neither do we want to avoid the wealth of information that may be lingering at the bottom of each page. After you have read and meditated on the text, make use of the wisdom of others who have provided those helpful footnotes for you.

We Have Something in Commentaries

If you get used to footnotes and discover that they just whet your appetite for learning about the background and supplemental information for biblical text, you might want to invest in a commentary. These are generally big, thick books that may appear intimidating at first. But as you begin to piece together not only what the Bible says, but also a between-the-lines understanding of the culture and setting at the time of writing, commentaries can help add to your comprehension.

Some commentaries deal with only a single book (or short section) of Scripture. Others will cover the entire Bible but aren't likely to be quite as detailed.

If you want to use a commentary in conjunction with your Bible reading, you'll probably want to choose one based on the same translation you are using. Otherwise, it won't necessarily address the words and phrases in your text. For example, if you're using *The New American Standard Bible,* and your commentary is based on the King James Version, it is likely to explain certain terms or phrases that have already been translated differently in your Bible text. You want your Bible version and your chosen commentary to match, or the commentary might be more confusing than helpful.

Also be aware that commentaries are written at vastly differing academic levels. Some are "easy reads" with popular language and simplified explanations. Others assume a deeper level of academic achievement and can be hard to understand for newcomers to Scripture—and more expensive as well. So before you invest a lot in a commentary (or even more in a *set* of commentaries), you might want to do some firsthand examination. Your local pastor will probably be glad to recommend something. Libraries, either church or public, might also have a decent selection.

WHAT'S THE GOOD WORD?

Let the wise listen and add to their learning, and let the discerning get guidance—for understanding proverbs and parables, the sayings and riddles of the wise.

–PROVERBS 1:5-6

BACKGROUND INFO

These days, most larger bookstores have well-stocked "Religion" sections which contain a number of good Bible commentaries and other products you can review at your leisure. Also be sure to check out your local Christian/family bookstores, where the employees may be able to better assist you in your selection.

Dictionaries Where You'll Find Noah, but Not Webster

If you aren't ready for a full-fledged commentary that tracks along with chapter and verse of the Bible text, you can still benefit from a good Bible dictionary. That way, you can stick primarily with straight Scripture, but when you discover a person, place, or thing you don't understand, you can look it up in the dictionary.

Bible dictionaries, like commentaries, can vary in their depth. Some may not contain references that others do. But what they do include is generally defined from the comprehensive scope of Scripture. Commentaries tend to deal with such things only in the context of a particular verse or passage.

For example, leprosy is mentioned numerous times throughout Scripture, and a commentary probably won't say a lot about it each and every time it is mentioned. The commentator may explain it in great detail in a place or two, but you may not happen to be at one of those places. Rather than scour the commentary for other passages where leprosy is mentioned, attempting to pick up bits of new information about the disease, a Bible dictionary will spell it out for you in one place.

Sometimes you can find what you're looking for in a regular dictionary, but a Bible dictionary usually frames the definition in a more helpful context. Let's say you've come across the word *concubine* and you want to know more about what kind of woman this might be. A recent copy of the *American Heritage Dictionary* will provide you with a contemporary legal definition and a cultural reference using imperial China as an example. Most Bible dictionaries, however, go into more detail about the rights and privileges, as well as the legal restrictions, of concubines. You're also likely to find sources for biblical guidelines that protected concubines as well as a list of prominent biblical characters who had concubines.

The people who compile Bible dictionaries usually have a good idea why you would be looking up the things listed and anticipate your questions.

Bible Atlases

Just as a Bible dictionary will be considerably more targeted for most of your word searches than a regular dictionary, so too will a Bible atlas be much more helpful than a contemporary map of the world when it comes to biblical geography.

SWORD DRILL

What biblical character had 300 concubines? (See 1 Kings 11:2–3. But if you were paying attention in chapter 8, you should already know the answer.)

For one thing, the names and boundaries of various countries are rarely permanent for long periods of time. Just think how the map of the United States has changed over the past two hundred years. We know better than to grab a brand-new Rand McNally map and go looking for the Louisiana Territory. So as we go back thousands (rather than hundreds) of years into Bible history, we need to consult maps that are appropriate for the time.

Perhaps your study Bible has maps in the back, and it is for good reason there are usually more than one. Moses roamed much of the same geographic area as Abraham, but many of the prominent cities in their life stories are different, necessitating different maps. That same region continued to change both ownership title and place names for Joshua, David and Solomon, and Daniel and later prophets. It changed even more for the New Testament residents who lived after the world-changing Greeks and Romans stormed into the area. On some maps Assyria is the prominent nation, but you'll miss it altogether on earlier maps, and it is but a distant memory in New Testament times.

A Bible atlas will cover all the primary stages of biblical history, allowing you to search and locate the cities and countries you encounter in your reading. And when it comes to Bible geography, it can be helpful to investigate beyond mere cities and countries. You'll get more out of some of the stories when you know which areas were deserts and which were mountainous, which were densely populated and which were isolated, and so forth.

For example, if you know that Jerusalem sat at a higher altitude than many of the surrounding cities, you may begin to notice references to this. Jesus spoke of going *up* to Jerusalem (Matthew 20:18), as had Zechariah (Zechariah 14:16) and others. Psalms 120 through 134 are designated "songs of ascents," so these may have been favorite tunes of pilgrims headed to annual festivals in Jerusalem.

WHAT'S THE GOOD WORD?

I lift up my eyes to the hills—where does my help come from? My help comes from the LORD, the Maker of heaven and earth. He will not let your foot slip.

—PSALM 121:1–3

Other portions of Scripture take on special meaning when we notice they take place on a mountain, crossing a lake, on a plain, or at some other specific geologic and geographic area. The story of Jesus calming the storm, for example, is more powerful when we notice He speaks from a rickety, sinking boat rather than with His feet planted firmly on shore (Luke 8:22–25). You don't need an atlas to appreciate each story, of course, but you may discover it is surprisingly helpful to track where people are moving to and from. Besides, pinpointing cities on a map helps ground the accounts in reality rather than letting them go by as merely good stories.

One Good Verse Deserves Another... and Another

Perhaps one of the most common, yet overlooked, resources is cross-references. When you first get a Bible, sometimes it's hard to miss all the tiny letters printed as superscripts to certain words. After a while, though, it becomes natural to simply ignore them altogether.

But if you've never bothered to check out why those tiny letters are there, you should know they correspond to the same letter somewhere else on the page— usually in a center column or at the bottom. These are cross-references, and each one will send you to another verse or passage.

For example, in one story where Jesus cast out a number of demons from a man, the evil spirits begged to be sent into a herd of pigs and not into "the Abyss" (Luke 8:30–33). This abrupt mention of the Abyss is not further addressed in this passage, which could be frustrating. Many study Bibles would be likely to include a footnote to provide additional information, as would a good commentary. But if all you have handy is a Bible, you might find a cross-reference to Revelation 9:1–2, where you'll find a bit more about the Abyss (and perhaps yet another footnote). You might also find a cross-reference from that passage to Revelation 9:11 where there is still another biblical mention of the Abyss.

When you're reading through the short but mysterious book of Jude, cross-references can help you track down many of the author's illustrations. If we don't know anything about "the archangel Michael" (v. 9), a cross-reference sends us to Daniel 10:13, 21; 12:1; and Revelation 12:7. A cross-reference to "Balaam's error" (Jude 11) sends us first to 2 Peter 2:15, and a cross-reference there sends us back to three different Old Testament sources (Numbers 22:4–20; 31:16; and Deuteronomy 23:4) as well as to another New Testament reference (Revelation 2:14). Jude's mention of Korah's rebellion (v. 11) is accompanied by a cross-reference that shoots you straight back to its origin in Numbers 16:1–3, 31–35. And these are just a few examples. (These particular cross-references are from *The New International Version* translation.)

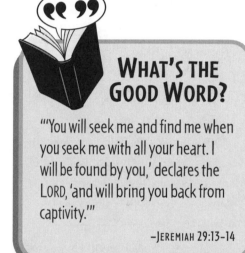

WHAT'S THE GOOD WORD?

"'You will seek me and find me when you seek me with all your heart. I will be found by you,' declares the LORD, 'and will bring you back from captivity.'"

—JEREMIAH 29:13–14

We think nothing of sitting down to surf the Internet and winding our way through dozens of interconnected sites searching for information. Cross-references work essentially the same way. We might get more information with a good footnote or by consulting a commentary, yet cross-references have the advantage of connecting Scripture with Scripture. With a little effort on our parts, we can discover many insights we might otherwise miss or misunderstand.

Try to Remember . . . or Use a Concordance

So cross-references are helpful if you happen to be at one point in the text and want to leap to a related area. But what if you're trying to find where you want to be in the first place? That's where you'll want to consult a trusty concordance.

Suppose you know you've read a verse that says something about Jesus knocking at a door. You can go to a concordance and search for key words that are specific to what you're looking for. Since Jesus is mentioned in a lot of verses throughout the New Testament, looking under "Jesus" might not be the best option. But if you were to look under "door" or "knock," either key word is likely to point you to Revelation 3:20 where Jesus is quoted as saying, "Here I am! I stand at the door and knock." You will also find other verses that contain the words *door* and *knock*, so you must read through the short segments of verses printed beneath each key word in order to tell which specific reference you're seeking.

> ## BACKGROUND INFO
>
> While the Gospels are a good place to **start** if you're looking for a quote from Jesus, keep in mind that other New Testament writers quote Jesus from time to time. (See Acts 20:35, for example.) And the entire New Testament is **about** Jesus. So if you don't find what you're looking for in the Gospels, expand your search to the later portions of the New Testament.

Not all concordances are complete. In fact, many contain only a limited list of key words with a short list of options after each one. So if you don't find what you're looking for, you can't assume it's not there. It simply might not be listed. So your next step would be to consult an *exhaustive* (complete) concordance that should pinpoint exactly what you want to find.

Be aware, however, that exhaustive concordances can be exhausting if you're looking for a particular word that appears in a lot of places throughout Scripture. In the previous example, for instance, *Strong's Exhaustive Concordance of the Bible* (based on the King James Version) lists 260 references to "door" or "doors," and since the one you were looking for is in Revelation, the last book of the Bible, you would be likely to skim through almost all of them before you found what you were seeking. (When you know the verse is in a particular book but don't recall exactly where, a concordance becomes very helpful in your detective work.)

As was suggested as a guideline for commentaries, use a concordance that matches the Bible version you're using. For example, suppose someone comments that, "Jesus promises we will have abundant life," and you want to look up the original source. If you start looking for *abundant* in a *New International Version* commentary, you'll find some listings but not the one you're looking for because the "abundant life" phrase is based on a King James Version translation. And if you look for the key word *life*, you'll find a much longer list to search through.

Since you're working under the assumption that this was a quote by Jesus, you're likely to find it in one of the Gospels: Matthew, Mark, Luke, or John. In this case you'll have to skim through Matthew, Mark, and Luke before you get to John 10:10 where your concordance gives you the clue, "I have come that they may have *l*." And when you look up John 10:10, you'll find what you were looking for: "I have come that they may have life, and have it to the full."

Even if you know that the "abundant life" phrase comes from the King James Version, and even if you begin with the reliable *Strong's Exhaustive Concordance*, your search may be no less a challenge. First of all, you still won't find what you're looking for under the word *abundant*. But if you check

BACKGROUND INFO

As you research what's available in the area of Bible study tools, don't forget about the electronic options. Computer software is available to provide Bible text in a number of translations (even comparing various versions side by side if you wish). You can also find a number of concordances which, once installed, don't take up additional space on your bookshelves. With the keying in of a single word, you can instantly have a list of all the places that word is found in Scripture.

alternative word forms (as you always should), you will move on to *abundantly*. There, under John 10:10, you will find, "and that they might have it more *a*." The word "abundantly" isn't connected to the word "life" in this short quotation from the verse. Unless you knew how Jesus phrased His statement to begin with, you might not even realize this is what you're looking for. And if you look for "life" in *Strong's*, you'll find a listing of 450 options. Even the section in the Gospels includes more than 80 listings because Jesus said a lot about *life*. But this time, if you make it all the way to John 10:10, you'll find, "I am come that they might have *l*, and." Even then, only by looking up the verse can you confirm that it is indeed the one you want.

SWORD DRILL

Since we're on the topic of **tools,** what biblical building was constructed with great care, so that no tool noises were heard on the construction site? (See 1 Kings 6:2, 7.)

BACKGROUND INFO

Oil is sometimes symbolic of the Holy Spirit in the Bible. Designated kings and other special people were anointed with oil, signifying God's blessing upon the person. God even provided a recipe for this special oil (Exodus 30:22–33). And if you don't think an "anointed one" was special, the term is the literal translation of the word **messiah.**

Many times, a concordance will help you turn right to the passage you're looking for. Other times, you'll need patience and perseverance as you run down that elusive verse.

As you get comfortable using concordances and other Bible study tools, you will know better what to look for when choosing a study Bible. Do you prefer lengthy, detailed footnotes or short and to-the-point ones? How extensive do you want the concordance to be? You might find that one person's viewpoint is helpful (such as in *The Ryrie Study Bible* or *The MacArthur Study Bible*), or you might go for one with notes provided by an extensive and scholarly team of researchers. In time, however, you are likely to find one particular study Bible among the dozens (maybe hundreds) of other options that seems to be just what you're looking for.

The Problem with Tools

As you can see, the use of concordances, as well as other Bible resources, can be a challenge. Like any other tools, their use becomes more natural and productive with practice. They require use of your mind, memory, logic, and determination. Yet it can pay off when you finally find what you're looking for, whether a definition, a cross-reference, a place on the map, a verse you're trying to recall, or whatever. It's a vastly satisfying experience to learn to navigate the Bible on your own, coming up not only with good questions, but also the means of answering many of those questions yourself.

Perhaps this chapter has seemed simplistic to you. Maybe you already know about all these resources and can use them like a pro. If so, the question for you is, *Do* you? Many of us have tools hanging around the garage or tucked-away musical instruments that we seldom touch. We don't get rid of them because we're always waiting for just the right opportunity when we might put them to use.

But if our goal is to really understand the Word of God better, we need to keep the related tools sharp by using them frequently. This is one area where we don't want inactivity to make them . . . or us . . . rusty. Perhaps we need the "oil" of the Holy Spirit to reduce friction and cause these tools to work more smoothly for us.

Another potential problem with tools is the cost. Numerous wives bemoan a husband's passion for accumulating tools until the garage looks like a showroom for Home Depot. And if you're just beginning to get serious about Bible study, this chapter's promotion of helpful "tools" might sound like a car salesperson's pitch you should by all means avoid. ("Yes, ma'am, you're going to want the full-color illustrated Bible dictionary, the exhaustive concordance, the book-by-book Bible commentary, the three-dimensional Bible atlas, and every other top-of-the-line item we sell. You could go with something cheaper, of course, but you don't want to shortchange God, do you?")

This is not the intention. Don't go overboard. In fact, it's probably wise to borrow these tools until you discover which ones you're going to use the most. Ask around and see what resources your friends can lend you, or check out local libraries. Maybe you even have access to a church library. When you find resources you like to use and think you'll need on a regular basis, then you can start accumulating. (By the way, keep these things in mind for when people start asking, "What do you want for your birthday?" or "What do you want for Christmas?" If your mother-in-law knew you wanted a Bible

BACKGROUND INFO

The Internet contains no shortage of Bible "resource" material. Just remember: You get what you pay for. Much of what you find is written from a personal or denominational slant—often an extreme one. Other information lacks any kind of sources to check out and should be read with some degree of skepticism. We should always be careful about thoughtlessly believing whatever we find on-line, but this is especially true when it comes to Christian resource material.

dictionary, she probably wouldn't have to spend as much on your gift and you wouldn't have yet another reindeer sweater in your closet.)

Like any other collection of tools, you're going to find other appealing resources once you start accumulating. For example, a lot of people enjoy using *An Expository Dictionary of New Testament Words* by W. E. Vine. Sounds like a real thriller, doesn't it? But suppose you come across a New Testament Bible verse using the word *love*. By looking up the reference in Vine's, you don't have to learn Greek to see if it's *agape* (a highest-level, godly degree of love), *phileo* (a term of tender affection), or something else.

Don't try to overdo it with Bible study aids to begin with. Use what is helpful, and forget about the rest for now. Just be aware of what is available when you get to the point where you want to know a bit more than what the Scripture text is telling you.

And now that you're aware of the tools at your disposal, we're about to turn our attention to various ways you might want to put them to use.

Chapter Flashback

Match the most appropriate Bible tool you would use for each of the following situations.

1. You have only your Bible, you've come across the word *atonement*, and you would like to find other places in the Bible that might help you understand this concept.

   A. Footnotes

2. You're trying to recall where to find that verse about being more than conquerors.

   B. Commentary

3. You read that Jesus went from Bethany to Jerusalem and you want to know which direction He was traveling.

   C. Bible dictionary

4. You'd like to know everything you can learn about the Philistines.

   D. Bible atlas

5. You have only your study Bible with you, but you want to learn as much background information as you can about Psalm 23.

   E. Cross-references

6. You've read the parable of the shrewd manager (Luke 16:1–9) and the available footnotes, but you are still a bit confused about what it really means.

   F. Concordance

Answers: (1) E, (2) F, (3) D, (4) C, (5) A, (6) B

Loaded with Options

DIFFERENT METHODS OF BIBLE STUDY

SNAPSHOT

"Okay, honey. We're here. You can take off your blindfold."

"Finally! Connor, this has been the strangest present ever. When I let you plan the vacation for our tenth anniversary, I never guessed you would fly us to *Nebraska*, then rent a car and drive . . . forever. Where are we, anyway?"

"Lebanon, Kansas."

"I give up. I don't see anything. What's the attraction?"

"There aren't any attractions here—not that I know of, anyway. But you are now parked at the geographic center of the conterminous United States."

"Excuse me?"

"We're in the very center of the U.S., not counting Alaska or Hawaii."

SNEAK PREVIEW

1. People enjoy many different methods in their pursuit of better Bible understanding.

2. All good Bible study begins with close observation of what the text says.

3. Using a variety of Bible study methods in different settings, over time, increases Scripture comprehension.

271

"Why, exactly?"

"Here's my thinking. I've brought you to the middle of this great land of ours. We've rented a comfortable car. Now we can go anywhere you want to go. If you want oceans, we'll head to the coast. Mountains? Desert? Land of 10,000 lakes? You name it, from West Quoddy Head, Maine, to Capa Alava, Washington—as far east or west as you can go. Or if you want to shoot for Alaska. . ."

"Slow down, big guy. I would be happy with any of those destinations, but you're saying we now have to spend half our vacation *getting* there?"

"Actually, we need to get there and back, because I'm supposed to return the car in Omaha."

"So *more than* half our hard-earned vacation/anniversary time off is going to be spent *on the road?*"

"Or we could stay right where we are if that's what you want to do. Just north of here I saw signs for the Willa Cather Pioneer Museum in Red Cloud, Nebraska. Who knows? That could be a wonderfully romantic place to spend a vacation."

"You're kidding, right?"

"I thought you'd be pleased to have so many choices."

"Right now I'm considering a choice I had ten years ago when I chose you. I'm seriously questioning that decision now."

"You seem upset."

"What clued you, Sherlock?"

"I don't understand what the problem is."

"Connor, you've had six months to plan a special trip. When you started talking about 'a surprise adventure,' I envisioned cruises, resorts, ranches, skiing, scuba diving, and probably everything—except this episode of 'Little Taurus on the Prairie,' that is."

"We can still do any of those things. Tell me where you want to go, and we'll begin our adventure."

"Who cares? Just quit talking and start driving."

"But which way?"

"Head for that museum. This 'pioneer' could use a bathroom right about now. And in the meantime, hand me that atlas. *Somebody* has to come up with a plan."

* * * * * * * * * * * * * *

As we approach the end of *The World's Easiest Guide to Understanding the Bible*, perhaps you're beginning to sense you're going to be abandoned in the middle of nowhere—left with a bit more comprehension of the Bible than before, but no plan for how to navigate it from here on. We've covered material *about* the Bible, we've gone *through* the Bible (rather quickly), and we've discussed a number of tools you might use to get *into* the Bible.

WHAT'S THE GOOD WORD?

The lions may grow weak and hungry, but those who seek the LORD lack no good thing.

–PSALM 34:10

But from now on, how does Bible learning happen? And when? If you put in fifteen to thirty minutes each day, will your eyes pop open one morning as you leap out of bed and shout, "Hey! I get it now!"?

When you finish the next couple of chapters of this guide, it's just going to be you and your Bible. Sixty-six books. Hundreds, maybe thousands, of pages. Here you are; go to it!

Whither Do We Go from Here?

Approaching Bible study without some kind of plan is not much different than plopping yourself down in Lebanon, Kansas, and improvising a vacation. Where to start? Where to plan to finish? What route? How fast? What do you hope to accomplish? The seemingly endless options can become mind numbing.

But don't worry, and don't start to feel overwhelmed. There are surely some people in Lebanon, Kansas, who will assure you it's not a bad place to pass some time. The same goes for Lebanon, Oregon, or Lebanon, Tennessee, or any other town in the country. Depending on your personal preferences, you may not want to spend as long in some places as others, but you can learn something from every place you pass through.

It is not the intention of this book to abandon you in a strange and unfamiliar place with miles to go before you find anything remotely interesting. So this chapter is devoted to the hows and whens of Bible study. Let's start with the whens.

Making Time for the Maker of Time

Bible study needs to become a regular practice. Since the Bible is a primary means by which God communicates with us, we need to consult it as frequently and naturally as we would call up a friend or converse with a spouse. God speaks through His Word. To neglect to crack the covers of our Bibles is like holding our hands over our ears and chanting, "I can't hear You."

SWORD DRILL

When it comes to Bible reading and/or spiritual things, it can be exciting (and maybe even a bit scary) to see things other people don't. One time Elisha and his assistant were surrounded by an entire enemy army out to get them. Elisha didn't panic. Why not? (See 2 Kings 6:15-23.)

Only after you get personally involved in something do you notice how prevalent that hobby or habit becomes. Until people get a new dog, they don't realize how many other dogs are in their neighborhood that they never noticed before. Couples with their first baby suddenly begin to field questions and receive child care tips from total strangers in grocery stores, office cubicles, and other unexpected places. And many people who begin to read the Bible every day are surprised to see how often a newly discovered passage comes to mind soon and unexpectedly—in a meaningful context.

Most valuable pursuits require regular attention over extended periods of time. When dieting, we don't expect to drop twenty pounds in a week (even if we are willing to buy any product that makes such claims). When we're learning to play a musical instrument, a good teacher can tell whether we spent time practicing every day or only practiced the day before the lesson. And to feed our physical bodies, most of us eat every day. We don't cram down seven days' worth of food on Monday, thinking, *There, that should do me for the week!*

God's Word also "digests" better if we "feed" on a daily basis rather than spiritually force-feeding ourselves once or twice a week. Jesus taught us to pray, "Give us today our daily bread" (Matthew 6:11), not, "Load us up with everything we need for a lifetime."

And your "minimum daily requirement" of Bible study need not be taxing. This kind of "study" doesn't demand term papers, dissertations, or even written homework. Your primary assignment is to read, absorb, and listen with your inner spirit to hear God speaking through the printed page. If you're like most people, some days you won't be able to hear much. Other days, the message comes through like a shout.

How Many in Your Party?

Personal Bible reading is of the utmost importance. Whether we're building model airplanes, building wreaths out of grapevines and evergreens, or building useful Bible study skills, we have better comprehension when we actually see and do something, in contrast to only hearing how it should be done. So involving ourselves in Scripture is certainly a positive step.

Still, you may also know from experience that unless you incorporate some kind of accountability, it is human nature to let your personal commitments slide when you get tired or lazy. It's a breeze to make a New Year's resolution to read through the Bible in a year, or to devote twenty minutes a day to Bible study. And it's also a breeze to give up by mid-February, if not mid-January, when no one is looking over your shoulder to enforce the resolution.

So in addition to your regular (almost daily) Bible reading, it's good to get involved with a Bible study *group* as well. A natural place to start is church and/or Sunday school. If your schedule precludes a regular Sunday morning involvement, many churches provide midweek studies, or even home study on various days and evenings of the week. You may need to look around to find a study that fits your schedule and your interests, but you probably won't have too much trouble. And when you find the right one, the shared experience of group Bible study becomes less of an obligation and more of a party.

BACKGROUND INFO

Bible study in a church setting has distinct advantages: You have direct access to pastors and/or teachers who can help with the questions you struggle with (because they've struggled with the same questions). And most of the other members can recommend good resources based on personal experience.

If you show up one week and don't have a clue what the group is talking about, don't feel intimidated. No one expects you to be "up to speed" right away. In fact, most groups will welcome your questions. New members can infuse life into a group.

The more persistently you pursue understanding of the Bible, the more aware you will become not only of what the Bible says, but also what it means. With consistent effort, any initial confusion and reluctance you feel will soon give way to insight, enthusiasm, and downright excitement.

We're about to examine a number of different options you might want to try as you begin Bible study on your own. But before we do, we need to understand one technique that will make most of these options work even better for you.

It's Inductive, My Dear Watson

WHAT'S THE GOOD WORD?

Let us not give up meeting together, as some are in the habit of doing, but let us encourage one another—and all the more as you see the Day approaching.

–HEBREWS 10:25

Bible study is the one place we need to put aside the "tricks" we learn in order to get by in the world. We're taught to "put the right spin" on negative information, operate on a "need to know basis," and do whatever it takes to come out on top in a dog-eat-dog world. So when trying to convince someone else to see things our way, we tend to present only the facts we feel are pertinent, and have the other person "deduce" the desired conclusion.

The literary patron saint of deductive reasoning is Sherlock Holmes. But if you read the Arthur Conan Doyle stories closely, you'll notice that Holmes's deductive reasoning worked so well because of something else—his observation of facts. Sherlock picked up on clues—sights, smells, sounds, inconsistencies, and so forth—that others missed. And when it came to solving the mystery, his deductive reasoning always sounded so "elementary" because he had observed a number of things undetected by his peers.

If we approach Scripture with a similar intense desire to observe every detail, we will develop a greatly expanded ability to come to valid conclusions about what we read. But before we dare attempt to "deduce" an interpretation or an application, we must discipline ourselves to observe, observe, observe.

This approach to Bible study is frequently called the *inductive* method. Simply put, this method begins with establishing basic facts and then drawing logical conclusions from them. Unfortunately, some people approach Scripture more like lawyers than detectives—they begin with a desired position and then seek only facts that will make their case. Such an approach is subjective and selective, not good inductive study, and can do more harm than good.

BACKGROUND INFO

Pause for just a moment and see how many successful movies and TV shows you can list that create intrigue because of the powers of observation of the main characters. If you need help getting started, think about detectives, coroners, crime scene investigators, and so forth.

For example, a good lawyer (or perhaps we should say an *experienced* lawyer) can present selective facts that cause the jury to use good deductive reasoning and still come to the wrong conclusion. For example, a lawyer defending an accused thief might create reasonable doubt to his client's guilt by establishing two clear facts: (1) The getaway car was green, and the defendant owns a red car; and (2) An eyewitness will testify to seeing his client in a store fifty miles away at the precise time of the robbery. A couple of facts he might *not* choose to include in his argument, however, are that the defendant has an identical twin who works at that particular store and that the client received a speeding ticket dated three minutes after the robbery while driving a borrowed green car.

When it comes to Bible study, we've already noted the importance of personal examination of Scripture. The next step is developing good, objective observation skills. To get the most out of Bible reading, we must approach the text like

SWORD DRILL

God helps us past initial feelings of reluctance when we want to get closer to Him. When Isaiah's feelings of unworthiness caused him to hesitate to respond to God's call, how did God remedy the situation? And what was the result? (See Isaiah 6:1–8.)

investigators. The inspired writers of Scripture have jam-packed it with details. If we're content to merely skim through the text for twenty minutes, we can pick up some valuable information, to be sure. But we might take away much more if we spend that same twenty minutes on a single verse, checking out the nuances of what it means.

Any Questions?

The previous chapter listed a number of tools that can help you better navigate difficult Bible passages, but nothing is as effective as regular, disciplined *observation*. You start questioning what you're reading—not because you doubt what is written, but because you want to know more. Here are a few questions to start with:

➤ *Who is the author, and why was he writing?* For example, when you realize that Paul was in prison when he wrote Philippians (and other letters), you get a different feel for the content.

➤ *Who was the author addressing?* Is the passage praise to God, or a message for God's people? Are those people Jews or Gentiles? Are they faithful followers, or have they rejected God?

➤ *What writing style is being used?* If it's a parable or allegory, we need to look for an underlying meaning. If it's a commandment, we need to respond one way; if it's a worship passage, we might respond differently.

➤ *Where does the passage fit on the Bible timeline?* Prophetic books, for example, may contain warnings of events that have by now already taken place (although we can still learn relevant and applicable lessons from such passages). Other portions, however, refer to events yet to come. Good observation helps us differentiate past, present, and future.

And these questions are just a beginning. Observation continues as we begin to detect details of the scene, emotions, geographical significance, cultural relevance, similarities and contrasts to other portions of Scripture, and much, much more.

We can't effectively cover all the aspects of inductive Bible study in a single chapter, but once you know what it's called you can read up on it to your heart's content. Many good books exist to challenge you to be more aware of the importance of good observation and to help you in this vital area of Bible study.

Only after we learn to observe what Scripture really says—all the details and contexts—should we move on to the next two steps of the inductive Bible study method: *interpretation* and *application*. Far too many people latch on to one or two Bible verses too quickly and jump to interpretation, right or wrong. Many of the widespread misconceptions about Christianity are due to zealous, though completely erroneous, Christians who attempt to emphasize portions of Scripture (out of context) and have no desire to use basic observation skills.

Skipping (or rushing through) the observation step will almost always create problems with accurate interpretation and application of Scripture. That's why you need to read the Bible for yourself instead of taking someone else's word for it. And that's why you need to do so on a regular basis. Each venture into the Word of God adds to your compilation of information and further clarifies the truth in your own mind.

Once you determine *when* are the best times for you to study the Bible, next you need to consider *what* and *how* you intend to study. As you establish your personal regimen of Bible study, be sure that somewhere you are involved in good inductive study. For instance, if you're trying to read through the Bible in a year, you're probably going to have a lot of questions, but you won't have much opportunity to answer them. You can't read three or four chapters each day and squeeze all the relevance out of such a large block of text. So you might want to add one or

BACKGROUND INFO

A skilled and experienced Bible teacher who has spent a few decades both teaching and writing on the topic is Dr. Howard Hendricks. He and his son Bill have written an excellent, easy-to-understand introduction to Bible study titled **Living by the Book** (Moody Press). An accompanying workbook includes dozens of structured Bible studies. Both products were written for "regular people" who have an interest in better understanding Scripture.

more of the following options. Different people enjoy different paces, different styles, and so forth, so choose what you think will work best for you—whether selecting one method to focus on, or combining a couple of different options.

Straight-Through-the-Bible Options

Many people are eager to read straight through the Bible—cover to cover. That is, they're eager until they hit the Leviticus/Numbers/Deuteronomy stretch or the lengthy string of Old Testament prophetic books. Many sincere and committed people have bogged down in the Old Testament and given up before ever reaching the New Testament.

Other people grit their teeth and approach this task sort of like taking medicine. They push themselves to read the whole Bible in a year so they can "get it over with." While there's absolutely nothing wrong with the goal of reading through the Bible in a year, the primary motivation shouldn't be merely the accomplishment of a long and dreaded task. Rather, it should be to see for ourselves what God has recorded for us to know about Him.

A straight read-through of the Bible is not likely to answer all our questions. On the contrary, it is certain to raise many, many more. So reading straight through the Bible doesn't mean anything is "over with"; it is merely a step that springboards us into an ongoing search for answers when we have more time. The search for God's truth never ends.

If you desire to read the whole Bible in a relatively short period of time, you have several options.

The One-Year Bible

If your goal is to read the Bible in a single year, you can now find Bibles that divide the text into dated daily readings—January 1 to December 31. One advantage of these Bibles is that they break up the longer, drier portions of Scripture. Rather than take you straight from Genesis to Revelation, they include daily readings from both the Old and

WHAT'S THE GOOD WORD?

Do your best to present yourself to God as one approved, a workman who does not need to be ashamed and who correctly handles the word of truth.

–2 Timothy 2:15

New Testaments, and even throw in short portions of Psalms and Proverbs to add variety.

But since the books are broken up and rearranged, don't expect to use a one-year Bible as your *only* Bible. The reordering of the books makes it awkward to use if, for instance, you're trying to turn from verse to verse during a group study or look up a list of references from a concordance. Also be aware that you may not find one-year Bibles in all translations or paraphrases if you're partial to a certain one.

WHAT'S THE GOOD WORD?

"Sow for yourselves righteousness, reap the fruit of unfailing love, and break up your unplowed ground; for it is time to seek the LORD, until he comes and showers righteousness on you."

–HOSEA 10:12

The Two-Year Bible

Reading the Bible in a single year is an ambitious goal, even for those who are somewhat familiar with Scripture. So recently the two-year Bible was produced to slow the pace a bit. The structure is the same as the one-year Bible, but the daily readings are only about half as long. This will provide a greater opportunity to reflect upon and apply the text.

Daily Reading Plans

If you don't want to buy a whole extra Bible just because it breaks down the text into convenient daily readings, you can find various plans to show you what to read in your own Bible that will take you through its entirety in a year. If you prefer a two-year stretch instead, it's easy enough to divide each recommended reading into two separate days. (One of these reading plans is included in the appendix at the back of this guide.)

Do-It-Yourself Plans

If you don't want to be bound to anyone else's reading plan, it's a simple matter to do the math yourself. The Bible contains a total of 1,189 chapters—929 in the Old Testament and 260 in the New Testament. If you want to read the whole thing in a year, you'll need to read just under twenty-three chapters each week. That breaks down to a bit over three and one-fourth chapters per day for a seven-day commitment, or just over four and one-half chapters per day if you want to take off Saturdays and Sundays.

You can read what you want to read. If you want to go straight through, you can. If you want to prorate Old Testament and New Testament, you can. Some people would much prefer to let someone else dictate their daily readings; others like to navigate for themselves.

Audio Options

These days you can find Scripture in numerous formats, one of which is audiocassette. Most such versions allow you to *hear* the entire Bible in a year, word for word, by listening less than a half hour daily. Many people have longer commutes than that. The challenge of an audio format, however, is staying mentally focused on what is being read. Paying attention to the narrator can be especially challenging if you're dodging debris on the interstate or trying to separate feuding children.

BACKGROUND INFO

Keep in mind that not all Bible chapters are the same length. For example, it's tempting to shout "Woohoo!" and knock off early when you get to a "chapter" like Psalm 117, which is only two verses long. But if you don't read a little extra on days like that, the next day or so you'll get to a chapter like Psalm 119, which more than compensates with a whopping 176 verses.

Other Bible Study Options

If you're not necessarily determined to read the whole Bible right away, then a number of other options open up for you. Below are some opportunities you might want to pursue.

Bible Book Studies

Among the most popular types of Bible study are book studies. Select a Bible book you would like to know more about and spend as long as it takes to acquire a thorough understanding of it. Then move on to another one.

The advantages of this type of study are numerous. Your daily reading is always in the context of what you've read on previous days. You can spend time grasping the significance of a verse or two instead of speed-reading through three or four chapters. You can read the same verse or passage over and over again until it makes sense. You get a coherent point of view from the same author over a period of time. And in addition to everything else, it's usually easy to find commentaries based on individual books. If you want to add the insight of Bible scholars to your own study, you'll find ample resources to accompany most Bible books.

If you're doing a book study in a group, you'll be expected to go at the pace determined by the leader, of course. It may be faster or slower than you would wish, but you have the advantage in such a setting to raise questions and get a lot of additional input you might otherwise miss.

Biographical Studies

Some people are naturally drawn to biographies of famous figures, and Bible studies can be structured around key characters of Scripture. Some of these will be short and sweet, and you can discover everything the Bible has to say about the person in a brief time. But if you want to examine the lives of Moses or David, for example, be prepared to spend weeks or months rather than days or hours. Again, any halfhearted search should turn up a number of existing Bible studies based on the lives of various Bible characters.

> **BACKGROUND INFO**
>
> Don't be overly ambitious if you're new to Bible book studies. Rather than beginning with Ezekiel or Revelation, try a Gospel. (Mark is the shortest, and it's relatively simple to understand.) James is a good practical book as well. If you're leaning toward the Old Testament, consider Ruth, Esther, or Jonah. You can move on to the longer and more complex books later.

Word Studies

Sometime you might want to sit down with just a Bible and a good concordance and do a word study. Follow the listings in your concordance and look up each reference to the theme you have selected.

Choose something basic but not too broad. For example, a topic such as *God* or *love* might require more time than you want to invest. But if you choose a theme such as *grace*, *mercy*, *justification*, or something similar, you can spend several days' worth of Bible study running down these essential aspects of your faith.

You might not find great relevance in each and every verse that mentions your chosen theme, but you're sure to accumulate a great deal of information that you can piece together and increase your understanding.

Daily Devotionals

Whatever other Bible study options you might choose, many people also recommend adding daily devotions. Several Christian organizations provide booklets on a quarterly basis for a minimal charge, if not for free. Or peruse bookstores to find devotional books on general or specific themes (business, women's concerns, men's issues, etc.).

Most daily readings are only a page or two, and can become a personal or family tradition to read first thing in the morning, at bedtime, or just before a meal. Since lifestyles vary so much, you need to determine what's best for you. But pausing for just a couple of minutes every day to focus on one simple thought from Scripture can easily add to one's comprehension of and appreciation for the Bible.

WHAT'S THE GOOD WORD?

My son, do not forget my teaching, but keep my commands in your heart, for they will prolong your life many years and bring you prosperity. Let love and faithfulness never leave you; bind them around your neck, write them on the tablet of your heart. Then you will win favor and a good name in the sight of God and man.

PROVERBS 3:1–4

Adult Education/Correspondence Courses

Maybe you've been involved in Bible study for a long while now and are looking for more of a challenge than the basic-level material you've been using. If so, you might be able to find academic courses that will continue to enrich your understanding of the Bible.

A local Christian college might offer adult education classes in Bible-related topics. If not, others may offer correspondence courses that provide a variety of learning opportunities. If you are connected to the Internet, you have access to "distance learning" courses—classes you take via computer that provide on-line feedback from your professor. These options are usually more costly than the average resources you would find on a bookstore shelf, but the tradeoff is the increased depth of the material—and perhaps even college credit if that's what you're looking for.

Enjoy Your Journey

There are no doubt numerous other options as well, but these should get you started. Without spending another cent, you can review part 2 of this guide ("Through the Bible"), single out a story or two you'd like to know more about, and then use the Bible resources discussed in the previous chapter (chapter 16) to locate and delve into the story.

If Bible study is brand new to you, just reading and absorbing the basic truths will probably be plenty to take on at first. But if you've already gotten that far in times past, you might want to stop at one book, one passage, or one verse to dig deeper into the meaning and see what you can find. No matter how much we think of our powers of observation, it is amazing how frequently new insights will arise from stories we thought we knew inside and out.

So in one sense, this book *is* taking you to a point from which you have a vast array of options and potential destinations. But that's a good thing. As we will see in the concluding chapter, Bible study is a discipline that should last you a lifetime. So set your course, establish a comfortable pace, and keep going. One day everything will "click" for you and you'll never want your journey to end.

WHAT'S THE GOOD WORD?

"But my salvation will last forever, my righteousness will never fail. Hear me, you who know what is right, you people who have my law in your hearts: Do not fear the reproach of men or be terrified by their insults."

–ISAIAH 51:6B-7

Chapter Flashback

1. When is a good time to study the Bible?

a. Every day
b. Every other Wednesday at 8:23 P.M.
c. Whenever you feel like it
d. All of the above

2. Reading through the whole Bible in a year is:
   a. A good start, but should not be the culmination of your Bible study
   b. An insane goal
   c. The first step everyone should take toward better Bible study
   d. A dreadful obligation

3. Try to be sure that your regular Bible reading always includes:
   a. Coffee and donuts
   b. Group participation
   c. Good inductive study
   d. Nap time

4. If you've never tried a Bible book study, a book you might not want to *begin* with is:
   a. Mark (16 chapters, almost entirely about Jesus)
   b. Jeremiah (52 chapters, with a higher word count than any other Bible book, containing a lot of detailed prophecy and history)
   c. Jonah (4 chapters, good fish story)
   d. Ruth (4 chapters, phenomenal love story)

5. Bible study will be more worthwhile as you train yourself to:
   a. Keep your eyes open no matter how sleepy you get.
   b. Find some kind of study every night of the week.
   c. Read while you're jogging, driving, attending business meetings, etc.
   d. Observe the many details contained in Scripture.

Answers: (1) d, (2) a, (3) c, (4) b, (5) d

PART FOUR

In Conclusion...

Save Room for Dessert

BIBLE STUDY AS A LIFELONG COMMITMENT

SNAPSHOT

The four friends had placed their order and were into light conversation. This time Tom had chosen the restaurant.

"Thanks for meeting me here, everyone. It's good to see all you guys again."

"Hey, Tom, this is a great restaurant!" Blake said. "We need to get together for lunch more often."

"Okay. Here are your drinks," the waitress interrupted as she placed a beverage in front of each person. "That's one coffee with cream, a Diet Sprite with a twist of lime, an unsweetened tea, and for Tom, the usual."

"How about that Notre Dame team this year?" Tom asked. "They look very good."

But the other three weren't exactly paying close attention to what Tom was saying. "Uh, Tom . . . what are you drinking?" asked Stu.

SNEAK PREVIEW

1. The ongoing desire to better understand the Bible should be a lifetime pursuit.
2. If not careful, it's easy to overcommit to Bible study and "burn out" before long.
3. While Bible study may seem difficult or confusing at first, with practice and experience it becomes a welcome habit that produces very real benefits.

"It's milk. I always get milk. So do you think the Fighting Irish can go all the way?"

"It's not the milk we're wondering about," said Paul. "Why are you drinking it out of a . . . a . . ."

"A sippy cup?" Tom said, completing Paul's question.

"You took the words right out of our mouths," said Stu.

Tom wasn't a bit defensive. "I use a sippy cup because I don't dribble as much. I still haven't gotten the hang of drinking out of glasses. I've almost mastered using a straw, but I didn't want to chance making a mess in front of all you guys. Is it a problem?"

"No," Blake answered. "It's just a bit strange to see one of the city's most influential lawyers drinking milk out of a sippy cup. But enough about that. What do you recommend we order, Tom?"

"Well, I hear everything is good—big salads, juicy burgers, and great ribs. But I always get the grilled cheese sandwich."

"Let me guess," said Paul. "You haven't mastered chewing yet?"

"Don't be ridiculous. Of course I can chew. But the knives here are very sharp and I still need practice learning to cut my own meat."

* * * * * * * * * * * * * *

A scene like this would be ridiculous in real life. Most of us would be embarrassed to be in public with an otherwise normal person incapable of basic adult eating skills—or even worse, to be that person. Yet on a spiritual level, this is exactly the picture provided for those who don't "grow up" in the area of Bible study and comprehension.

Before You Can Become a Hot Dog Bible Scholar, You Have to Be a Wean-er

For infants just starting out, milk is a natural source of nourishment—not only for human beings, but all mammals. Before animals start hunting or gathering, they must be nurtured on milk for a period of time. As the ads say, it does a body good.

Spiritually, many of the truths of Scripture are as easily digested as milk—simple to understand and apply. And we're expected to lap them up as eagerly as any newborn seeking nourishment. Peter, for one, encourages us to do so: "Like newborn babies, crave pure spiritual milk, so that by it you may grow up in your salvation, now that you have tasted that the Lord is good" (1 Peter 2:2).

Whenever a person places faith in God and has the "born again" experience described by Jesus (John 3:3), the next step after spiritual birth is spiritual feeding on the "pure spiritual milk" of God's Word. It's no easier to skip this spiritual stage than it would be for an infant to skip formula and baby food and try instead to gum his way through a steak dinner.

Yet just as that infant will soon enough grow teeth and will want to sink them into something more substantial than the nipple on a bottle of milk, so too should born-again believers in Jesus move from a milk stage to something meatier.

WHAT'S THE GOOD WORD?

"Come, all you who are thirsty, come to the waters; and you who have no money, come, buy and eat! Come, buy wine and milk without money and without cost."

ISAIAH 55:1

This was the very symbolism used by more than one New Testament writer. Paul chastised those in the Corinthian church: "Brothers, I could not address you as spiritual but as worldly—mere infants in Christ. I gave you milk, not solid food, for you were not yet ready for it. Indeed, you are still not ready. You are still worldly" (1 Corinthians 3:1–3).

And the author of Hebrews expresses a similar complaint: "We have much to say about this, but it is hard to explain because you are slow to learn. In fact, though by this time you ought to be teachers, you need someone to teach you the elementary truths of God's word all over again. You need milk, not solid food! Anyone who lives on milk, being still an infant, is not acquainted with the teaching about righteousness. But solid food is for the mature, who by constant use have trained themselves to distinguish good from evil" (Hebrews 5:11–14).

Got Meat?

Just as human beings are expected to be physically weaned off milk and move on to other more varied food sources, so too are we to desire deeper spiritual truths that are a bit tougher to chew. But this doesn't always happen. You may know people who have been Christians and regular church attenders for decades yet are still "on the bottle" when it comes to spiritual maturity and personal comprehension of the Bible. (It's not usually a pretty sight.)

So as you approach the final pages of this guide, your final challenge will be to plan your spiritual diet, so to speak. If you're new to the Bible, drink in its contents like a hungry baby going after a bottle—even if you're a ninety-year-old great-great-grandparent. But if you've already been at the milk stage long enough, it's time to start tackling some of the meatier portions of Scripture. By now you should know where to find them and how to approach them. You have the tools and the meal is laid out before you. It's just a matter of sitting down at the table and preparing your spiritual taste buds. Take your time, chew before swallowing, and you may be surprised at how much spiritual nutrition you will receive from more serious and intentional study of the Bible.

BACKGROUND INFO

The concept of eating is significant throughout the Bible. Eating is how Adam and Eve specifically disobeyed God in the first sin. God provided daily manna for His people during their wilderness travels. Much attention was given to which foods were "clean" (okay to eat) versus "unclean." Peter's vision revealing the inclusion of the Gentiles in the newly forming church was food-related. And even today, the church continues to eat bread and wine in representation of Jesus' body and blood. It should not seem odd, then, that spiritual maturity is also symbolized with food items, such as milk and meat.

Start to Finish

Lots of people begin Bible study with the best of intentions and the anticipation of a long and productive habit. The first days and weeks go very well, yet for some reason the regularity of study begins to dwindle. Perhaps a new job, a new child, or some other commitment forces a temporary decline in Bible study, and before long the temporary decline has become a permanent halt.

Several biblical references to the Christian life compare it to a race, which might tend to confuse us. If that race were the Kentucky Derby, we could expect to go as hard and fast as possible for a couple of minutes, and it would all be over. If it were the Indianapolis 500, our goal would be 200 laps around a 2 1/2-mile track until we saw a checkered flag. We would set a pace to finish the race and then, win or lose, move on to something else.

But since this spiritual "race" of ours involves reading and understanding the Bible in order to maintain a strong relationship with God, it's never over. How do we run a race where the finish line is the drawing of our final breath?

Because the Christian "race" is lifelong, many people give up along the way. To avoid such failure, and to ensure that we complete this important event, we need to set an appropriate pace for Bible study, spiritual maturity, and related matters. In addition, we are to obey the rules along the way so we don't get disqualified. No shortcuts. No tripping up the other runners. No "pinch runners" while we trot back to the dugout for a little nap.

Starting this race is important. As you read and study the Bible, the time will come to put down the bottle, get to the meat of the message, and join the race. Then the goal becomes to finish. Even as you begin to plan your course of Bible study for the immediate future—to *start* something wonderful and rewarding—be sure to pace yourself for a good *finish* as well.

SWORD DRILL

Speaking of eating, which biblical character asked the following riddle: "Out of the eater, something to eat; out of the strong, something sweet"? And what was the riddle's solution? (See Judges 14.)

WHAT'S THE GOOD WORD?

Do you not know that in a race all the runners run, but only one gets the prize? Run in such a way as to get the prize. Everyone who competes in the games goes into strict training. They do it to get a crown that will not last; but we do it to get a crown that will last forever.

1 CORINTHIANS 9:24-25

WHAT'S THE GOOD WORD?

How sweet are your words to my taste, sweeter than honey to my mouth!

PSALM 119:103

If you perceive Bible study to be a lifetime pursuit, you shouldn't feel the need to overdo it right away. What's your hurry? If you were hoping to get through the Bible in a year, but running down the answers to all your important questions is slowing you down, you go right ahead and answer those questions. The rest of the Bible will still be there next year, and the next, if you don't get to it this year.

If you find you aren't enjoying your Bible study, try varying the pace. Perhaps you're in a group that's plodding slower than you wish to go. If so, do more on your own. If your pace is so fast that you aren't getting anything out of the exercise, slow down. Like anything else, what works for someone else might not be right for you.

SWORD DRILL

A man named Demas is mentioned three times in the Bible. A couple of times Paul names him as a friend and fellow worker, and sends greetings in his name (Colossians 4:14; Philemon 24). However, in one of Paul's final letters, how is Demas ultimately remembered? (See 2 Timothy 4:9-10.)

One More Trip to the Bible Buffet

When it comes to Bible study, we might find new inspiration to finish what we start if we go back to the food analogy. If we begin with milk and move on to meat, what's left? If we're faithful in our regular pursuit of what the Bible has to say, the next phase is *dessert*.

Yes, Bible study can be difficult and inconvenient at times. The transition from those simple truths and stories to doctrines and meatier matters can be awkward and complicated. Some days you won't feel like keeping up the pace. You may feel like you're behind the pack, and you'll simply want to quit. Or just as dangerous, you might feel you're so far ahead that you can coast for a while. (Remember the little story about the tortoise and the hare?)

But in this day-to-day race that never ends, if you find a reasonable pace that keeps propelling you ahead a little at a time, you're in for a surprise. You're going to discover, perhaps to your shock, that you *enjoy* it! You'll be learning new and applicable truths. You'll be coping better with the problems and anxieties of life. And more than anything else, you'll be discovering a relationship with God that is more natural and comfortable than you ever thought possible. And as a consequence, many of your other relationships will be growing stronger as well.

If we discipline ourselves to stay in the race—to get beyond the milk and on to the meat of Scripture—the rewards start becoming evident. More than simply finishing the race and receiving heavenly crowns (which is certainly nothing to scoff at), we also discover great enjoyment simply in *running*. All the love/peace/ joy promises in Scripture begin to become realities rather than merely nice little sayings.

SWORD DRILL

What two people were at one point commanded to actually **eat** God's Word, and found it to be sweet? (See Ezekiel 3:1–3 and Revelation 10:9–10.)

Any physical exercise is difficult at first with soreness, cramps, and other problems to be expected, yet beyond the initial pains are great benefits. Similarly, regular Bible study takes some getting used to. But once you get past any initial reluctance and resistance, the Bible becomes a spiritual dessert cart. It's not that you'll leave behind all your problems—indeed, you may have more than ever. But as you encounter future problems, you'll take with you a resource greater than any obstacle you'll ever face.

Perhaps you have known an elderly person facing death who, after a lifetime of Bible study, showed no fear about stepping from this world into the next. Maybe you've seen people experience the gravest of injustices or personal injuries, yet extend forgiveness to those who harmed them. Maybe you've seen someone persevere and continue with life even while facing situations that would have made Job's experiences look like a trip to Club Med. If so, watch and learn from such people. From them we see that understanding the Bible—*really* understanding the Bible—has very real benefits. Truly understanding Scripture includes so much more than just knowing names, stories, and other such trivia.

When God's Word goes from being just a book on your coffee table to being your personal source of direction and comfort, you'll find yourself doing things you never before thought possible. After the milk . . . after the meat . . . as you keep running the race and approaching the finish line . . . only then will you discover how truly sweet God' s Word can be.

So even as you begin to pursue a greater understanding of the Bible, be sure to save room for dessert. You won't be sorry.

Chapter Flashback

This time, instead of a chapter flashback, let's do a flash *forward*. Consider the following questions if you're seriously interested in pursuing a personal plan of better understanding the Bible.

1. Three portions of the Bible I would really like to know more about are:

2. The best time for me to devote to Bible study on a daily basis is:

3. What are my best options for getting involved in regular group study?

4. What obstacles should I expect if I really want to get serious about regular Bible study? What will I do when faced with such things?

5. What resources could I use to help me get more out of future study?

6. What promises from Scripture can I cling to as I begin this important discipline in my life?

If you are interested in information about
other books written from a biblical perspective,
please write to the following address:

Northfield Publishing
215 West Locust Street
Chicago, IL 60610

APPENDIX

Reading Through the Bible in One Year

Bible Reading Schedule

DAY	DATE	TEXT	DAY	DATE	TEXT
1	*Jan. 1*	Gen. 1–3	32	*Feb. 1*	Ex. 1–4
2	*Jan. 2*	Gen. 4:1–6:8	33	*Feb. 2*	Ex. 5–8
3	*Jan. 3*	Gen. 6:9–9:29	34	*Feb. 3*	Ex. 9–11
4	*Jan. 4*	Gen. 10–11	35	*Feb. 4*	Ex. 12–13
5	*Jan. 5*	Gen. 12–14	36	*Feb. 5*	Ex. 14–15
6	*Jan. 6*	Gen. 15–17	37	*Feb. 6*	Ex. 16–18
7	*Jan. 7*	Gen. 18–19	38	*Feb. 7*	Ex. 19–21
8	*Jan. 8*	Gen. 20–22	39	*Feb. 8*	Ex. 22–24
9	*Jan. 9*	Gen. 23–24	40	*Feb. 9*	Ex. 25–27
10	*Jan. 10*	Gen. 25–26	41	*Feb. 10*	Ex. 28–29
11	*Jan. 11*	Gen. 27–28	42	*Feb. 11*	Ex. 30–31
12	*Jan. 12*	Gen. 29–30	43	*Feb. 12*	Ex. 32–34
13	*Jan. 13*	Gen. 31–32	44	*Feb. 13*	Ex. 35–36
14	*Jan. 14*	Gen. 33–35	45	*Feb. 14*	Ex. 37–38
15	*Jan. 15*	Gen. 36–37	46	*Feb. 15*	Ex. 39–40
16	*Jan. 16*	Gen. 38–40	47	*Feb. 16*	Lev. 1:1–5:13
17	*Jan. 17*	Gen. 41–42	48	*Feb. 17*	Lev. 5:14–7:38
18	*Jan. 18*	Gen. 43–45	49	*Feb. 18*	Lev. 8–10
19	*Jan. 19*	Gen. 46–47	50	*Feb. 19*	Lev. 11–12
20	*Jan. 20*	Gen. 48–50	51	*Feb. 20*	Lev. 13–14
21	*Jan. 21*	Job 1–3	52	*Feb. 21*	Lev. 15–17
22	*Jan. 22*	Job 4–7	53	*Feb. 22*	Lev. 18–20
23	*Jan. 23*	Job 8–11	54	*Feb. 23*	Lev. 21–23
24	*Jan. 24*	Job 12–15	55	*Feb. 24*	Lev. 24–25
25	*Jan. 25*	Job 16–19	56	*Feb. 25*	Lev. 26–27
26	*Jan. 26*	Job 20–22	57	*Feb. 26*	Num. 1–2
27	*Jan. 27*	Job 23–28	58	*Feb. 27*	Num. 3–4
28	*Jan. 28*	Job 29–31	59	*Feb. 28*	Num. 5–6
29	*Jan. 29*	Job 32–34	60	*Mar. 1*	Num. 7
30	*Jan. 30*	Job 35–37	61	*Mar. 2*	Num. 8–10
31	*Jan. 31*	Job 38–42	62	*Mar. 3*	Num. 11–13

Day	Date	Text
63	*Mar. 4*	Num. 14–15
64	*Mar. 5*	Num. 16–18
65	*Mar. 6*	Num. 19–21
66	*Mar. 7*	Num. 22–24
67	*Mar. 8*	Num. 25–26
68	*Mar. 9*	Num. 27–29
69	*Mar. 10*	Num. 30–31
70	*Mar. 11*	Num. 32–33
71	*Mar. 12*	Num. 34–36
72	*Mar. 13*	Deut. 1–2
73	*Mar. 14*	Deut. 3–4
74	*Mar. 15*	Deut. 5–7
75	*Mar. 16*	Deut. 8–10
76	*Mar. 17*	Deut. 11–13
77	*Mar. 18*	Deut. 14–17
78	*Mar. 19*	Deut. 18–21
79	*Mar. 20*	Deut. 22–25
80	*Mar. 21*	Deut. 26–28
81	*Mar. 22*	Deut. 29:1–31:29
82	*Mar. 23*	Deut. 31:30–34:12
83	*Mar. 24*	Josh. 1–4
84	*Mar. 25*	Josh. 5–8
85	*Mar. 26*	Josh. 9–11
86	*Mar. 27*	Josh. 12–14
87	*Mar. 28*	Josh. 15–17
88	*Mar. 29*	Josh. 18–19
89	*Mar. 30*	Josh. 20–22
90	*Mar. 31*	Josh. 23–Judg. 1
91	*Apr. 1*	Judg. 2–5
92	*Apr. 2*	Judg. 6–8
93	*Apr. 3*	Judg. 9
94	*Apr. 4*	Judg. 10–12

Day	Date	Text
95	*Apr. 5*	Judg. 13–16
96	*Apr. 6*	Judg. 17–19
97	*Apr. 7*	Judg. 20–21
98	*Apr. 8*	Ruth
99	*Apr. 9*	1 Sam. 1–3
100	*Apr. 10*	1 Sam. 4–7
101	*Apr. 11*	1 Sam. 8–10
102	*Apr. 12*	1 Sam. 11–13
103	*Apr. 13*	1 Sam. 14–15
104	*Apr. 14*	1 Sam. 16–17
105	*Apr. 15*	1 Sam. 18–19 Ps. 59
106	*Apr. 16*	1 Sam. 20–21 Pss. 56; 34
107	*Apr. 17*	1 Sam. 22–23 1 Chron. 12:8–18 Pss. 52; 54; 63; 142
108	*Apr. 18*	1 Sam. 24; Ps. 57 1 Sam. 25
109	*Apr. 19*	1 Sam. 26–29 1 Chron. 12:1–7, 19–22
110	*Apr. 20*	1 Sam. 30–31 1 Chron. 10 2 Sam. 1
111	*Apr. 21*	2 Sam. 2–4
112	*Apr. 22*	2 Sam. 5:1–6:11 1 Chron. 11:1–9; 12:23–40; 13:1–14:17
113	*Apr. 23*	2 Sam. 22 Ps. 18
114	*Apr. 24*	1 Chron. 15–16 2 Sam. 6:12–23 Ps. 96

Day	Date	Text
115	*Apr. 25*	Ps. 105 2 Sam. 7 1 Chron. 17
116	*Apr. 26*	2 Sam. 8–10 1 Chron. 18–19 Ps. 60
117	*Apr. 27*	2 Sam. 11–12 1 Chron. 20:1–3 Ps. 51
118	*Apr. 28*	2 Sam. 13–14
119	*Apr. 29*	2 Sam. 15–17
120	*Apr. 30*	Ps. 3 2 Sam. 18–19
121	*May 1*	2 Sam. 20–21; 23:8–23 1 Chron. 20:4–8; 11:10–25
122	*May 2*	2 Sam. 23:24–24:25 1 Chron. 11:26–47; 21:1–30
123	*May 3*	1 Chron. 22–24
124	*May 4*	Ps. 30; 1 Chron. 25–26
125	*May 5*	1 Chron. 27–29
126	*May 6*	Pss. 5–7; 10; 11; 13; 17
127	*May 7*	Pss. 23; 26; 28; 31; 35
128	*May 8*	Pss. 41; 43; 46; 55; 61; 62; 64
129	*May 9*	Pss. 69–71; 77
130	*May 10*	Pss. 83; 86; 88; 91; 95
131	*May 11*	Pss. 108–9; 120–21; 140; 143–44
132	*May 12*	Pss. 1; 14–15; 36–37; 39
133	*May 13*	Pss. 40; 49–50; 73
134	*May 14*	Pss. 76; 82; 84; 90; 92; 112; 115
135	*May 15*	Pss. 8–9; 16; 19; 21; 24; 29
136	*May 16*	Pss. 33; 65–68
137	*May 17*	Pss. 75; 93–94; 97–100
138	*May 18*	Pss. 103–4; 113–14; 117
139	*May 19*	Pss. 119:1–88
140	*May 20*	Pss. 119: 89–176
141	*May 21*	Pss. 122; 124; 133–36
142	*May 22*	Pss. 138–39; 145; 148; 150
143	*May 23*	Pss. 4; 12; 20; 25; 32; 38
144	*May 24*	Pss. 42; 53; 58; 81; 101; 111; 130–31; 141; 146
145	*May 25*	Pss. 2; 22; 27
146	*May 26*	Pss. 45; 47–48; 87; 110
147	*May 27*	1 Kings 1:1–2:12 2 Sam. 23:1–7
148	*May 28*	1 Kings 2:13–3:28 2 Chron. 1:1–13
149	*May 29*	1 Kings 5–6 2 Chron. 2–3
150	*May 30*	1 Kings 7 2 Chron. 4
151	*May 31*	1 Kings 8; 2 Chron. 5:1–7:10
152	*June 1*	1 Kings 9:1–10:13 2 Chron. 7:11–9:12
153	*June 2*	1 Kings 4; 10:14–29 2 Chron. 1:14–17; 9:13–28; Ps. 72

Day	Date	Text
154	*June 3*	Prov. 1–3
155	*June 4*	Prov. 4–6
156	*June 5*	Prov. 7–7
157	*June 6*	Prov. 10–12
158	*June 7*	Prov. 13–15
159	*June 8*	Prov. 16–18
160	*June 9*	Prov. 19–21
161	*June 10*	Prov. 22–24
162	*June 11*	Prov. 25–27
163	*June 12*	Prov. 28–29
164	*June 13*	Prov. 30–31
		Ps. 127
165	*June 14*	Song of Songs
166	*June 15*	1 Kings 11:1–40
		Eccles. 1–2
167	*June 16*	Eccles. 3–7
168	*June 17*	Eccles. 8–12;
		1 Kings 11:41–43
		2 Chron. 9:29–31
169	*June 18*	1 Kings 12
		2 Chron. 10:1–11:17
170	*June 19*	1 Kings 13–14
		2 Chron. 11:18–12:16
171	*June 20*	1 Kings 15:1–24
		2 Chron. 13–16
172	*June 21*	1 Kings 15:25–16:34
		2 Chron. 17
		1 Kings 17
173	*June 22*	1 Kings 18–19
174	*June 23*	1 Kings 20–21
175	*June 24*	1 Kings 22:1–40
		2 Chron. 18

Day	Date	Text
176	*June 25*	1 Kings 22: 41–53
		2 Kings 1
		2 Chron. 19:1–21:3
177	*June 26*	2 Kings 2–4
178	*June 27*	2 Kings 5–7
179	*June 28*	2 Kings 8–9
		2 Chron. 21:4–22:9
180	*June 29*	2 Kings 10–11
		2 Chron. 22:10–23:21
181	*June 30*	Joel
182	*July 1*	2 Kings 12–13
		2 Chron. 24
183	*July 2*	2 Kings 14
		2 Chron. 25
		Jonah
184	*July 3*	Hos. 1–7
185	*July 4*	Hos. 8–14
186	*July 5*	2 Kings 15:1–7
		2 Chron. 26
		Amos 1–4
187	*July 6*	Amos 5–9
		2 Kings 15:8–18
188	*July 7*	Isa. 1–4
189	*July 8*	2 Kings 15:19–38
		2 Chron. 27
		Isa. 5–6
190	*July 9*	Micah
191	*July 10*	2 Kings 16
		2 Chron. 28
		Isa. 7–8
192	*July 11*	Isa. 9–12
193	*July 12*	Isa. 13–16
194	*July 13*	Isa. 17–22

Day	Date	Text
195	*July 14*	Isa. 23–27
196	*July 15*	Isa. 28–30
197	*July 16*	Isa. 31–35
198	*July 17*	2 Kings 18:1–8
		2 Chron. 29–31
199	*July 18*	2 Kings 17; 18:9–37
		2 Chron. 32:1–19
		Isa. 36
200	*July 19*	2 Kings 19
		2 Chron. 32:20–23
		Isa. 37
201	*July 20*	2 Kings 20
		2 Chron. 32:24–33
		Isa. 38–39
202	*July 21*	2 Kings 21:1–18
		2 Chron. 33:1–20
		Isa. 40
203	*July 22*	Isa. 41–43
204	*July 23*	Isa. 44–47
205	*July 24*	Isa. 48–51
206	*July 25*	Isa. 52–57
207	*July 26*	Isa. 58–62
208	*July 27*	Isa. 63–66
209	*July 28*	2 Kings 21:19–26
		2 Chron. 33:21–34:7
		Zephaniah
210	*July 29*	Jer. 1–3
211	*July 30*	Jer. 4–6
212	*July 31*	Jer. 7–9
213	*Aug. 1*	Jer. 10–13
214	*Aug. 2*	Jer. 14–16
215	*Aug. 3*	Jer. 17–20
216	*Aug. 4*	2 Kings 22:1–23:28
		2 Chron. 34:8–35:19

Day	Date	Text
217	*Aug. 5*	Nahum
		2 Kings 23:29–37
		2 Chron. 35:20–36:5
		Jer. 22:10–17
218	*Aug. 6*	Jer. 26; Habakkuk
219	*Aug. 7*	Jer. 46–47
		2 Kings 24:1–4, 7
		2 Chron. 36:6–7
		Jer. 25, 35
220	*Aug. 8*	Jer. 36; 45; 48
221	*Aug. 9*	Jer. 49:1–33
		Dan. 1–2
222	*Aug. 10*	Jer. 22:18–30
		2 Kings 24:5–20
		2 Chron. 36:8–12
		Jer. 37:1–2; 52:1–3; 24; 29
223	*Aug. 11*	Jer. 27–28; 23
224	*Aug. 12*	Jer. 50–51
225	*Aug. 13*	Jer. 49:34–39; 34:1–22
		Ezek. 1–3
226	*Aug. 14*	Ezek. 4–7
227	*Aug. 15*	Ezek. 8–11
228	*Aug. 16*	Ezek. 12–14
229	*Aug. 17*	Ezek. 15–17
230	*Aug. 18*	Ezek. 18–20
231	*Aug. 19*	Ezek. 21–23
232	*Aug. 20*	2 Kings 25:1
		2 Chron. 36:13–16
		Jer. 39:1; 52:4
		Ezek. 24;
		Jer. 21:1–22:9; 32:1–44
233	*Aug. 21*	Jer. 30–31; 33
234	*Aug. 22*	Ezek. 25; 29:1–16; 30; 31

Day	Date	Text
235	*Aug. 23*	Ezek. 26–28
236	*Aug. 24*	Jer. 37:3–39:10; 52:5–30
		2 Kings 25:2–21
		2 Chron. 36:17–21
237	*Aug. 25*	2 Kings 25:22
		Jer. 39:11–40:6
		Lam. 1–3
238	*Aug. 26*	Lam. 4–5
		Obadiah
239	*Aug. 27*	Jer. 40:7–44:30
		2 Kings 25:23–26
240	*Aug. 28*	Ezek. 33:21–36:38
241	*Aug. 29*	Ezek. 37–39
242	*Aug. 30*	Ezek. 32:1–33:20
		Dan. 3
243	*Aug. 31*	Ezek. 40–42
244	*Sept. 1*	Ezek. 43–45
245	*Sept. 2*	Ezek. 46–48
246	*Sept. 3*	Ezek. 29:17–21
		Dan. 4
		Jer. 52:31–34
		2 Kings 25:27–30
		Ps. 44
247	*Sept. 4*	Pss. 74; 79–80; 89
248	*Sept. 5*	Pss. 85; 102; 106; 123; 137
249	*Sept. 6*	Dan. 7–8; 5
250	*Sept. 7*	Dan. 9; 6
251	*Sept. 8*	2 Chron. 36:22–23
		Ezra 1:1–4:5
252	*Sept. 9*	Dan. 10–12
253	*Sept. 10*	Ezra 4:6–6:13
		Haggai

Day	Date	Text
254	*Sept. 11*	Zech. 1–6
255	*Sept. 12*	Zech. 7–8
		Ezra 6:14–22
		Ps. 78
256	*Sept. 13*	Pss. 107, 116, 118
257	*Sept. 14*	Pss. 125–26; 128–29;
		132; 147; 149
258	*Sept. 15*	Zech. 9–14
259	*Sept. 16*	Esther 1–4
260	*Sept. 17*	Esther 5–10
261	*Sept. 18*	Ezra 7–8
262	*Sept. 19*	Ezra 9–10
263	*Sept. 20*	Neh. 1–5
264	*Sept. 21*	Neh. 6–7
265	*Sept. 22*	Neh. 8–10
266	*Sept. 23*	Neh. 11–13
267	*Sept. 24*	Malachi
268	*Sept. 25*	1 Chron. 1–2
269	*Sept. 26*	1 Chron. 3–5
270	*Sept. 27*	1 Chron. 6
271	*Sept. 28*	1 Chron. 7:1–8:27
272	*Sept. 29*	1 Chron. 8:28–9:44
273	*Sept. 30*	John 1:1–18
		Mark 1:1
		Luke 1:1–4; 3:23–38
		Matt. 1:1–17
274	*Oct. 1*	Luke 1:5–80
275	*Oct. 2*	Matt. 1:18–2:23
		Luke 2
276	*Oct. 3*	Matt. 3:1–4:11
		Mark 1:2–13
		Luke 3:1–23; 4:1–13
		John 1:19–34

DAY	DATE	TEXT	DAY	DATE	TEXT
277	*Oct. 4*	John 1:35–3:36	288	*Oct. 15*	Mark 6:1–30
278	*Oct. 5*	John 4			Matt. 13:54–58;
		Matt. 4:12–17			9:35–11:1; 14:1–12
		Mark 1:14–15			Luke 9:1–10
		Luke 4:14–30	289	*Oct. 16*	Matt. 14:13–36
279	*Oct. 6*	Mark 1:16–45			Mark 31–56
		Matt. 4:18–25; 4; 14–17			Luke 9:11–17
		Luke 4:31–5:16			John 6:1–21
280	*Oct. 7*	Matt. 9:1–17	290	*Oct. 17*	John 6:22–7:1
		Mark 2:1–22			Matt. 15:1–20
		Luke 5:17–39			Mark 7:1–23
281	Oct. 8	John 5;	291	*Oct. 18*	Matt.15:21–16:20
		Matt. 12:1–21			Mark 7:24–8:30
		Mark 2:23–3:12			Luke 9:18–21
		Luke 6:1–11	292	*Oct. 19*	Matt.16:21–17:27
282	*Oct. 9*	Matt. 5;			Mark 8:31–9:32
		Mark 3:13–19			Luke 9:22–45
		Luke 6:12–36	293	*Oct. 20*	Matt. 18;8:19–22
283	*Oct. 10*	Matt. 6–7			Mark 9:33–50
		Luke 6:37–49			Luke 9:46–62
284	*Oct. 11*	Luke 7;			John 7:2–10
		Matt. 8:1, 5–13; 11:2–30	294	*Oct. 21*	John 7:1–8:59
285	*Oct. 12*	Matt. 12:22–50	295	*Oct. 22*	Luke 10:1–11:36
		Mark 3:20–35	296	*Oct. 23*	Luke 11:37–13:21
		Luke 8:1–21	297	*Oct. 24*	John 9–10
286	*Oct. 13*	Mark 4:1–34	298	*Oct. 25*	Luke 13:22–15:32
		Matt. 13:1–53	299	*Oct. 26*	Luke 16:1–17:10
287	*Oct. 14*	Mark 4:35–5:43			John 11:1–54
		Matt. 8:18, 23–34;	300	*Oct. 27*	Luke 17:11–18:17
		9:18–34			Matt. 19:1–15
		Luke 8:22–56			Mark 10:1–16

Day	Date	Text
301	*Oct. 28*	Matt. 19:16–20:28
		Mark 10:17–45
		Luke 18:18–34
302	*Oct. 29*	Matt. 20:29–34; 26:6–13
		Mark 10:46–52; 14:3–9
		Luke 18:35–9:28
		John 11:55–12:11
303	*Oct. 30*	Matt. 21:1–22
		Mark 11:1–26
		Luke 19:29–48
		John 12:12–50
304	*Oct. 31*	Matt. 21:23–22:14
		Mark 11:27–12:12
		Luke 20:1–19
305	*Nov. 1*	Matt. 22:15–46
		Mark 12:13–3
		Luke 20:20–44
306	*Nov. 2*	Matt. 23;
		Mark 12:38–44
		Luke 20:45–21:4
307	*Nov. 3*	Matt. 24:1–31
		Mark 13:1–27
		Luke 21:5–27
308	*Nov. 4*	Matt. 24:32–26:5,14–16
		Mark 13:28–14:2, 10–11
		Luke 21:28–22:6
309	*Nov. 5*	Matt. 26:17–29
		Mark 14:12–25
		Luke 22:7–38
		John 13
310	*Nov. 6*	John 14–16
311	*Nov. 7*	John 17:1–18:1
		Matt. 26:30–46
		Mark 14:26–42
		Luke 22:39–46
312	*Nov. 8*	Matt. 26:47–75
		Mark 14:43–72
		Luke 22:47–65
		John 18:2–27
313	*Nov. 9*	Matt. 27:1–26
		Mark 15:1–15
		Luke 22:66–23:25
		John 18:28–19:16
314	*Nov. 10*	Matt. 27:27–56
		Mark 15:16–41
		Luke 23:26–49
		John 19:17–30
315	*Nov. 11*	Matt. 27:57–28:8
		Mark 15:42–16:8
		Luke 23:50–24:12
		John 19:31–20:10
316	*Nov. 12*	Matt. 28:9–20
		Mark 16:9–20
		Luke 24:13–53
		John 20:11–21:25
317	*Nov. 13*	Acts 1–2
318	*Nov. 14*	Acts 3–5
319	*Nov. 15*	Acts 6:1–8:1
320	*Nov. 16*	Acts 8:2–9:43
321	*Nov. 17*	Acts 10–11
322	*Nov. 18*	Acts 12–13
323	*Nov. 19*	Acts 14–15
324	*Nov. 20*	Gal. 1–3

Day	Date	Text
325	*Nov. 21*	Gal. 4–6
326	*Nov. 22*	James
327	*Nov. 23*	Acts 16:1–18:11
328	*Nov. 24*	1 Thessalonians
329	*Nov. 25*	2 Thessalonians
		Acts 18:12–19:22
330	*Nov. 26*	1 Cor. 1–4
331	*Nov. 27*	1 Cor. 5–8
332	*Nov. 28*	1 Cor. 9–11
333	*Nov. 29*	1 Cor. 12–14
334	*Nov. 30*	1 Cor. 15–16
335	*Dec. 1*	Acts 19:23–20:1
		2 Cor. 1–4
336	*Dec. 2*	2 Cor. 5–9
337	*Dec. 3*	2 Cor. 10–13
338	*Dec. 4*	Rom. 1–3
339	*Dec. 5*	Rom. 4–6
340	*Dec. 6*	Rom. 7–8
341	*Dec. 7*	Rom. 9–11
342	*Dec. 8*	Rom. 12–15
343	*Dec. 9*	Rom. 16
		Acts 20:2–21:16
344	*Dec. 10*	Acts 21:17–23:35
345	*Dec. 11*	Acts 24–26
346	*Dec. 12*	Acts 27–28
347	*Dec. 13*	Eph. 1–3
348	*Dec. 14*	Eph. 4–6
349	*Dec. 15*	Colossians
350	*Dec. 16*	Philippians
351	*Dec. 17*	Philemon
		1 Tim. 1–3

Day	Date	Text
352	*Dec. 18*	1 Tim. 4–6
		Titus
353	*Dec. 19*	2 Timothy
354	*Dec. 20*	1 Peter
355	*Dec. 21*	Jude
		2 Peter
356	*Dec. 22*	Heb. 1:1–5:10
357	*Dec. 23*	Heb. 5:11–9:28
358	*Dec. 24*	Heb. 10–11
359	*Dec. 25*	Heb. 12–13
		2 John
		3 John
360	*Dec. 26*	1 John
361	*Dec. 27*	Rev. 1–3
362	*Dec. 28*	Rev. 4–9
363	*Dec. 29*	Rev. 10–14
364	*Dec. 30*	Rev. 15–18
365	*Dec. 31*	Rev. 19–22

Index